75 Best
Business Practices for
Socially Responsible
Companies

75 Best Business Practices for Socially Responsible Companies

ALAN REDER FOR
THE SOCIAL VENTURE NETWORK

A JEREMY P. TARCHER/PUTNAM BOOK
published by G. P. PUTNAM'S SONS New York

To *the business leaders and companies for whom profits are the ticket, not the event;*

To *the entrepreneurs who light the way by creating social solutions instead of problems;*

Finally, to all the women and men everywhere who take their citizenship to work with them.

A Jeremy P. Tarcher/Putnam Book
Published by G. P. Putnam's Sons
Publishers Since 1838
200 Madison Avenue
New York, NY 10016

Library of Congress Cataloging-in-Publication Data
Reder, Alan.
    75 best business practices for socially responsible companies /
Alan Reder for the Social Venture Network.
        p.   cm.
    "A Jeremy P. Tarcher/Putnam Book."
    ISBN 0-87477-783-6
    1. Social responsibility of business—United States—Case studies.
    2. Business enterprises—Social aspects—United States—Case
studies.   I. Social Venture Network.   II. Title.
HD60.5.U5R44   1995   95-13772 CIP
658.4'08—dc20

Cover and interior design by Mauna Eichner

Printed in the United States of America

10   9   8   7   6   5   4   3   2   1

This book is printed on acid-free recycled paper. ∞

Acknowledgments

I take no credit whatsoever for the original conception of this book — for that phase of the project, I was merely one of those applauding from the sidelines. Chuck Blitz, then executive director of the Social Venture Network (SVN), and Jeremy Tarcher developed the book idea to a high state of maturity before putting it in my hands. In effect, I adopted a healthy, very promising child.

It is entirely appropriate, of course, that this title be housed under Jeremy Tarcher's roof. His is one of the few remaining values-driven operations in publishing; I feel honored to be once again represented in his catalog. Editor Dan Malvin's attunement to the issues discussed within as well as his superior editorial sensibilities buffed the draft to a high state of polish. The editorial relationship was also the most congenial I have ever enjoyed.

The current work, by the way, grows out of the ongoing "best practices" information project that SVN maintains for its members. SVN has published two best-practices collections for the membership, and continues to describe member businesses' practices in its newsletter as well. All of those publications were valuable sources for *75 Best Practices,* so thank you, Eric Weaver and Suzanne Joyal, for your superior work in pulling the information and the publications themselves together. And I am especially indebted to SVN member and Stanford University professor Kirk Hanson, whose articulation of the concept of socially responsible best practices informed this volume as well as the previous two. The works of

SVN members and authors Milton Moskowitz and Bob Rosen also served as important references.

Jennifer Chapman, SVN's associate director, was my liaison at SVN for the book project. Whenever some arrangement or another needed to be hammered out, she rolled up her sleeves and hammered. At various points along the way, SVN board member Mark Albion was mentor, consultant, and buddy, and usually all three at once. Suzanne Joyal kept me abreast of best-practices information from members as it arrived in the SVN office. A packet she annotated and supplied to me on Vatex of America spurred me to investigate what turned out to be one of the best stories in the book. Kare Anderson also provided research for this project.

Some 100 executives, managers, and frontline employees generously shared their thoughts and experiences with me in lengthy interviews. They are quoted in the vignettes themselves so, with a couple of exceptions, I won't repeat their names here, but I am deeply grateful for their contributions. I do want to extend a special thank-you to Monica Milstead of Xerox and Jim Metts of H. B. Fuller, who went way beyond the call of duty, or my request, by supplying written statements in support of their verbal comments.

Not quoted in the book but essential to its preparation were the many media relations and administrative assistants who arranged interviews, sent me documentation, and otherwise did whatever I requested. Those people included Stephen Peeples of Rhino Entertainment; Patty Jacobs of Beth Israel Hospital Boston; Kerry Efigenio of Morrison & Foerster; Sonja Whitemon of Federal Express; Steve Sanchez of 3M; Jim May of S C Johnson Wax; Bill Belknap of H. B. Fuller; Rob Michalak of Ben & Jerry's; Honey Siegel of Fel-Pro; Mary-Anne Hines of Shaman Pharmaceuticals; Sheryl Battles of Pitney Bowes; Danny Krauss of Esprit; Jeff Leebaw of Johnson & Johnson; Leigh Gott of Marquette Electronics; Peter Jeff of Steelcase; Susanna Knapp of Tabra; Brian Simmons of Lotus Development; John Berry and Mark Schurman of Herman Miller; Cheryl Engstrom of Nordstrom; Melanie Jones and Ginger Hardage of Southwest Airlines; Lynne Fountain of SAS

Institute; Lynn Greenwood of A. G. Edwards; Susan Silver of Vitas Healthcare; Diane Wisdom and Hank Rusman of J. C. Penney; Sean Fitzgerald of Levi Strauss; Gary Lachow of Merck; Brian Williams of The Body Shop USA; Nancy Vetstein of Mullen (for Ryka); Lynne Turner of Stonyfield Farm; Jonathan Radigan of Seventh Generation; Lindsay McNamar of Fenton Communications; Nancy Fulginiti of Southwire; Joni Martin of Odwalla; Steve Roman of Bank One; Judd Everhart of Xerox; and especially Lori Fenimore of DuPont. I'm sure I've missed a name or two, so please accept my apology and consider yourself included in the above.

Because no one in management was available for interviews, Susan Alcorn of Finast referred me to the Business Enterprise Trust (BET), which had conducted a detailed study of Finast's operation in downtown Cleveland. BET's Marilyn Turner and Kathleen Meyer had exhaustive materials sent to me, from which I prepared the Finast vignette. They asked that the following paragraph about the BET be included in the book:

My neighbor and dear friend Denise Buck transcribed the interview tapes, doing whatever it took to get me material as I needed it. Her enthusiasm for the substance of the interviews was an early indication that the material was working.

I can't let the opportunity pass to again thank Josh Mailman for his phone call several years ago inviting me to apply for SVN membership, and to acknowledge him and the other

SVN founders and board members for the phenomenal organization they've created. It's an honor to preside at your coming-out party.

Trust, by the way, that the several SVN companies mentioned inside are just a small sample of the hundreds of business pioneers that comprise the membership. While not mentioned specifically, the other members, individually and in aggregate, are an indispensable part of the book's spirit.

I owe my greatest debt on this project to my family — my wife, Hyiah, my daughter Ariel, and my new son, Ajene — who permitted and endured my virtual disappearance from the healthy life of our family over the final months of the book's preparation. They bore the strain heroically, as always. This book is as much their contribution as the Network's or mine.

Contents

✸ *Indicates a Social Venture Network Associated Company*

About Best Practices, Social Responsibility, and Other Introductory Matters

As I was preparing to interview Ben & Jerry's co-founder Ben Cohen for this project, the company's publicity director warned me that Ben likes to "cut right to the chase." Indeed, he does. In the September/October 1993 issue of the *Utne Reader,* Ben and a number of other business leaders and social commentators shared their thoughts on the role of social responsibility in business. Ben wrote: "Businesses have created most of our social and environmental problems. If business were instead trying to solve these problems, they would be solved in short order."

I hope you take a similar conclusion with you from this book. Inside, you will find fascinating business answers to some of our greatest social dilemmas — job insecurity, the widening gap between haves and have-nots, environmental degradation, economic disempowerment of minorities and women, even the rising cost of health care. Certainly, some of those answers were created by generous-spirited managers at some cost to their own company — either its great surpluses or its precious operating margin. But many others not only address social issues in creative and impactful ways but also return dollars, directly or otherwise, to the bottom line.

We in the progressive business movement place great faith in the power of entrepreneurial initiative. The examples in this book prove that the same inventiveness used historically to create great wealth can be applied to social issues as well, so that all those affected by a company's decisions, not just the stockholders, either benefit from its actions or at least are not harmed. In fact, as the Social Venture Network's co-chair, Stonyfield Farm CEO Gary Hirshberg, has put it, a socially responsible business practice ought to be financially viable as well, for that's the only way it will ever be put to widespread use.

We in no way intend to imply that socially responsible practices constitute the only way to run a company. They are one way to run a company and they have worked well for many, many organizations. The message here, as real as it is modest, is that businesses don't have to make their profits at society's expense. In addition, many things — for example, improved employee retention and productivity, better customer goodwill, and cost savings from environmental efficiencies, to name just a few — will go better for a company as a result of practices such as those described within.

That said, this book probably should have come with a red label reading WARNING: EXTREME DANGER OF GETTING MISTAKEN IMPRESSION. While a few of these "best practices" could probably be lifted wholesale from these pages and applied to most any workplace, most cannot. In general, socially responsible business practices are not add-ons. You can't just drop these practices into a company like food coloring into water and expect they'll change anything. They work best together — that is, synergistically — in a socially reflective and responsive culture. Like delicate seeds, they will not survive in hostile soil, nor will they thrive without attention and support from the top of the company.

This is true, of course, not only of socially responsible practices but also of best practices in the traditional sense. As Jim Clarkson of Southwire said to me when I was interviewing him for this project, it's generally the good companies that do the good things. In other words, best practices aren't inoculations.

While we're at it, a few other cautions as well: First of all, because almost nothing in society changes faster than business, it is possible that by the time this book appears in stores, some companies will have dropped or modified the practices attributed to them. We have tried in most cases to find practices with some record of durability and/or commitment but we can't predict the future other than to say that nothing lasts forever. Remember that IBM was until quite recently a no-layoff company.

We also caution readers against measuring these companies against perfection. The downside of being considered socially responsible in any area is that the public and the media tend to place you on a pedestal from where you have nowhere to go but down. Should any company featured within stumble in the future, or at least receive negative press, ask yourself how it stacks up against the rest of its competition in American business, not just against its own reputation. Also scrutinize the press coverage with extreme skepticism — the press gets a lot of mileage out of publicizing quirky companies and feel-good practices but once it has built the company up to impossible heights, the only way to get more mileage out of the story is to tear the company back down again.

Readers should also be aware that we've taken great liberties with the term *best practice*. Some vignettes in this book are probably better described as best approaches that encompass a number of specific practices. Some represent noble but not wholly successful attempts rather than finished practices; they've been included because they address social issues in admirable and interesting ways and because they have good teaching value even in their current flawed form.

Finally, we remind readers that this is a book of socially responsible practices, not companies. Being listed in this book because of a particular admirable practice is no endorsement of a company's overall ethical behavior. Some of America's better employers are major polluters or otherwise produce goods or services that would never make this book's responsible product/service section. By the same token, some of the country's most philanthropic or community-minded companies run sweatshop-like workplaces.

In fact, as many of us in the progressive business movement have long realized, the term *social responsibility* — despite its presence on this book cover — has pretty much outlived its usefulness, for it implies a standard to which no business citizen can measure up. Ah, but socially *responsive* or socially *reflective* — now, that's another story. Reflect and respond. Try to improve in every way. In a perfectly imperfect world, that's all we can expect. And if enough of us in business take up that pledge — perhaps with the help of the examples herein — it will be perfectly good enough.

Employees

Empowerment, Egalitarianism, and Sharing the Wealth

Company: Reflexite

Policy/Practice: Combining employee stock ownership with participatory management.

Bottom Line: In 1992, *Inc.* magazine named Reflexite's entire workforce its Entrepreneur of the Year.

Every CEO in America dreams about what Reflexite has in spades: employees who act like owners. Then again, while most executives merely fantasize about that level of workforce dedication, Reflexite took the direct route — made its employees owners and involved them in important decisions. Spurred by their contributions, this relatively modest-sized outfit, a technology-based company in New Britain, Connecticut, continues to expand and thrive in a daunting competitive climate in which its major rival is none other than industrial behemoth 3M.

While the business press now abounds with stories of spectacular company turnarounds based on the potent motivational combo of employee stock ownership programs (ESOPs) and participatory management, the Reflexite story begins elsewhere. Yale-trained engineers Hugh and Bill Rowland had built a solid-performing enterprise after Bill's late-1960s invention of an improved method for producing *retroreflexive* material, the stuff that makes highway signs and barricades, life preservers, fire-fighting gear, and other safety products visible from long distances. The Rowlands ran a good shop in the old paternalistic sense, providing their employees solid benefits, generally secure employment, and a safe work environment.

However, by 1983 the company, then doing a profitable $3.5 million in sales, was on the verge of being devoured by its own success. That year, the Rowland brothers, now in their sixties and anxious to establish successors to themselves as owners/managers, received the first of a series of tempting, but troubling, offers — a forty-two-times-earnings bid from 3M. Hugh and Bill had seen other absentee owners milk local businesses for their key assets — in Reflexite's case, its technology and patents — and then shut down the operation. They didn't want to see their baby die and their workers and community suffer. Then again, their accountants and attorneys were urging them to provide liquidity for their estates, and the $5 million they would clear from 3M was nothing to sniff at.

Just prior to the 3M proposal, Hugh Rowland had recruited Cecil Ursprung, a customer company's marketing executive, to be Reflexite's next president. Ursprung, anxious to test his mettle in what he viewed as a potentially world-class outfit, helped persuade the board to reject 3M and give him the reins instead. The decision solved the Rowlands' succession worries but not their cash problem. And that created a problem for Ursprung, who noticed that the Rowlands were continuing to entertain offers for the company. So in mid-1984, he suggested to them that an ESOP, a legal device for transferring stock to employees, might resolve their concerns about their personal finances and the company's future all at once.

Today, Ursprung can cite study after study showing that ESOP companies that give employee/owners decision-making input usually outperform the competition — and that ESOPs without employee empowerment haven't produced nearly the same results. That research wasn't available when Reflexite installed its ESOP in 1985 but, Ursprung recalls, "it made intu-itive sense that if you established an ESOP as a pension plan, it wasn't going to motivate our workforce because our average age back then was about thirty-one. But combining ownership in an entrepreneurial sense with sharing power with people made a lot of sense to me." As the new president from out of town, he also realized that an empowered ESOP might be just the hook he needed to rally the workforce behind his leadership.

Still, Reflexite began its ESOP venture cautiously, trans-ferring less than one percent of the company. However, with regular allocations increasing employee ownership, the ESOP began to pay off as a motivator, and the company began to fund it more aggressively. As of mid-1994, the ESOP had grown in appraised value from the original $150,000 in 1985 to $19 million, the combined effect of the program's owner-ship increasing to 42 percent of the company and the stock growing at a compound rate of about 30 percent annually over that period. Employees can also buy stock directly as the founders make it available or participate in a stock-option program; as of this writing, an additional 24 percent of Re-flexite was in employees' hands through direct stock purchase.

In many ESOP companies that haven't taken full advan-tage of the program as a management tool, employees never embrace their ownership stake. It's just another benefit they'll realize when they retire. Reflexite makes sure employees' spe-cial status stays at the front of their minds. Company letter-head, inspection cards, and promotional videos all declare to the world that employees co-own the company. Employees re-ceive monthly and quarterly financial data, annotated to ex-plain such bean-counter lingo as "deferred liabilities" and "accumulated depreciation." They also attend meetings held at least quarterly where, says Ursprung, "we go over not only the financial statement, but news of the day, the kinds of busi-ness things that every owner would be interested in knowing."

Reflexite has also passed through to employees the vote on their ESOP shares, another unusual feature for an ESOP company. Ursprung notes that, considering the additional shares that employees directly own and vote, the workforce "literally has the power to throw me out of the office, as I reminded them the other day in a plant-wide meeting. I don't remind them of that every day. But we wanted to make a serious statement about who ultimately controls the destiny of this corporation and, I'm sorry, it was not about to be a trustee in a bank someplace who didn't know a damn thing about this company." Should employees harbor remaining doubts about who's ultimately in charge, there's the hard-cash reminder — stock dividends. In 1993, Reflexite distributed a total of $600,000 to about 275 employees, in addition to more conventional incentive bonuses. (All employees participate in incentive-pay programs.)

Although committed to employee empowerment from the start, Ursprung admits that management struggled with how to transform Reflexite into an empowerment culture. Employee participation was largely ad hoc until 1989, when the company instituted a quality-improvement program that involved every department and employee, as individuals and in teams, in making a difference for Reflexite. In retrospect, Ursprung sees that structured participation was crucial: "This stuff has to be a regular part of what it's like to come to work. Otherwise, people don't take you seriously. And you've got to be willing to not only live with but support the results."

Wearing two hats does force Reflexite employee/owners to make some tough decisions when their immediate welfare conflicts with the long-term interests of their company. In one recent case, management became concerned that the company's 100 percent prepaid health plan was out of line with current practice, burdening the company with costs that its competitors weren't bearing. A nine-employee committee ultimately agreed, recommending to the board that the employees start kicking in 20 percent, as other companies were requiring. The decision taxed all workers and their families but saved their company hundreds of thousands of dollars.

One cost reduction you won't often see in participatory cultures like Reflexite's is the savage laying off of employees that many other companies use to solve financial problems or increase profits. Reflexite had suffered through a 20 percent layoff during a business downturn in the pre-ESOP winter of 1982–83 and Ursprung says that the current employees who survived that cut won't ever forget the pain and anxiety it spread. The company grew so rapidly for nearly a decade afterward, however, that a sales dropoff in summer 1991 caught it with more employees than it could profitably support.

This time, management and employees worked together to find a more creative solution to the crisis. Making job saving its first priority, management imposed a graduated pay cut that hit them as the highest-paid employees first and hardest. Acting on an employee suggestion, the company also constructed a voluntary-leave program that guaranteed takers that they wouldn't lose either seniority or benefits while they were gone. Remembers Ursprung, "we ended up having ninety people participate in that program and over a period of six months the company lowered its labor costs by 16 percent without a single layoff."

Finally, teams of employees generated so many cost-saving ideas in their work areas that the company saved over $600,000 more. Says Ursprung, "When business started to return to normal in the spring, we had come out of that experience a much stronger organization, like a sports team after a big win."

In fact, Ursprung says that without job security, all of Reflexite's other motivational attributes would amount to zip. One of the company's ten profit centers recently produced a 40 percent throughput increase. Notes Ursprung, "They won't let you have that 40 percent increase if they know that all they're doing is working themselves out of a job."

For all the performance advantages of the Reflexite style, Ursprung points out one flat note, literally, that he didn't anticipate in 1985: "To get the maximum amount of participation in decision making, you have to have the flattest organization possible, because the main purpose of managers and supervisors is to tell people what to do. And so the growth in managerial and supervisory jobs in this company hasn't matched the company's growth overall. There are people at Reflexite who in a very traditional sense have difficulty seeing their next step up the ladder, and their perception is accurate.

"You counteract that by emphasizing the attractiveness of ownership and having power in an organization — maybe not managerial, territorial-type power, but access to decision making power and the financial rewards that come to owners of successful companies." In addition, Reflexite is implementing an incentive-pay program for employees who expand their skills horizontally, since opportunities for vertical advancing are limited.

Ursprung also cautious business leaders contemplating a Reflexite-ian makeover to let go of their old notions of executive power: "In 1989, I came up with a reorganization scheme for the company. The folks tried to make it work for six months, but it didn't and confusion reigned. If I were a normal CEO in a normal situation, I probably would've stuck this out because my ego wouldn't have allowed otherwise. No one would have questioned my decision, but they would have complained behind my back about how stupid it was. Here, people let me know as I walked around the company that they were genuinely concerned, not only about their own jobs but about the viability of this solution to a growth situation. I concluded that however brilliant the plan was on paper, it wasn't working on the floor and we undid it."

Not that Ursprung feels in any way usurped: "What I tell CEOs who are considering participation, is 'Don't worry, nobody wants your job. People by and large don't want to deal with the kinds of complex decisions you deal with. They do want to know that your job is being done competently. They do want to be able to ask you questions. But it's been my observation that people are much more interested in working on problems that have a nearer impact on their own work situation, and guess what, that's very convenient, because who knows more about the work and how it can be improved than the people who are doing it.'"

Like many companies, Reflexite charts improvement and progress wherever it can. Still, Ursprung notes that it's not easy to separate out the contributions of turned-on worker/owners from, say, improved technology or a successful marketing approach. But his gut feelings tell him that the contributions have been great indeed: "I still remember one woman who didn't realize that I was within earshot saying after we first established the ESOP, 'My gosh, now that I'm an owner, I'm gonna have to cut down on these personal telephone calls.' Over time, the fact that we are employee owned and the fact that we have had success has affected the behavior of a majority of Reflexite people. We don't have everybody, but we do have a critical mass."

COMPANY: RHINO ENTERTAINMENT

Policy/Practice: A combined goal completion/profit-sharing program.

Bottom Line: You eat really well here if you don't bite off more than you can chew.

The Spike Jones Anthology — Musical Depreciation Revue. Dr. Demento Presents Spooky Tunes and Scary Melodies. Ed Wood — Look Back in Angora. Cat Women of the Moon — 3D. A quick glance at these Rhino Records audio and Rhino Home Video titles and you conclude that, whatever the company's other merits, this is not a place for orderly minds.

Well, so much for first impressions. Despite the lunatic edge of much of its catalog, Los Angeles, California–based Rhino Entertainment is in its day-to-day operations one of the more logically managed companies in the country. After all, what makes more motivational sense than giving employees a generous piece of the action contingent on their productivity, encouraging even frontline staff to contribute ideas about fundamental company processes, and creating a community-minded enterprise in which all involved can take unending pride?

Central to the general logic of this pro-employee, pro-community culture is a specifically rational practice called Rhino By Objective. Appropriately for a company that specializes in music and video reissues, Rhino By Objective is itself a reissue — vice president for human resources Sharon Foster suggested the program to company founder/president Richard Foos after experiencing something similar with her previous employer. Here's how it works:

At the beginning of each year, top management communicates its business and social goals to the various department heads, who in turn present them to their respective staffs. Within departments, employees dialogue about how they can contribute, developing in the process their own departmental objectives. From that list they then choose projects — called RBOs — that they would like to take on, with the understanding that they will be held accountable for accomplishing them. With their supervisors, they articulate the goals in writing and define action steps and timelines. Several times over the succeeding 120 days, they will meet with their supervisor to discuss their progress. Managers who supervise two or more employees also commit to a management RBO — to manage their employees to a successful completion of their RBO projects.

Of course, what keeps the game at high pitch are the stakes, which are twofold, says Foster. Employees determine the degree to which they will participate in the company's biannual profit sharing by how they score on their RBO evaluation, a self-rating approved by the supervisor. But Foster says that for some Rhino-ites, the emotional stakes are higher still: "The times when it doesn't happen or you only get halfway there are real down times for some people, not due to the money necessarily but due to disappointing themselves."

On the plus side, of course, many employees experience tremendous personal and professional growth from completing a challenging project. Foster's favorite such story concerns an employee under her supervision who volunteered to re-vamp a bloated mailing list with well over 17,000 names: "I don't think she had a clue about what she was getting into. I think she thought, If it's in the computer, it can't be that bad." Because the list was a composite of several departments' lists, she broke the master list back down and sent each part to the appropriate department head with a memo asking them to re-turn an updated version to her by the stated date. "Of course, that date came around," Foster recalls, "and she didn't have a thing in her mailbox."

At Foster's urging, the employee began showing up at each offender's office and demanding attention: "That was a pretty hard thing for her to do. She's an administrative assis-tant and she was going up against vice presidents, even though nobody's going to pull rank here. So that really snapped them to because she said, 'I'm trying to do something here that's worthwhile and I feel that you don't really care.'" With guilt trips properly distributed, the revised lists began rolling in. But then, Foster says, "she really began to panic because her timeline was staring her in the face. I'm saying all along, 'I have all the faith in the world in you and we will pull it off.' I ended up bringing in two temps whom she supervised, and she brought the project in three days before due date."

What Rhino gained from all that far exceeded some saved postage, asserts Foster: "It gave her tremendous self-confidence. She was able to step up to the department heads and get her needs met, and for the first time she was able to su-pervise two people, which really helped her to grow. You men-tion that mailing list to her now and I mean she is all aglow because all the negative stuff is gone — 'I did it, and it was perfect!'"

Rhino By Objective, by contrast, is not yet perfect, but it continues to improve as the company tinkers with it. Manage-ment made an early mistake by putting all the profit-sharing money into a big pot with, in hindsight, predictably unfortu-nate results. Foster: "Instead of creating a team spirit — 'Let me help you with your RBO because I need help with mine' — people were saying, 'Nuts to you, I get a bigger piece if you don't.'" Now every employee competes against her/himself. For each employee, the company sets a maximum share of profits as a fixed percentage of base salary, with the self-evaluation determining the percentage of that share earned. Based on a four-part rating — timeliness, completion of action plan, product quality, and completion of objective for which the plan was designed — most employees qualify for 80 to 100 percent shares, says Foster.

Which is not to imply that goals are always met in their original form. "Sometimes things occur that are completely out of not only the employee's but the manager's control," says Foster, "and those are all taken into consideration. One of the biggest things that happens here is because we're all so enthusiastic, we underestimate our time frames, forgetting that we have other work to do, too." In those cases, employees renegotiate the goals with their supervisor so that, for example, the original time frame becomes the research phase, with completion rescheduled for the next 120-day cycle. "The only real failure," says Foster, "is the employee who throws his hands up and says, 'I don't know why I picked this, I don't want to do this.' Those are few and far between."

Despite the ante, the self-rating system has worked well from the start. Foster says that "employees are usually harder on themselves than the manager is." And although managers are responsible for employees' RBOs, "amazingly enough we're pretty darn fair and we'll admit that they didn't do well in this area or the end product doesn't look as shiny and sparkly as they said it was going to."

Including social goals in the program goes straight to the heart of what Rhino is about. For instance, since the early 1990s, Rhino has sent financial assistance and employee volunteers to the Al Wooten, Jr., Heritage Center, a nonprofit education/recreation center in Los Angeles's inner city that provides a positive after-school refuge for neighborhood youth. When Foster and I spoke in early 1995, several employees had also elected as their RBOs the investigation of such social upgrades to the workplace as expanded work/family benefits, increased representation of women and minorities in management, diversity training for the workforce, and increasing company support for continuing education of employees. (For more on Rhino's employee teams, see page 298.)

Rhino may not have planned it this way, but RBOs have engendered considerable cross training in the company as well, a huge side benefit in a modern organization. Says Foster, "We've had, for instance, A & R [artists and repertoire] people who've taken on RBOs with marketing people because they want to understand the marketing side of the business. It's also helped in developing relationships with people whom you don't have a daily contact with, which is really important."

Overall, says Foster, despite occasional missed deadlines and depressed visages at bonus time, "I think this process has been very influential in moving the company forward. It truly gives the employees a real connection to what they do and where the company goes, and that by itself has been very powerful for Rhino. I mean, our employees feel a tremendous sense of pride in being here and they feel a tremendous responsibility about the performance of their jobs." As if getting Spike Jones to the people wasn't motivation enough.

COMPANY: BETH ISRAEL HOSPITAL BOSTON

> ***Policy/Practice:*** Combining employee empowerment and gain sharing based on a concept called the Scanlon Plan.

> ***Bottom Line:*** In an ailing health-care system, a hospital with a proven wellness strategy.

The factory that employed him, as well as his job, were dying when steelworker and union leader Joe Scanlon figured out a way to rescue both: Define some simple measure of costs, pay employees regular bonuses for knocking down those costs through their own suggestions or efforts, and workers will pull together with managers to save the company. Desperate, the factory's executives decided to give Scanlon's idea a try. To their great surprise and relief, it did what he predicted, and the company recovered.

Although Scanlon spurred that turnaround back in the 1930s and went on to teach at the Massachusetts Institute of Technology, American organizations have been slow to adopt his concepts. However, where the so-called Scanlon Plan has taken hold, it has worked wonders. Case in point: Beth Israel Hospital, a famous teaching hospital located just south of Fenway Park in Boston. Beth Israel dubbed its version of the plan Prepare 21 (for Participation, Responsibility, Education, Production, Accountability, Recognition, and Excellence for the 21st Century). In each of the initiative's first two years — 1989–90 and 1990–91 — employee ideas saved near $2 million. Through the Prepare 21 contract with staff, the hospital split the savings with them in the form of regular bonus checks.

Beth Israel wasn't ailing like Joe Scanlon's steel company when in the mid-1980s its executives began investigating new ways to organize work there. But president/CEO Dr. Mitchell Rabkin did worry about the continuous cost cutting forced on the hospital by changes in the health-care industry. He'd been painstakingly building Beth Israel's quality and morale since he took the reins in 1966. Now both were threatened unless staff at all levels joined management in embracing the hospital's business challenges. He hoped that some sort of empowerment scheme would be the magic elixir.

Rabkin's careful research into the matter took him and other Beth Israel managers to Zeeland, Michigan, where furniture maker Herman Miller, Inc., had operated under a Scanlon Plan since 1950. On a tour of the Miller plant, they asked a brawny, tattooed loading dock worker to tell them what he thought was important about his job. To their astonishment, he lectured them in great detail about his role in ensuring quality and reducing costs. As Rabkin and human resources director Laura Avakian recalled in a journal article, "He turned to us and said, 'Do you know that overseas they can make this same stuff, same quality, and ship it to the U.S. for 35 percent less than we're doing it right now? So the real question about my job is, do we want to be a company that manufactures furniture [and] employs 2,000 people, or do we want to be a company that imports furniture and employs only 20?' We finally understood what 'owning the problem' meant."

Although suitably impressed with Miller's operation, Rabkin wasn't sold yet that the Scanlon Plan would work at Beth Israel. No one had ever tried the plan in a complex service organization, only in manufacturing companies where employees' roles in quality and productivity were more clearcut. Sure, empowerment made sense intuitively, but would it provide enough of an incentive in a place where output depended more upon the interplay between large departments and complex systems than on individual effort?

The only way to answer the question was to plunge ahead. Effectively, Beth Israel's leadership empowered the workforce to decide the empowerment issue. Dividing the huge staff into small groups, they educated them about the project and solicited their opinions in secret ballots. Overwhelmingly, employees voted Yes.

Prepare 21 continues to evolve as the staff works with it, but it has transformed problem solving at Beth Israel from the beginning. Explains Rabkin: "Because not everything goes on in one's own department, it is usual in a conventional hospital to have everybody blame everybody else and nothing much change. Here, groups start out representing nursing or transportation or what have you. But through processes like those of Total Quality Management, where you see numerically what's going on, these separate groups tend to coalesce into one work team which ultimately solves the problem. That has worked out very, very well."

Still, Prepare 21 works differently than does Herman Miller's Scanlon Plan because Beth Israel's financial gains aren't big enough to do much for employees. As a nonprofit organization, the hospital doesn't generate the financial surpluses that Miller does. Impressive as the seven-figure savings generated by Prepare 21 seem, the staff's half of the take generally amounts to less than one percent of pay for the average employee once distributed to the thousands on Beth Israel's payroll.

But make no mistake, Prepare 21 motivates. Employees still realize their welfare is tied to the hospital's. Notes Prepare 21 coordinator Luanne Selk, "When times are tough, people here aren't surprised, because we share the information on an ongoing basis. That builds a high level of trust instead of the sense that, 'Oh, management is just making this up.' And then people are more ready to make changes that need to be made."

Perhaps the most dramatic demonstration of Prepare 21's worth came in 1993, when patient volumes dropped throughout Boston's hospital system, including at Beth Israel. Based on the first four months, management projected a $16 million loss by year's end. Options were clear: Beth Israel had to somehow simultaneously boost quality to attract more patients and slash costs, or face massive layoffs. At a grim meeting, the hospital's executive vice president requested that all managers and team leaders ask their team members for ideas and report back in ten days. They returned with 3,000 ideas from employees at every level of the organization. "The exciting thing for me," recalls Selk, "was that the senior management was able to make more informed decisions because of that input." Those decisions saved an immediate $5 million. By year's end, the hospital was $745,000 in the black and no jobs were cut.

For all its advantages, Prepare 21 also begets some unique challenges. For one thing, the medical staff tends to get riled whenever quality improvement is discussed, until they realize it isn't *their* quality that's being questioned. In fact, just getting physicians to play team ball is a continuing challenge, suggests Rabkin delicately. Figuring out how to measure for quality-control processes that aren't easily quantified is no day in the park, either.

Historically, empowerment plans that don't include meaningful gain sharing haven't paid off the way Beth Israel's has. The key to the hospital's success may lie in its nonprofit status. Employees at the hospital have no reason to feel management is grabbing too big a piece of the pie, particularly because with Prepare 21's open-book style, they know exactly how big that pie is. Selk adds that Prepare 21 helps create the kind of workplace where people want to work: "That's very difficult to quantify, too, but we know from employee-relations feedback that people really appreciate being asked for their ideas." Of course, given the value of those ideas, management is only too happy to oblige.

COMPANY: VATEX AMERICA

Policy/Practice: Educating employees about the business to increase the effectiveness of a profit-sharing plan.

Bottom Line: Those who know, do and those who don't, teach — a wise division of labor in Vatex's experience.

When Jerry Gorde started Vatex America, a Richmond, Virginia–based textile and specialty-item screen-printing outfit, he wanted to accomplish one modest goal besides selling T-shirts: reinventing capitalism. "This is like the Marxist political organizer of the sixties deciding to go into the belly of the monster," he explains as he introduces the original Vatex fantasy: providing decent urban jobs for those with few or no skills; sharing the wealth and power so equitably as to be almost unpatriotic; and teaching everyone on the floor to be just as much of a capitalist as the owner/CEO, or "chief ego officer," as Gorde refers to himself. "And thus we'd create a legitimate model for the Ph.D. candidates to study so we could announce to the world that we'd succeeded in shaping a humanistic capitalism."

Effectively, of course, the whole project pivoted on its toughest challenge: educating workers about how the business worked. The idea, it seems, was that with a little financial enlightenment, they would act — and benefit — like the co-owners that Vatex's employee stock ownership plan (ESOP) would make them. But as Gorde would painfully discover, you can lead Vatexians into the classroom but you can't make them learn economics.

Gorde made his first mistake by trying to teach the course himself: "I assumed that if I spoke in the most simplistic terms that I knew how to, that I would be on the level with the folks that had to absorb this information. I'm a 'street'-looking guy. When I walk through here, it's 'Hi, Jerry,' and I'm of the people. Well, yeah, I am but I'm not, and point in fact is that I did this for ten years not knowing it was over the heads of the majority of people here. I was going home thinking I really had succeeded where others failed, until I sat down and started having conversations with people about what they understood, and they didn't know crap."

Essentially, Gorde tripped over class divisions in his supposedly classless workplace. The production-line folks, mainly from Richmond's black and white underclass, dutifully nodded their heads during lectures but, unbeknownst to Gorde, didn't see why they should be there and were absorbing virtually nothing. Meanwhile, a number of the sales staff, who came from middle-class backgrounds, were absorbing far more than Gorde would have wanted them to, had he known what was about to happen. Says Gorde, "The few that really learned all of those lessons left because they finally had the last piece of information that they needed on how to build a rival business. Not all, but certainly 50 percent of the lifers, people that came on board and said 'I will make my economic life here at Vatex.'"

Gorde didn't get it at first, but the production workers had a point in thinking that the course didn't really apply to them. Although the compensation ratio at Vatex was, and is, one of the country's fairest, with the top salary paid (Gorde's) limited to five times the Vatex average, production people still made incomes far too marginal for stock ownership to mean anything to them. They needed cash for food, rent, and Saturday night, not investments in the future of some street corner factory that was being torn apart from the inside anyway. In fact, even the salespeople, who were starting to raise families and think about buying homes, realized the stock wasn't helping them raise a down payment or even qualify for a mortgage.

Fortunately, one of those who was learning something at Vatex was Gorde himself. He traded in the ten-year-old ESOP on an exceptionally generous, performance-based profit-sharing system that paid bonuses monthly and at year's end, and hired an educational consultant to teach "Vatexomics" to the troops. The consultant built a curriculum that tested employees after each segment to measure whether the information was getting through. And it was, says Gorde: "People were passing the test, so they obviously had to understand things like 'capital' and 'income statement' and balance-sheet information and so on."

So far, so good, but then to save money, Gorde asked the consultant to teach management how to teach the course themselves. Once Vatex took the course over, it was "right back to the soup again," Gorde says, sighing. "The road to hell is paved with good intentions. I'm not of the socioeconomically disadvantaged class. I haven't had a miserable experience with education, I'm not turned off to the process, and I'm not sure how to teach people who are."

If you've followed the story up to here, you know that Vatex is one company that both studies its mistakes and holds to its ideals. The next step the company took — hiring a junior college to develop and teach Vatexomics on-site — is the one that's stuck. Employees take the course on their own time and participation is entirely voluntary, but those who don't pass the course don't get to share in profits. That makes for a powerful incentive, because the profit-sharing system now in place reserves a hefty 10 percent of company profits — 5 percent monthly, and another 5 percent at year's end — for those who qualify, as determined by a combination of attendance and performance factors in addition to the course requirement.

How's it all working? Pretty nicely, admits the usually self-deprecating Gorde, especially after the company began issuing profit-sharing checks separately from paychecks so resistant employees could see what it cost them not to play the Vatex game full-out. Virtually every one of his 120 employees has taken the course, and while he's never numerically measured how Vatex policy changes have changed performance, he's seen attendance — previously a major problem — improve as employees see how it relates to their chunk of profits.

But he's not ready to invite in the doctoral candidates and announce the new millennium quite yet: "I have a sense that we're continually moving toward what we feel are more economically just processes. Whether or not we can actually say that this model should be adopted by other people because it improves the bottom-line result beats the hell out of me. But I know that I have a greater sense of relationship with people that I haven't shared common experiences in life with, because it's a more open, caring, and sharing environment. And I know that I feel more like a *mensch* doing it this way."

COMPANIES: BETH ISRAEL HOSPITAL BOSTON AND MORRISON & FOERSTER

Policy/Practice: Promoting egalitarianism in the workplace.

Bottom Line: Level the playing field and you don't waste as much energy running up hill.

When authors Milton Moskowitz and Robert Levering profiled Beth Israel Hospital Boston and San Francisco–based law firm Morrison & Foerster in their book, *The 100 Best Companies to Work for in America,* they noted that both outfits seemed impressively egalitarian in both policy and practice. That's not unusual for the type of workplace that passes muster for *100 Best,* but it's far from the norm where professional "royalty" like doctors or lawyers are involved. What's different here is that each organization is led by people that don't buy the usual dichotomies between management and staff or between professional and non-.

Dr. Mitchell Rabkin, an endocrinologist, became president of Beth Israel, a leading teaching hospital for Harvard Medical School, in 1966. Although he speaks with the detached precision of an academic, all signs point to his leadership as the place where the hospital's person-centered approach begins. On his first day as president, he eliminated the doctors' dining room, a small space sequestered off the main dining area. All employees wear the same type of pins, and Rabkin makes certain that all information in the physicians' newsletter not uniquely pertinent to them, such as schedules of rounds, is repeated in the employees' edition.

But egalitarianism at Beth Israel runs much deeper than

symbols. Although Rabkin insists that Beth Israel enjoyed a culture of openness long before he took over, he has guided into place participatory management programs that for the first time actively sought input from staff at all levels. Today, improving the hospital's efficiency, quality, and productivity is everyone's job, and the management style is suggestions-from-below, not edicts-from-on-high.

Central to this effort is Prepare 21, a gain-sharing/empowerment program that Rabkin helped institute in the late 1980s (see page 13). But Beth Israel also uses focus groups and other group processes to solicit employee ideas. Manager of training and organizational development Luanne Selk, who had previously worked for a large banking corporation, was shocked at the lack of authoritarianism when she first joined the staff. Asked to design a management development course, "I did that thinking I would just design it and roll it out." Instead, she had to pass it by a group of managers for their feedback.

"At the bank, once I had the vice president's approval, I just did it and everybody fell in line. Here it was clear that the managers were going to have as much say as I did in what the training would look like. The benefit of that of course is that, longer term, you have much higher commitment and a better product. Where I had worked before, people would come and sit in the training session but nothing would change."

Beth Israel is no less fair-minded in the way it carries out its medical functions. That's because in Rabkin's scheme the patient's needs and comfort come first, not the doctor's desire for obeisance. Rabkin: "We don't have, for instance, omni-persons. Everybody here is a patient advocate, and that I think makes a tremendous difference in feeling."

Beth Israel enjoys an unmatched reputation not only for the quality of its nursing but also for the way nurses are treated. The hospital assigns every patient to a registered nurse, who then manages the patient's care in consultation with — not under orders of — the physician. The system affords patients a continuity of care not usually possible in more hierarchical institutions, and nurses a unique measure of respect. Says Rabkin: "We allow and encourage nurses to do what in fact they are trained to do. That doesn't take place in many hospitals."

Rabkin is the first to admit that not every physician immediately buys into Beth Israel's way of viewing things. But in general, "physicians, the chiefs of service, the professors of medicine and surgery etcetera, etcetera, have all been very supportive."

Selk observes that the same culture of mutual respect affects relationships between medical and non–medical professionals: "I have expertise in certain kinds of things, and the clinician has theirs and we rely on and appreciate each other."

Morrison & Foerster has accomplished a comparable culture shift with its own professional aristocracy, its attorneys. Acknowledges chief administrative officer Penelope Douglas, "We aren't perfect in this regard, but we're acutely aware of the value that the firm has held deeply for over one hundred years: respect for every individual in the firm. Clearly, when you have high-pressure situations and a professional environment, there are going to be times when staff feel they're not being regarded as equals. But I think we try very hard through a number of means to make sure that we do the best job that we can in this regard."

Those means extend from such formal steps as making benefits similar for all "MoFo" employees and partners (with some exceptions where MoFo has enhanced the attorney package for competitive recruiting reasons) to the informal custom of calling everyone, regardless of position, by their first names. The firm also shares all organizational information with the entire staff at give-and-take sessions called town meetings. By bringing in some non-attorneys to help manage the firm, MoFo has headed off potential professional conceit from another angle. Says Douglas, "I think that kind of spirit of respect for what people can bring to the party at the top probably helps the feeling going down through the organization."

The firm's long-standing commitment to social justice (see page 184) has also played a part in creating a more equitable work environment. Then again, not all businesses centered on high social ideals spend as much energy as does MoFo on ensuring that the same values carry through inside the company walls. To break down both hierarchical and diversity barriers, for instance, the Los Angeles office solicited feedback from staff in personal interviews, followed that with an office workshop where action plans were formed, and then reviewed progress a year later at a staff-wide retreat.

Only one form of intolerance flies at MoFo — intolerance for violations of core MoFO ideals. And that's as much for pragmatic as humane reasons. Big-league law is a high-pressure, high-stakes game where results can pivot as much on the timely competence of support people as on attorneys' brilliance. Says Douglas, "We're not a public-interest group, we're a business, a very much for-profit business. We want to maintain a set of values that we feel helps us, so we make sure that young attorneys who are thinking of joining us really understand that combination is very important to us."

COMPANY: FEDERAL EXPRESS

Policy/Practice: A multilevel grievance procedure by which employees can get their case heard by top executives and, in some cases, decided by a panel of their peers.

Bottom Line: The ultimate form of employee input: the right to appeal a manager's decision.

When he founded Federal Express in 1973, Frederick W. Smith set out to create something special, not just for management, stockholders, and customers, but for employees as well. He wanted FedEx to be an enlightened workplace where employees were exceptionally well treated, in return for which they would, as the company's *Manager's Guide* reads, "deliver the impeccable service demanded by our customers who will reward us with the profitability to secure our future." "People-Service-Profit" is how they abbreviate this core FedEx strategy, and it works much as Smith drew it up. Profits are an up-and-down matter for any company, especially an airline, but the service is tops, and the people on the whole seem happy to be on board.

What FedEx employees apparently appreciate most about the place is management's commitment to giving them not just a good deal — through generous compensation and a no-layoff policy — but also a fair shake, via a unique procedure called Guaranteed Fair Treatment Process (GFTP). GFTP enables any employee who feels wronged to appeal a manager's decision all the way to the top of the company if need be. A second outstanding feature: of the appeals ladder's three basic rungs, the top two offer the possibility of a trial by peers. Obviously, employees trust the system because they give it a real workout — about 2,000 cases per year in the mid-1990s out of about 88,000 domestic employees. GFTP works like this:

Miffed employees first file a complaint with their immediate manager, initiating what's called a management review in which the first two levels of management get a crack at settling the dispute with the employee. If not satisfied with the management review decision, the employee can file to the next level, where the most senior officer of the employee's operating division presides. Based on his/her investigation of the case's merits, that officer can choose either to grant a peer board of review or uphold or overturn the decision. The peer board is so called because the employee selects three of the five people impaneled to vote on the case.

If the employee still feels improperly judged, he/she effectively gets to knock on Fred Smith's door, because the CEO sits on the board at the final level of appeal, along with the COO, CPO, and two other senior officers on a rotating basis. The appeals board, as it's called, meets every Tuesday and, as the previous level, chooses to either send the case to peer review or make the decision itself.

Although the test in any case is whether the original decision against the employee was according to policy, evidence suggests that FedEx judges on terms more liberal than strictly by the book. Take the case of an employee who was terminated for showing up at work with a rifle in his truck, a violation of FedEx policy forbidding firearms on the premises. The employee had been hunting the day before and had killed a deer, which he left in the truck so he could have it processed after work the next day. When he arrived at work at 6:30 A.M., he asked a dispatcher to move the truck inside the company garage to keep the deer cool. The dispatcher discovered the gun and reported it to management.

When called in to explain himself, the employee claimed to his manager that in his excitement over the deer the previous evening he had forgotten about his rifle. Although the rifle wasn't loaded and there was no ammunition in the vehicle, the manager fired him, stating that he believed the employee's story but that company rules were unequivocal on the matter.

The employee's appeal went all the way to the appeals-board level, where the termination was overturned. The board found the employee's explanation entirely credible — there was a dead deer in the truck, after all, and no ammunition — although it issued him a warning letter and suspended him for thirty days without pay.

Although the appeals board in this case bailed out a manager from a decision he hadn't wanted to make, how do FedEx managers in general take to having their authority and judgment second-guessed? Says James Perkins, senior vice president of personnel/CPO: "Initially, as one might expect, the management people were a little concerned about someone looking over their shoulders, but the impact that it has had is that our management people go out of their way to ensure that our employees are treated fairly."

And should the sense of fair play fail a manager whose decision is reversed in GFTP, says Perkins, "We take a very strong stand that if we can prove retaliation, the person that is guilty of retaliation would be summarily terminated. But I'm certainly not aware of any retaliation that has transpired as a result of any employee using the process. We handle this in our management-training classes."

In 1992, FedEx made a rather major adjustment to GFTP, subsuming under the program's jurisdiction the company's EEO (equal employment opportunity) complaints, few though they were. Perkins explains that most major companies maintain a separate EEO department that receives and investigates complaints "so it gets to be a we/they sort of situation. The only way we felt we could ensure that unfair treatment never entered our environment was for the management people to be responsible and more knowledgeable so they would recognize and eliminate its systemic costs. We provide the necessary training and the consultation of the employee relations, EEO, and legal people where necessary, but it's the upper-level director who's responsible for conducting the investigation. We've found this makes our management people more aware of situations that constitute discrimination or might be perceived as discrimination."

The change goes to the heart of the philosophy that spawned GFTP in the first place, says Perkins: "We think that in a mature organization, that management people need to be responsible for not only the profit and service aspect of the business but also the people aspects. It's a mind-set. When management is responsible, things really start happening if that responsibility is clarified and they're held accountable for the outcome."

COMPANY: 3M

Policy/Practice: Empowering employees to innovate.

Bottom Line: A team that wins by letting everyone play quarterback.

For over two decades now, millions of Americans have been writing reminders to themselves on little adhesive-backed pieces of paper called Post-it Notes. For the 3M corporation, Post-it Notes serve as a different kind of reminder — that empowering employees to spend a chunk of their work time on projects of their own continues to pay huge dividends to the corporation. Post-it Notes, a 3M product, arose from just such an employee-initiated effort; sales now total in the hundreds of millions of dollars annually.

"One of the key goals of the company is that 30 percent of our sales will come from products that did not exist at 3M four years ago," explains Geoffrey Nicholson, vice president of international technical operations and, coincidentally, one of the people who first championed Post-it Notes through 3M's system. To feed that many projects into the pipeline takes a rather comprehensive company-wide effort, which 3M encourages through a variety of means.

Primary among those is the policy that allows employees to spend 15 percent of their time — roughly one day a week — working at whatever they think will move the company forward. Whether that's a new product idea or some way to improve one of their job functions, they don't have to get anyone's permission first. "As a matter of fact," says Nicholson, "if a supervisor comes along and asks, 'What are you doing?,' you can say 'Well, at this point I'm not going to tell you.'"

That may sound like a chaotic way to manage a company, but Nicholson says the policy fits the creative process — "the very initial, chaotic stage of innovation where you're trying out ideas, or perhaps combining technologies to form something new and different." The latter points to the fact that product innovation at 3M doesn't always mean inventing something from scratch. The company also encourages employees to find new uses for old products. Nicholson mentions one 3M item called a hinged flip frame, which is used to hold transparencies for overhead projectors; the hinge, which allows the user to easily insert and remove transparencies from the frame, is made from 3M white medical tape, also a good surface for penning notes. A 3M salesman in Sweden invented the product because he was tired of lugging around the heavy cardboard frames that were the standard way of enclosing transparencies prior to his little invention.

The emphasis on resourcefulness has started to pay environmental dividends as well. For instance, a dozen employees at a 3M factory in Manila came up with a way to make toilet-bowl brushes from the plastic fibers left over from the production of Scotch-Brite cleaning cloths.

Of course, it often takes money as well as time and ingenuity to develop a product idea. Toward that end, 3M's management initiated in the mid-1980s the Genesis and Alpha grant programs, which enable employees to apply for funding for project ideas that may have the potential to do substantial business. Only technical staff may apply for the former but the latter is open to all staff across the company internationally. Grants can reach $150,000, with $25,000 for a two-year span typical, says Nicholson.

While 3M will fund the development of good ideas, it doesn't monetarily reward the inventor if his/her project proves itself out in the marketplace. The inventors of the Post-it Note haven't seen a dime in royalties from it. However, there isn't much evidence that employees resent the absence of cash awards. In fact, claims Nicholson, "Our technical people say they prefer that there isn't any direct compensation, because it would tend to promote people slamming their notebooks to protect their ideas and stopping sharing with each other. One of the key elements of success here is the continuous sharing of technology and information. Not only that, but employees sometimes team up on projects with each one using their 15 percent of [discretionary] time." Nor does the evidence suggest that the cashless acknowledgment system has stifled creativity — the company markets some 60,000 products.

The flip side of not gracing employee-inventors with royalties is not penalizing them for failure. Says Nicholson, "If you want to have your people create some truly radically different things, then you have to accept that failure will be a part of that process, and we fail in about 50 percent of our formal new product programs. We believe that that is an acceptable risk in order to be successful."

In fact, involving non-technical employees in product development has salvaged some potential snafus. 3M packages its Scotch-Brite cleaning cloths in green squares for cleaning floors, but when the company tried to launch the product in the Philippines market, it bombed. The sales and marketing folks suspected that cultural factors might be at play. Sure enough, when they investigated the matter, they discovered that many Filipino women clean floors by pushing half a coconut, brown husk side up, back and forth over the floor with their feet. Nicholson: "So the guy in the sales and marketing area said, 'Well, maybe we should make our Scotch-Brite brown, the color of a coconut, and cut it into the shape of a foot.' Guess what? The sales took off like crazy.

"That certainly wasn't a laboratory development. It's easier for people outside the technical area to think in terms of things like that. So we expect all functions to contribute because they all can do that kind of thing and are challenged to do it. A secretary might just as well have come up with the idea for the Post-it Note. My point is that we shouldn't box them in, because we want people to have that freedom to think of good ideas."

For all the emphasis on innovation, 3M's sales growth slowed to a crawl in the early 1990s — 2 percent from 1991 to 1993 — after a 60 percent rise in the second half of the preceding decade. Management's diagnosis: the company wasn't inventing or getting products to the marketplace fast enough to overcome the drag of recession. So don't expect a rollback in the license given employees to invent.

Besides, the 3M attitude — which goes back to W. L. McKnight, chairman from 1949 to 1966 — is like religion here, says Nicholson: "The McKnight philosophy is that you have more to lose if you start telling people what to do instead of telling them what you want and then allowing them to do it in their own way. As a matter of fact, we tell our people that it's better to ask forgiveness than to ask permission. If they really believe in something, we in management will become the excuse if it doesn't work out."

COMPANY: ZYTEC

> *Policy/Practice:* Reimbursing employees for purchases made to enhance customer service.

> *Bottom Line:* For a thousand bucks, the kind of workforce and customer satisfaction that money can't buy.

On an alphabetical list of companies that empower their employers, Zytec would bring up the rear. But when it comes to putting its money where its rhetoric is, Zytec leads the pack. That's because this Eden Prairie, Minnesota–based electronics supplies manufacturer authorizes its employees — from production workers and part-timers on up — to spend up to

$1,000 any time they think the expenditure will improve customer service. The operative word here is *authorize,* for employees don't need to first obtain anybody's approval, or even fill out a requisition form. And if their manager or supervisor won't pay the bill, vice president for marketing and sales John Steel will.

Since 1984 or so, Steel recalls, Zytec had followed the gospel of the late W. Edwards Demings, who preached that the key to improving quality and productivity, and thus growth and success, was to, as Steel paraphrases, "give the tools to the employees closest to the problem and get out of their way." Then Steel read a book, Ron Zemke's *Service America,* that so crystallized Zytec's Deming-ish service strategy that he and some other managers fashioned a course for employees named for it.

Steel remembers, "We were trying to get them to understand customer needs and how to respond to them — 'When in doubt, say yes' and all that good stuff. And then somebody in the group said if we really believe this, why don't we give employees the tools to say yes, and one of those tools is money."

In Zytec's egalitarian culture, the logic of the proposal was hard to refute. Steel arbitrarily set the amount at $1,000, established the no-rules rules, and informed the accounting department, which, Steel says, chuckling, "almost had a coronary, as you can well imagine. They wanted all kinds of restrictions. 'They should at least talk to their boss' or 'We should have a budget and when the budget is low, we tell them the program's dead until we get more money in the budget.'"

Employees, of course, received the idea more positively, but many still found it hard to believe that management would place so much faith in them. Part-time quotations analyst Becky Miller had been with the company only a couple of months when her son became seriously ill, needing periodic hospitalization and long periods of home care. Steel allowed her to work at home so she could be with her son, but the constant transiting between there and the office to pick up documents quickly wore thin and also made it hard to service customers in a timely fashion. She knew a fax machine could make all the difference, but balked at purchasing one until co-workers assured her that Steel meant what he said about the Service America initiative: "When I brought the receipt in, John signed it with no questions and said 'What a great way to use the program!' He was so supportive."

Today, Miller's son is fine and she does most of her work at the office. But the fax machine stays home, receiving late-evening messages from customers in Ireland and Austria. Miller is often firing information back across the Atlantic by 6:00 A.M., three hours before she arrives at Zytec. The customers are happy, and so is Miller: "If something came up where I needed to make another purchase to do my job better, I wouldn't hesitate."

Not all employees have been as quick as Miller to implement Service America. Because Zytec doesn't track the money spent through the initiative, Steel can't measure the effectiveness of the program, or even how often employees use it, but, he says, "My sense is, the policy is used far less than we had expected and, to be quite frank, probably far less than what I wish. When you've got 600 or 700 employees who think they have the power to make a yes decision providing customer service, you've got a powerful company with a distinct advantage in the marketplace."

Steel doesn't know of specific instances where the Service America initiative has been abused, but, he says, "I'm sure it has been. Our sick-leave policy gets abused. Our vacation policy gets abused. We used to write policies and procedures to catch the 2 percent of abusers and we ended up with a manual big enough to break your desk. We threw that out and wrote a manual to satisfy the 98 percent. So I'm sure that some Service America money has been misspent.

"But I'll tell you," he adds, laughing, "that we in management have misspent considerably more of the company's money, by buying the wrong equipment or hiring the wrong person. Somebody misspending $1,000 in a $100 million-plus company is peanuts compared to what we in management have screwed up."

When companies newly empower employees, middle managers feeling correspondingly disempowered may strike back at their charges if senior management doesn't take preventive steps. Service America weathered one such stormy episode. "An employee went to our class and then made a decision two or three weeks later to do something that cost about $450," Steel recalls. "The employee was loudly and publicly berated by his manager. The other employees saw this and said 'If that's what happens, what is this stuff John Steel talks about? Here somebody tries the program and he gets called on the carpet.' I heard about it through the grapevine and had to spend a whole bunch of time doing damage control. We've probably only had one incident like that but it takes a lot of effort to undo the harm."

The fact that the snafu was so isolated underscores Zytec's deep commitment to empowerment, well established there long before Steel birthed the Service America program. Self-managed teams organize the company's work, nobody punches a time clock, and employees manage their own time off as well, with vacation and sick leave lumped together for their use. Hundreds of workers at all levels also participate in Zytec's long-range strategic planning sessions and travel around the world to meet with customers. Irish customer Stratus was so satisfied with Zytec's quality that it asked the company to send a couple of representatives to receive a special reward. Zytec sent the account manager and a woman whose name had been drawn from a hat containing the names of all factory workers who had helped build the Stratus product.

So the reimbursement program simply reinforces what was already a pro-employee tradition. Says Steel, "The policy works for Zytec. I wouldn't be so presumptuous as to say it would work for another company. You have to have a culture and a value system of trust. I graduated from the University of Minnesota in 1968, where I learned that you never ask non-managers to think, to add value, or to contribute on the job because only college graduates are smart enough. Before I could accept Deming and some of the others, I had to erase some of the old tapes, and that's tough to do. But once you do it, you never go back."

Job Security

Company: S C Johnson Wax

Policy/Practice: Compassionate downsizing and restructuring.

Bottom Line: One of the best places to work in America is also one of the best places from which to lose a job.

In late 1994, a wire-service story defending the corporate downsizing trend appeared in newspaper business sections across the country. According to the article, a majority of corporations surveyed after amputating large chunks of their workforce claimed that their productivity rose as a result. Toward the end of the piece, almost as an afterthought, the writer noted that nearly 90 percent of the downsized companies also reported substantial drops in employee morale. Several conclusions may be drawn from this information, but one that is inescapable is that a number of major employers no longer seem to weigh the importance of employee goodwill.

They see things differently at household product maker S C Johnson Wax in Racine, Wisconsin. In 1976, the company — a generous, caring employer for well over a century — articulated its core philosophy in an employee and manager handbook titled "This We Believe." Central to that philosophy is a pledge, paraphrases Garvin Shankster, senior vice president of human resources, "to manage our business in such a way that we can provide security for all the employees and also our retirees." In the company's view, that's just good business, Shankster explains: "We believe that the commitment of our people to our company and to our business objectives is not only important but can be a competitive advantage, and therefore we want to do things that maintain that commitment."

Which is not to say that Johnson Wax hasn't done its own share of employee shuffling. Like many corporations of its size — Johnson Wax is one of America's 150 biggest — the company has downsized and restructured in recent years. But true to the company's core values, Shankster's department has gone to near-exhaustive lengths to find displaced employees decent employment, either at Johnson Wax or elsewhere.

Shankster recalls one of the rare times in recent years where the company felt compelled to close an operation, a manufacturing facility in France. The company had no other jobs in the country to offer the employees, he adds, so "we communicated clearly the rationale of why we had to take the action. We put together a very generous compensation arrangement for the employees, and then we actually developed some small businesses that we had one of our key executives help oversee for individuals that didn't have employment. This was a way for them to transcend and have some income over and above this separation until they got employment. Then we worked with them and all the local industries until we placed all of our employees, so it was a combination of efforts. We are not a company, even in those situations, that tells employees 'We're closing the door, here's your money, now you go and solve your problems.'"

Although it wasn't possible in the French situation, Johnson Wax normally attempts to place as many uprooted employees as possible within the company, through a variety of approaches. For instance, after selling off a skin- and hair-care business, it brought back in-house business that it had outsourced to create jobs for those who were displaced by the sale. In other cases, management will invest in retraining, "although obviously employees have to be willing to accept the retraining and the new job responsibilities," says Shankster.

If need be, Shankster and his staff can also search a company employment database that identifies positions opening up through normal attrition. However, people rarely depart Johnson Wax except to retire or because they've chosen to relocate, says Shankster, so the search isn't always that fertile. Employees who can't be placed through any of the above efforts are carried at full compensation on what is called "displaced status, meaning they're available for placement for several months until we can appropriately get them repositioned within our company," Shankster explains. In the meantime, management gives them temporary assignments.

"The last option that we ever look at to solve our problem," asserts Shankster, "is having people leave the company. If we get into a situation where we don't think we'll be able to appropriately absorb the displaced personnel in a year or two, we'll go to offering a voluntary separation plan. In many cases, people will voluntarily elect to take that offer because they think it might be a better option for their career, given the fact that we don't have an appropriate placement for them here. The separation arrangement is very competitive [and] on the generous side, and we think that is very, very appropriate to have it that way."

In one situation in the 1980s, the company did have trouble placing all of the employees at a restructured factory, so it offered a $20,000 check to any factory worker who volunteered to leave the company. Shankster: "The actual separation payment that even new hires get would still have to be sufficient to help them transcend from this employment situation to another one. Irrespective of service, we will give everybody the resources they need to help find another job if they're voluntarily leaving."

Certainly, the fact that Johnson Wax has been family owned and managed since its founding in 1886 explains much of the company's benevolence toward its workforce. Nobody here is trying to impress Wall Street with how savagely they can control costs. Still, the competitive climate is such today that Johnson Wax might well get away with some savagery of its own if it had the inclination. But the company — which didn't lay anyone off during the Great Depression, either — doesn't seem to be the least bit tempted. In an era when even highly profitable companies are dumping workers by the thousands, this is one place where employers have history on their side.

COMPANY: RHINO FOODS

Policy/Practice: Loaning temporarily unneeded employees to other companies instead of laying them off.

Bottom Line: An elastic workforce that stretches and contracts with company fortunes, while boosting — not decimating — company morale.

Production workers at specialty-dessert maker Rhino Foods were feeling pretty smug about their job security in the spring of 1993. The Burlington, Vermont–based company makes the dough pellets for Ben & Jerry's hugely popular Chocolate Chip Cookie Dough ice cream. It had supplied 3.5 million pounds of cookie dough in 1992 alone. Now the weather was warming up again and customers would be buying more ice cream to beat the heat. If anything, they figured, the company would soon be adding employees.

They'd figured wrong. Rhino's new facility and equipment, plus innovations made by process-improvement teams, were enabling the company to produce far more product, and with greater efficiency, than before. And Ben & Jerry's was debuting seven new flavors for the upcoming summer, cutting into their Chocolate Chip Cookie Dough ice cream output. That meant smaller orders from Rhino.

In most other companies, management would have decreed a layoff to fit the workforce to the changed conditions, wreaking havoc on the lives of employees and their families. Rhino, too, had cut its workforce as recently as the preceding fall.

Despite its own layoff history, however, Rhino is a progressive employer, committed to its employees' personal growth and empowerment (see page 113), its local community's needs, and ultimately the desire to "impact the manner in which business is done," as its mission statement declares. The mission statement also defines the company as one "whose actions are inspired by the spirit of discovery, innovation, and creativity." True to that spirit, founder/president Ted Castle and human resources director Marlene Dailey resolved to address *this* overcapacity problem inventively. And the deepest pool of company inventiveness lay within the workforce itself.

Recalls Castle, "We have a company meeting at least every other week, so I asked who would like to work on this approaching situation. I think we had then fifty employees and twenty-six people raised their hands."

The volunteers represented every department at Rhino. But despite their gratitude about being asked for ideas, few believed the inquiry would lead anywhere besides job cuts. They soon saw that Castle and Dailey meant what they said — they wanted a permanent solution for downturns in the business cycle and they wanted that solution to both protect profits and the Rhino-ites who had helped build them.

The committee met twice a week for four weeks. Dozens of worthy ideas emerged, but one — loaning employees to companies with a need for temporary help — seemed to uniquely meet the test of a permanent policy that preserved jobs. The only drawback: no one knew of another company that had attempted such a thing, so they were navigating uncharted waters.

Nevertheless, the committee pressed ahead, supported on the administrative end by Dailey and Toni Cook, who oversees the company's social and community endeavors. To make the experience as satisfactory as possible for the loaned workers, the committee decided that the alternative work sites should have values and employment policies similar to Rhino's. Although the alternative sites would pay employees' salaries, Rhino would pay any difference to prevent workers from losing pay, and would maintain benefits and profit sharing as well. The company would also reserve the right to recall its employees with two weeks' notice.

While Dailey found several companies interested in taking Rhino employees. However, only two — Gardener's Supply, Rhino's neighbor in Burlington, and Ben & Jerry's in nearby Waterbury — were able to act quickly enough to meet Rhino's needs. But those two were plenty. After reassurance by Castle that their jobs were secure, eleven employees — about 20 percent of the Rhino workforce — volunteered to take part and were soon packing gardening supplies or working the ice-cream side of Chocolate Chip Cookie Dough production.

Results of the "Great Employee Exchange Experiment" were in two months later. Final score: win-win. Rhino saved valued employees, salaries, and increased unemployment insurance fees in one fell swoop. At least as important, the company also cemented its bond of trust with its workforce. And the employees returned with new ideas and skills to share. For example, those who worked at Ben & Jerry's saw how their staff rotates lunches and breaks instead of shutting down the production line. The idea had been proposed at Rhino; it now had backing from employees who had seen it work firsthand.

The borrowing companies also liked the way the program played out, both in getting work done and the unintended but welcome side effect of cultural exchange. Ellen DesJardin, production supervisor at Gardener Supply, informed Rhino that their employees did a far better job for Gardener than the usual seasonal workers: "They were production oriented, so they came up to speed much quicker. On their first day, whenever there was some time between packing jobs, they found things to do that needed to be done. They were great at suggesting better and faster ways we might do things."

As of this writing, Rhino hasn't needed to negotiate a second exchange (Gardener Supply called twice after the first go-around to request more loaned employees, but with its orders back to normal Rhino had to decline). However, the company now has a smoothly functioning program in place should the need arise again. "The employee exchange is part of who we are now," says Castle. "We knew how to hire people. Now we also know how to exchange employees."

In both directions, as it turns out. In 1994, Rhino found itself temporarily needing more, not fewer, production workers and borrowed some from a landscaping company that had earlier shown interest in the exchange program. Nor does Castle see any reason why future exchanges need be limited to the production line: "I think you could do it with anybody — sales, marketing, accounting people, whoever."

For a company that has always tried to do business more humanely, the exchange experience has been especially gratifying. Castle and Dailey consider their original intuition — that employees can usually find creative solutions to problems, particularly those that threaten their jobs — thoroughly confirmed. "That doesn't mean that we wouldn't lay people off in the future," Castle acknowledges, "but we're going to try a bunch of other things first."

COMPANY: H. B. FULLER

Policy/Practice: Going several extra miles to protect employees' jobs.

> ***Bottom Line:*** Rewarding employees' allegiance is also an investment in it.

"There's a genuine commitment and concern for people here which is considered sort of outdated these days. We hear a lot about downsizing, reengineering, and the fact that employers no longer repay the loyalties of their employees, but things are just different here at H. B. Fuller."

The speaker is Jim Metts, vice president of human resources for the St. Paul, Minnesota–based specialty-chemical company and thus not exactly an unbiased observer. But then you open a company annual report, and there in the frontispiece, in print so large that no one can miss it, is the company's mission statement, which declares, "H. B. Fuller Company is committed to its responsibilities, *in order of priority* [my emphasis], to its customers, employees, shareholders and communities." When was the last time you saw a major corporation publicly subordinate the interests of investors to those of its workers, particularly in a document prepared primarily for the former's consumption?

You understand even more about the company's commitment to employment security when you examine the policies and heritage behind the rhetoric. In 1978, the company comprehensively examined its overall social responsibility. That effort produced among other things a document entitled "H. B. Fuller's Responsibility to its Employees," which included an employment-security policy declaring that "in the event of a work shortage at a facility, non-sales employees with two or more years of service with the company will not be laid off *nor* [*sic*] have their hours worked and paid reduced to less than 32 hours per week unless the *total Company* actually reports a loss (negative earnings) at fiscal year end." To date, Fuller has more than kept its pledge. It has never ordered a layoff.

The above implies that Fuller has also never had a losing year, which also is true as of this writing. But it's not as if the policy hasn't been tested. Profits declined in the two consecutive years prior to 1990, and dropped 39 percent in fiscal

1993. And between 1982 and 1993, the company condensed thirty plants into twenty. The plant closings were particularly trying for Fuller, since it hadn't closed many before and had no established practices for implementing its promise to save jobs. What it did have was a commitment to its people and its culture. Management gave the affected employees six months' notice and notified them of all available Fuller positions in the United States. The company then relocated those who wished with the same benefits due Fuller professionals, including a moving bonus of 120 percent of a month's pay. It helped the others find local jobs.

The procedures apparently worked for all concerned because most are in effect today (one exception — minimum notice is ninety days after a cease-production date has been set), along with several others that insulate employees as much as possible from the vagaries of the business cycle. For example, the company covers both the sales commission cost on the current home and closing costs on the new one for relocating employees who own their homes. The company also pays all usual expenses for house hunting, travel to the new location, and transport of household goods, and otherwise helps ease the hardships of moving.

Of course, modern workers face almost as much threat from new technology as they do from ax-wielding accountants, but Fuller has thought that one through as well: its employee responsibility document promises that the company will retrain all employees whose jobs become obsolete. If an employee can't handle the new job due to a mismatch of interests, abilities, or skills, the company endeavors to place him/her in a more suitable position.

Clearly, Fuller's leaders feels that its people-oriented approach makes good business sense, but they also take the company's stakeholder pledges to heart. For instance, Fuller gives generously — 5 percent of pretax profits — to communities where its plants are located. In fact, employees in factories with work slowdowns are paid to do community service when the company can't find enough work for them at the plant.

The impressive profits turned in by corporate America in

the early and mid-1990s were built in large part on the backs of severed workers. Obviously, the savagery of the competitive climate has made life tougher for Fuller and other corporate holdouts that refuse to feed off the pain of their own. In fact, Bill Belknap, Fuller's public relations director, carefully points out that H. B. Fuller does not have a no-layoff policy, just a no-layoff history. But that in itself stands out in an era when several other well-known corporate giants can't even claim the reverse.

PAY

COMPANY: BLACK BOX

Policy/Practice: Providing positive pay incentives to employees.

Bottom Line: A compensation game that everyone can win and productivity that can't be beat.

A few years ago, Pittsburgh–based Black Box Corporation, which markets computer network and other communications devices, found itself nose to nose with an all-too-contemporary dilemma. Like other American companies, it was eliminating layers of management to flatten its organization. Yes, the new structure put more responsibility and decision-making ability in the hands of frontline employees, which they welcomed. But it also knocked several rungs off the career ladder, leaving those same frontliners depressed about their future prospects with the company.

Fortunately, management responded with a solution as smart as the technology it deals. With the company unable to offer the range of promotions it once had, it effectively gave employees the ability to advance themselves, in skills and compensation. Today, an order-entry clerk who starts out at the $17,000 to $20,000 level can make as much as $35,000 in the same job by increasing his/her value to the company, as measured by a number of objective tests. And that base-pay increase is only one of several ways employees can enhance their earnings. Pay for performance has worked so well for Black Box as both a motivator and productivity booster that the company has built positive incentives into nearly every aspect of its culture, including the opportunity to make some unusually lucrative bonuses.

The heart of the Black Box system is a set of objective criteria by which management can measure both employee and company performance. The company divides employees into three classes — developmental, competent, and premium — according to their impact on the company and then pays them according to a range within those categories as determined by, again, strictly objective evaluations. For example, because Black Box does considerable international business, order entry clerks directly increase their value to the company as they gain the ability to speak to customers in the latter's native tongue, which customers greatly appreciate.

The company also monitors and tests clerks on the number of calls they can field and how well they handle them, the number of errors they make in entering the order, and so on. Each of these measures comes with pay consequences, because each contributes to productivity and, again, customer satisfaction. Black Box gives employees every chance to win the compensation game because when they win the company does, too. So for instance, the company reimburses 100 percent of tuition for job-related course work — if the employee can demonstrate competency when the course is completed — and teaches languages on-site.

Unusually able employees love the objective system because by demonstrating their ability, they can leapfrog over several pay grades even if they just joined the company. Explains president Jeff Boetticher, "We've had some people in the 'developmental' category actually manifest skills in the 'competent' category. A traditional company would say, 'Well, Mary Jane Jones can't possibly be that good because she hasn't been here long enough.' Here, if you can perform consistently to the next level of expectation, then you've earned the right to be at the next level and to be compensated accordingly."

By the same token, says Boetticher, objectivity is a two-edged sword. Employees who don't perform up to the level of their compensation category can be downgraded. However, the company first gives them a set period of time to raise their performance level and, notes Boetticher, "I'm pleased to report that in the time that we've been doing this, I've only seen one instance that somebody didn't rise to that challenge."

Black Box refers to its workers as "team members," and rewards them for team wins as well. As a baseline incentive, the company matches thirty cents on the dollar for employee contributions to their 401(k) plan, but the match can more than double based upon the revenue growth and profitability of the company. Black Box team members obviously know a good deal when they see one, because about 85 percent of the workforce participates in the plan. All team members except for commission salespeople are also eligible for annual bonuses, which — again, based on revenue growth and profitability — can increase an employee's compensation by anywhere from 4 to 40 percent of base salary.

In fact, in some special cases, employees can do far better than that, says Boetticher: "In 1993, we tied our warehouse guys' compensation specifically to the performance of their group against certain objectives with the understanding that they got nothing unless the company made it. Well, the company obviously made it but these guys did an exceptional job of reducing the errors per thousand boxes shipped, reducing the cost per box shipped, and meeting their on-time delivery criteria. They got a 160 percent bonus payout that year."

Then again, your fellow employees may send you home in a black box if you're perceived as letting down the team. Boetticher: "The last quarter of the fiscal year, depending where we are in our growth cycle, can get pretty interesting because of peer pressure and things like that. Sometimes our salespeople are the most popular people on the planet and sometimes our salespeople would benefit from someone else starting their car."

Incentive payouts have worked so well for this solidly successful company that Boetticher is always hunting for new ways to issue them. In 1992, he initiated something called the Premier Achievement Club award, which pays, yes, yet more bonus money to employees offering productive suggestions — from 2 to 6 percent of base salary based on the suggestion's merit and effect on the company. "It keeps us on top of our game," he says, "and throughout the year, there are probably fifteen, twenty, thirty people who participate in that, whose suggestions and recommendations are scrutinized and implemented." As you might have guessed by now, Black Box also uses incentives to keep its team members healthy — subsidizing gym memberships, paying for smoking-cessation courses for employees who successfully complete them, and so on.

For all the incentive system's advantages for team member and employer alike, Boetticher admits that many employees were upset about the new approach at first. The fact that employees are being measured puts the onus on them to measure up. When the new criteria were put in place, some team members got immediate raises. But others didn't, based on those same criteria, and mourned the more subjective system of the past. "Change is painful," Boetticher admits with a shrug, "but I think because everybody realized that we were treating them on a level playing field, people embraced it and they knew it wasn't going to be a moving target."

One of the most impressive results of the Black Box system, says Boetticher, has been the way it has enabled the company to grow without increasing head count. And it's not too hard to figure out why: with everybody chasing pay-grade increases and fatter bonuses, productivity rises like floodwaters. As Boetticher points out, "The guy who used to run from the building at 5:00 says, 'If I make a few more phone calls or I work on this project and invest another hour or two, I'll see that manifest itself in real-life compensation.'" Perhaps Boetticher should consider changing the company's name because there's no mystery about what makes Black Box work.

COMPANY: BEN & JERRY'S

Policy/Practice: A fundamental commitment to pay equity.

Bottom Line: A heartfelt goal but some remaining uncertainty about how to get there.

Author's note: Most practices described in this book have a far more stable record of success than this one. But Ben & Jerry's resolve to bring some sanity to the compensation spread in American corporations has received so much attention, and been the model for so many other idealistic companies, that its managers' internal struggles with the issue deserve closer examination. Besides, the company's efforts to align its compensation values with its ever-shifting reality still instruct. Even when Ben & Jerry's gets it wrong, the company breaks new and important ground.

In mid-1994, Ben & Jerry's announced that CEO Ben Cohen was stepping down so the company could hire a more experienced hand to grow the business. Oh yes, the press release continued, the company would be dropping its famed salary ratio because it might have to pay market rates — several times the $100,000-plus that Cohen pulls down — to lure a properly seasoned executive to the job.

The subsequent search unfolded in typical B & J style. Applicants were asked to submit with their résumés a 100-word essay on "Why I Would Be a Great CEO for Ben & Jerry's." Anxious to impress, an ad exec attached his résumé to a Superman's costume; a woman sent a near-nude photo with hers.

But the comic sideshow couldn't mask some serious concerns. To longtime fans of the company, the ratio — which limited executive salary and benefits value, including the compensation paid to founders Ben and Jerry themselves, to seven times that of the lowest-paid employee — had been a pillar of the company's commitment to just management. Media cynics had always regarded the company's progressive social initiatives as hopelessly idealistic. But maybe they had a point. Perhaps unforgiving realities were forcing Ben & Jerry's to start singing a less liberal tune.

Not to worry, says Cohen: "The numerical ratio has been abandoned. The value has been maintained. The plan going forward is to pay upper-level people at the bottom end of market rates and pay lower-level people at the top end of market rates. The plan at this point is not to change the compensation of anybody in the company except for paying the new CEO above the seven-to-one ratio."

Placing the matter in context shows that even a worst-case scenario leaves Ben & Jerry's firmly planted on the right side of the issue. In the typical corporation, notes *Business Week,* the CEO makes 157 times what average factory workers earn. Recruiters estimate that the CEO market rate for a company Ben & Jerry's size — about $154 million in sales — to be $300,000 to $500,000. The company's top possible salary in mid-1994 was $140,000 (of which Ben and Jerry themselves only take $132,000, says Cohen.) A $300,000 CEO would widen the Ben & Jerry's salary gap to fifteen to one; paying an executive $500,000 would only bump the ratio to twenty-five to one, still exemplary. By comparison, Herman Miller, Inc., the originator of "salary compression" among substantial U.S. companies, limits top compensation to twenty times the average Miller salary. To my knowledge, no other major company is close.

The obvious lesson from Ben & Jerry's experience is that if you plan to get a salary ratio, do some long-term thinking first. Ben & Jerry's directors — Ben Cohen, co-founder Jerry Greenfield, Jeff Furman, and Fred "Chico" Lager — set theirs arbitrarily at five to one in the early years of the company, after Furman, enamored of a group of Spanish cooperatives called Mondragon that operated under a three-to-one ratio, suggested the idea.

At the time, Ben & Jerry's was a $4 million company, and although top management all paid themselves well below going rates, the difference wasn't as great as it would be after a few years' worth of explosive growth. Despite the firm statement the policy made to the outside world, the quartet had never agreed amongst themselves if the ratio was the proper vehicle to accomplish the pay equity that was its goal. When the need arose to hire more professional business types to help manage the increasingly complex organization, dissension grew in lockstep.

As Greenfield sums up, "Clearly, the salary ratio has been the most difficult issue for us to resolve at the board level that we've ever had." But analysis of the ratio's problems shift depending upon whom you talk to at the company. Although Greenfield now counts himself among those that consider the ratio a failed experiment, the loudest dissenter all along has been former CEO Lager, still a director. "I was opposed to the policy because I thought it would be an obstacle to recruiting," he says, maintaining that the company's past difficulties in filling positions that would be highly compensated in other companies has proved him right. The company did increase the ratio to seven to one in 1990, when it was a $77 million business, but blunted the effect by changing the ratio from salary-only to total compensation.

Lager: "Essentially we were saying to people, not only take a 30, 40, 50 percent pay cut from what you're making, but if you work your heart out — which is what it takes, sixty to seventy hours a week — a year from now we'll give you a $5,000 raise if we can give our scoopers another fifty cents an hour. There was no payoff from [stock], from a bonus, from anything. Some people would say, 'Sure, I'll come in for less salary if there's a payoff for doing a great job,' but there was no carrot, either."

Lager also feels the ratio became a crutch that kept management from reflecting deeply about other ways to acknowledge its frontline people's contribution, such as through gain sharing or more input into decisions. "The bottom line is how well people get treated and whether or not you have a commitment to their personal well-being, and I think we had that. The aspect of the company that I think really conveys its commitment to sharing is its benefits, which are very much across-the-board. We are a perkless company." Indeed, Ben & Jerry's even gives its on-site child-care staff a regular company compensation package, highly unusual in American business.

Furman and Cohen continue to be the ratio's firmest advocates, but even Greenfield feels that the company's previous recruiting difficulties "were much more a result of lack of recruiting expertise." And all three remain optimistic that the company will find a CEO willing to work within the company's previous compensation culture. Furman: "I'm chair of the search committee and I'm looking for someone whose values are very much in line with the company. If their rhetoric is 'Our values are aligned and make sure I'm getting my half a million dollars a year,' then I don't see how that person really fits into the organization."

Interestingly, Herman Miller seems to have avoided much of the turmoil seen at Ben & Jerry's by setting its ratio higher. J. Kermit Campbell eagerly joined Miller in 1992 as its CEO, even though his roughly $500,000 salary was far below market for this near-billion-dollar outfit and the twenty-to-one requirement would severely limit his raises. Admits Lager, "I think if [the ratio] had been set at a different level, it could have accomplished the same thing without being so restrictive." (Postscript: In early 1995, Ben & Jerry's hired Robert Holland, Jr., as its new CEO. As reported in *Business Ethics,* he will be paid $250,000 per year plus stock options.)

Benefits

Company: Fel-Pro

Policy/Practice: Perhaps the best all-around benefit package in America.

Bottom Line: The gifts that keep on giving, the investment that keeps on paying off.

In the intensely competitive world of business, staying in step with your rivals is supposed to be a minimum requirement for survival. Yet one of the nation's most out-of-step companies remains one of its best. Fel-Pro, a Skokie, Illinois, maker of automotive and industrial gaskets, sealants, lubricants, and adhesives, offers its workers one of America's most lavish total compensation packages in an era when employee wages and benefits have been shrinking for two decades. So explain how a company with such high fixed costs has never suffered an unprofitable quarter in over thirty years of operation?

Employee morale and longevity certainly seem to supply part of the answer. As of late 1994, crane operator Andrew Collins had worked for Fel-Pro for nearly seven years after trying to find a home at half a dozen previous employers: "I feel more respected here than at other companies. It's like a family here."

Indeed, start with the benefits for employees' children. Those begin literally the day the child is born, when the company enters a $1,000 Treasury bond in the child's name, payable on his or her twenty-first birthday. (Mom, by the way, receives flowers from the company and a pair of inscribed shoes for baby.) At two, kids can start coming to the company's on-site day-care center. When they reach school age, Fel-Pro provides subsidized professional in-home care if they get sick (parent's cost: sixteen dollars per day). As they approach high school graduation, professional counselors paid for by Fel-Pro will help them and their parents choose a college; once enrolled, Fel-Pro assists them with up to $3,300 per year to offset tuition costs!

Other child and family benefits include $100 toward diapers or diaper service for parents who attend the company's free prenatal program; subsidized in-home tutoring for children with functional or emotional disabilities; and an elder-care resource-and-referral service. Then there's summer day camp for kids and family recreation for employees at the company's 220-acre Triple R ("rest, relaxation, and recreation") recreation area in wooded rolling hills forty miles from headquarters; parents pay twenty-five dollars per child per week for the day camp. The company provides summer jobs for employees' kids as well, hiring them to fill temporary positions and paying them above minimum wage.

Nor do the profuse family programs come at the expense of adult benefits and perks, traditional or non-. Besides the basic medical and dental plan, the package includes a liberal profit-sharing plan, on-site physical fitness facilities and wellness classes, full tuition reimbursement for employees continuing their education, group auto insurance, free annual eye exam and a pair of glasses, and a $1,000 check upon retirement.

And the above doesn't count the frills around the edges: an attorney who visits the work site weekly to consult with employees on their legal matters; a voucher for professional income tax preparation; a $100 check as a wedding gift; $250 when a family member dies; an extra day's pay on birthdays, employment anniversaries, and on June 1 (spending cash for summer vacations); two free changes of work clothes each year; special holiday gifts (for instance, a canned ham at Easter and a turkey each Christmas); and even a twenty-by-twenty-foot gardening plot at Triple R plus free gardening tools, water, and plowing for employees who want to grow food there.

According to co-chairman Ken Lehman, the Fel-Pro formula justifies itself in terms of simple enlightened self-interest: "Our founders, who were my grandfather and my great-grandfather, brought to business the idea that if you treat people fairly and give them as congenial a place to work as you can, they're going to more than repay you in terms of their loyalty, their creativity, their dedication."

A study of Fel-Pro's workforce by University of Chicago researchers confirms the founders' intuition. Between 1990 and 1992, the researchers queried 882 of the company's then-2,000-person workforce about Fel-Pro's family-responsive benefits. The results showed that the policies improved job performance across the board, and particularly affected "voluntary behaviors conducive to organizational change."

For instance, high benefit users were the most likely to make quality improvement suggestions and otherwise participate in the company's quality programs; were the employees most open to change, including the transition from traditional departments to teams; and were more likely to report helping out co-workers and their supervisor. They had the highest performance evaluations as well as the lowest intentions of leaving Fel-Pro. The study also measured how Fel-Pro employees valued the benefits, best illustrated by the fact that 66 percent of the 882 respondents disagreed or strongly disagreed with the statement, "I'd rather have more profit sharing and fewer benefits."

But there's more than method to Fel-Pro's "madness." Lehman says that the founders believed employers are obligated "to provide what can be provided within the size and scope and economics of their business." And so whenever someone in management or ownership (the company is 100 percent owned and controlled by the founding families) gets an idea for a new benefit, the company is likely to try it if it judges it can afford the expense. For instance, the Triple R facility was suggested by Lehman's aunt, a principal stockholder who's never worked for Fel-Pro.

Some critics see Fel-Pro's generosity as no more than a cynical attempt to keep employees from organizing. Lehman, a Peace Corps volunteer in the 1960s, flatly rejects the notion: "We aren't an anti-union company. If companies had taken the attitude at their inception that we've taken, there wouldn't have been the crying need for unions that there once was. Our attitude is that if we can't work with our employees and give them a workplace that speaks to their needs and serves our customers and if we can't do it together in partnership, then they deserve a union." Milton Moskowitz and Robert Levering interviewed several Fel-Pro workers while reviewing the company for *The 100 Best Companies to Work for in America*. "None of the employees we talked with felt they had been bought off by the benefits," they wrote.

As if to underscore the point, management's benevolence is manifested in many ways besides compensation. The open communication style and involvement of employees in problem solving and suggestions signify a heartfelt commitment to worker-centered business, as does the company's Better Neighborhood fund, an employee-administered grants program that has donated $2 million over the last couple of decades to local community organizations in the neighborhoods where employees live and raise their families. And Collins and director of administrative services Deborah Morrin seem even more impressed by Fel-Pro's walk than its talk. States Collins: "Everybody works together here instead of individually." An equally reverent Morrin extols the congeniality and accessibility of senior management and the lack of executive perks or other elitism.

Lehman admits that management has felt the heat in recent years from rivals with lower compensation costs: "It's not driving us to abandon our philosophy or any of our programs, but it is placing a lot of pressure on us to work smarter. But we still subscribe to our basic belief that we have to treat our people fairly. The benefit structure that we provide gives them things that they couldn't do on their own. It also puts their mind at rest and brings them to work in an optimal frame of mind to devote themselves to the job at hand."

It keeps them at Fel-Pro as well. If this company sounds like a place you'd like to work, you'll have to stand in a long line. At any one time, the waiting list of applicants numbers in the thousands. That gives management the ability to pick the best people around. It also creates a workforce and company that clearly deserve each other, in the best sense of those words.

COMPANY: SHAMAN PHARMACEUTICALS

Policy/Practice: Providing groceries so employees can prepare meals at work.

Bottom Line: Great for camaraderie and tougher on the belt line than the balance sheet.

Shaman Pharmaceuticals' free meals program began modestly enough. There wasn't a good place nearby to run out for eats at the company's original location in San Carlos, California, recalls founder and president/CEO Lisa Conte, especially with the late hours everyone was keeping to get the fledgling drug company off the ground. So one of the quartet of folks that composed Shaman at that point would hustle over to Safeway for sandwich makings and cookies. Before long, what had been a gastric necessity became policy. Staff made the food runs and the company paid the tab.

Today, says Conte with a chuckle, the program "is totally

out of hand" — the company feeds 110 people daily, at an annual cost in the low six figures, she estimates — and she couldn't be happier about it. What better way, she says, to unite Shaman's support staff and highly credentialed researchers than over a good meal? The bonding power of the program became especially apparent in 1992, when the three-year-old company moved into beautiful new digs in South San Francisco that included a large kitchen. Soon, Shaman's food shoppers were stocking not just cold cuts but, per staff requests, the ingredients for exotic hot entrees. It's not unusual now to find thirty or forty people collaborating on a single, spectacular repast. Says Conte, "It gives people from all levels of the company a chance to sit down and talk with each other, people who normally would have no reason to do so."

Of course, it takes more than food to win the hearts and minds of a workforce. Work-related games played at company-wide meetings at Conte's house, social events that include employees' spouses and kids, annual softball games, and problem-solving groups involving employees at all levels help keep spirits high.

And the sense of commitment you feel from the moment you enter Shaman's appealing, southwesternish building begins with an intertwined business and social mission that employees find easy to embrace. Unlike its competitors, which synthesize most of their products in laboratories, Shaman finds its drugs exclusively amongst medicinal plants that native peoples have used successfully for centuries, the theory being that such substances will have minimal side effects and be far more likely to prove themselves in clinical trials. It's not the only drug company to search the tropics for products, but no other drug company maintains such intimate ties with native healers (hence the company name) and their communities, so equitably rewards them for their collaboration, or so caringly ensures that native ecosystems will be sustained during its activity there.

Over its five-year history, the meals program has endured a few lumps in the gravy — besides all the bad "free lunch" jokes, that is. Periodically, some employees have taken the program for granted. Not everyone was thrilled when their turn came up to do the food shopping, and the more fastidious amongst the staff moaned about the state in which others left the kitchen. The company now hires out both tasks, and staff concentrates on working and eating.

Shaman went public in 1993 but it has yet to hear grief from its new shareholders about its not inconsiderable food bills. Indeed, Wall Street is fascinated with the company because its naturalistic scientific strategy has produced perhaps the most promising product pipeline in industry history. The meals program plays a part in the productivity because as researchers will, scientists often work around the clock here, stopping only to eat. The food on hand not only shortens their stops but keeps support staff around for more hours as well. For instance, one work group meets regularly on Friday mornings over breakfast.

Besides, Conte says, the biggest damage done by the program isn't to the bottom line but to the *waistline*. Conte says, laughing, "You know how when people go to an all-you-can-eat salad bar, they sometimes feel they have to eat as much as they possibly can? New employees here are like that — you see them walking back to their desks with pocketfuls of muffins and they'll put on like ten pounds."

COMPANY: ESPRIT

Policy/Practice: Subsidizing employees' attendance at cultural events.

Bottom Line: A great way to combine an employee benefit and support of community cultural institutions.

Consider this practice one that may work better at your company than it did at the one that invented it. In the early 1980s at San Francisco–based Esprit, when cash practically flowed out the water taps, headquarters created a lavish slate of employee benefits including an innovative little policy called the Culture Club. Designed to simultaneously develop a more well rounded workforce for the woman's sportswear company and maybe help cultural organizations and the arts besides, the policy allowed any employee to obtain reimbursement for half of the price of tickets to museums, art exhibits, classical music performances, and other cultural events (pop culture such as rock concerts excluded).

The Culture Club also added some class to employees' social lives, because the policy allowed them to take a date or friend with them and get one of the tickets fully paid for (that is, up to the reimbursement limit of $200 per employee per year). Public relations director Cassie Ederer thought she'd died and gone to Bay Area heaven when she first joined the company in 1990 as a PR assistant: "I'm a real theater fanatic, so the policy allowed me to go see any new Broadway musicals that were playing here in San Francisco. Actually, you could submit the tickets from anywhere, so if you were in New York and you wanted to go see a Broadway show, that was fine, too. I also attended a lot of museum exhibits and special openings that maybe were thirty dollars to go to when I didn't have the money to spend. The reimbursement made it a lot more enticing to go and try new things."

To paraphrase the Buddha, all good things come to an end, and at Esprit they came to a near screeching halt in the early 1990s. As Ederer describes it, both new competition and sweeping changes in the fashion industry caught the company at a time when it was too unwieldy to adapt. Sales plummeted, and management was suddenly forced to reexamine every unnecessary expense. Long a humanistic and otherwise socially proactive employer, Esprit decided to save jobs and eliminate extravagances in its benefit package instead.

Thus, the Culture Club died a quiet death as a benefit for

employees at headquarters. Participation had faded anyway, as Esprit's workforce — average age twenty-four in 1985 — grew older, started raising families, and stayed home more, so cutting the program wasn't a tough decision. As Ederer says, "The employees were disappointed but it wasn't anything that made people go away. If anything, it made them happier that benefits were being dropped, not people."

Management did, however, keep the program alive for retail managers and those working at Esprit showrooms around the country. Ederer points out that regional employees in the showrooms and retail stores don't get to enjoy the perks available at headquarters, and several perks did survive the cutbacks, including subsidized meals at the company cafeteria, an on-site gym, and big company parties. Offering the outside employees the Culture Club was a way of leveling things a bit.

Of course, the outside employees' participation hasn't been terrific, either — about 5 to 8 percent of eligible employees (that is, full-timers) during 1994. But management still believes in the Culture Club concept, and continues to encourage employees to take advantage of it. As the company bounces back from its slump of recent years, Ederer for one looks forward to the day when the Culture Club will be restored at headquarters. After all, things may have slowed down at Esprit for a while, but not in the cultural scene, so there are always new plays to catch, art exhibits opening, museums. . . .

SUPPORT *for* WORKING PARENTS

COMPANY: JOHNSON & JOHNSON

Policy/Practice: State-of-the-art support for working parents.

Bottom Line: An insurance policy on retention and productivity of the company's talented workforce.

Johnson & Johnson has long nurtured a reputation as a company that cares about the family. During the 1980s, however, caring of another kind was an important factor in the company's all but neglecting some crucial family issues — the dependent-care concerns of its own employees. In 1982, eight people died after ingesting a best-selling Johnson & Johnson product, Extra-Strength Tylenol capsules, that a psychopath had laced with cyanide. The manner in which the company mobilized to ensure public safety will long be remembered as an exemplary display of corporate citizenship. But "that really took its toll on certain resources that might have been available at that time," acknowledges Chris Kjeldsen, J & J headquarter's vice president of human resources, "and, quite honestly, on our focus as well."

Unfortunately, during the same years that management was preoccupied with repair work from the Tylenol incident and other internal matters, many large corporations were waking up to the work/family issue, spurred by a massive shift in the demographics of the labor force. Unprecedented numbers of women were entering the job market along with both spouses in many families. Single parenthood was also on the rise. Johnson & Johnson had always prided itself on its ability to attract and keep top talent. However, both potential recruits and its own employees were suddenly inquiring about flexible work arrangements, assistance with dependent care, and so on, and the company had no good answers for them. What was worse, many of its competitors did.

Of course, the Tylenol situation also proved how nimbly this industrial behemoth could move when pressed. In 1986, having recovered from the Tylenol affair, Johnson & Johnson began surveying its employees, about half of which were female, on their work/family needs. The results so energized management that they not only began planning a broad array of new work/family initiatives but even added a new plank to their hallowed credo: "We must be mindful of ways to help our employees fulfill their family responsibilities." By 1991, the New York–based Families and Work Institute was rating the company's new program first among the 188 it evaluated for its guide. The next year, a leading human resources trade journal named the total program one of the five benchmark work and family programs in corporate America and called J & J's on-site child-care center at its New Brunswick, New Jersey, headquarters "the Taj Mahal of corporate day care."

Indisputably, the headquarters' child-care center sets an intimidating standard. To match the new building to the rest of the complex, the company rehired the complex's architect, the world-renowned I. M. Pei. Final cost of the structure: $5 million.

But there's as much "go" as show to the company's "Balancing Work and Family" program. Benefits include up to one year unpaid family leave; paid time off for emergency family care or parent/teacher conferences; a resource-and-referral program to help employees find quality child- and elder-care help; child-care subsidies, based on family income, for employees of lesser means; dependent care accounts that enable employees to pay for care on a pretax basis; services to help relocating employees find appropriate schools for their children and jobs for their spouses; alternative job arrangements, including job sharing, flex time, and telecommuting; up to $3,000 assistance for adopting parents; individualized benefit plans; and on-site child care at four J & J sites besides headquarters. (A fifth was being considered when this was written in late 1994.)

And the company hasn't stopped there, adding to the program in recent years to meet unanticipated needs, such as providing care for school-age children during times when they're off from school and their parents are still working. In New Jersey, the company not only has reserved slots for about 100 children in local summer camps but shuttles them back and forth to the camp from their parents' work site. J & J has made provisions for school vacation and holiday backup care as well. Sure, such operations cost, says Kjeldsen, but they keep parents on the job.

In fact, Kjeldsen now possesses clear evidence that his company is getting its money's worth. Beginning in 1990, J & J allowed the Families and Work Institute to query workers about the program. The findings confirmed the wisdom of J & J's better-late-than-never work/family investment. Program users cited the initiative as "very important" in their decision to stay with the company, and those who used the flexible time and leave benefits had less absenteeism than average J & J employees. The study didn't measure the number of employees now working productively instead of fretting at their desks about their kids, but that surely has been a major plus as well.

Of course, after all the effort and cost to put the program in place, the company discovered that some hard-driving managers and supervisors were subverting their charges' desires to fully use it. Fortunately, the problem — common in workplaces with dependent care benefits — has an obvious solution and Johnson & Johnson applied it. The company now puts managerial personnel through training that explains the business reasons for the program and enlists their support in promoting the program to employees. "Every once in a while you still get somebody who's a hardcase," admits Kjeldsen. "So we sit down with them and make them understand." Because of the company's open-door policy, an employee with a resistant supervisor can also file a complaint over the supervisor's head through a variety of channels.

Johnson & Johnson runs a decentralized organization, with twenty-eight major affiliates in the United States. While the outlines of the program remain the same throughout J & J, the affiliates approach the child-care issue in a variety of ways. Three of the on-site centers are in New Jersey and nine of the affiliates use them, Kjeldsen says. But in more far-flung outposts of the company, some affiliates have needed to take more creative approaches to caring for their employees' dependents. For instance, Vistakon, the company's contact lens manufacturer in Florida, reserved a number of slots for its employees' children at a community center near its plant. Other affiliates have formed consortiums with companies in their area to address their needs jointly (for more on dependent-care consortiums, see page 67). J & J has also worked to expand the number of certified in-home day-care centers in communities where it has employees, a far more cost-effective way to add slots than building new child-care space.

In addition to becoming a national leader in serving its own working parents, Johnson & Johnson has helped lead multicorporate efforts to address the shortage of quality day care in America. With ten other major corporations, it cofounded the American Business Collaboration for Quality Dependent Care. Collectively, the companies have committed $26 million to expanding day-care alternatives in forty-four target communities.

Of course, the problem of ensuring quality day care stems in large part from massive turnover due to low wages and few or no benefits paid to most care personnel. Like many companies with on-site dependent care, J & J hires an outside contractor to manage the care in its facilities. However, it pays the contractor to provide above-market wages and benefits to the teachers, although Kjeldsen still feels the compensation is low and admits it hasn't completely solved the turnover problem.

Like its rivals, Johnson & Johnson has downsized and restructured in recent years; the company now, Kjeldsen acknowledges, expects employees "to do more with less." But he insists that "Balancing Work and Family" is here to stay: "We recognize that these support programs are more important than ever, both for those here and those who are considering working for us. It's clearly a nationally known program and it helps us keep and attract the quality employee that J & J has had for 108 years."

COMPANIES: VARIOUS (SEE BELOW).

Policy/Practice: Smaller companies joining together in a consortium to offer big-company-sized work/family benefits.

Bottom Line: An anyone-can-play solution to program costs for working parents.

The Johnson & Johnson story told above is a fine example of what a deep-pockets employer can do to keep its working parents on the job and productive. But how many companies can afford to do what Johnson & Johnson, a $14 billion outfit in 1993, did? Most, as it turns out, now that a resourceful work/family benefits consultant and a number of companies — many with as few as 100 employees — in Boulder, Colorado, have shown the way.

Take Exabyte, a small computer tape drive maker. Having formed a dependent-care consortium with consultant Cindy

Carrillo and eight other Boulder companies, Exabyte can now offer its workers benefits competitive with many employers a hundred times its size. The menu includes a child-care resource-and-referral service; a subsidized summer camp program in partnership with the YMCA; a subsidized school vacation program for elementary school–aged children; in-home sick care for employees' children at a cost to the employee of $1.50 to $5.00 per hour, with lowest-salaried workers charged the least; and a full slate of workshops on child and elder care. Total cost to the company: $20,000, or about $22 per each of its 900 Boulder employees.

That number is particularly astonishing in light of Exabyte's first estimate for a far less complete program. In 1989, Exabyte had investigated with Carrillo's help the possibility of building an infant-care center in league with other employers facing similar work/family issues. Recalls Exabyte's human resources director Dick Shinton, his company's portion of that project was going to cost it about $300,000 to create slots for ten infants, or about $30,000 per *slot,* even though the building they had lined up was available dirt cheap. That approach was not only prohibitively expensive, but also woefully inadequate — a survey that Carrillo had conducted of Exabyte's then-400 employees showed that they planned to have about 250 babies in the next eighteen months! And, of course, infant care only addressed one of Exabyte's several dependent-care challenges. Much the same was true for the other companies.

At this point, many companies would have totally abandoned the project of providing for their working parents. Says Carrillo, "I can't tell you how many times people say 'I'm just calling around to find out what it would cost to do a center.' Oftentimes, it takes a whole lot of money so they don't look any further." However, this group of human resources directors was determined to solve its companies' dependent-care issues. They also liked the process of brainstorming on their problems together, so they asked Carrillo to come up with a proposal for a dependent-care consortium.

The result was the Boulder Business Dependent Care Association (BBDCA), a separate corporation that, Carrillo says, "helped to shield them from liability, and helped to formalize how they were going to make decisions. It also helped with money because they were combining their resources and building a bigger employee population together. That justifies certain programs while spreading the cost. They could be the decision makers, but the corporation could be the contractor of services and my Work Options group could help administer it. They loved it and it grew from there."

Carrillo acknowledges that BBDCA members sometimes bring conflicting agendas to meetings, but they've established effective means of resolving their differences. For one thing, they've written by-laws that allow for orderly decision making. For another, they pay Carrillo to lead them through the decision-making process. Carrillo says, "I work with groups that I haven't charged anything on the front end and they don't get anywhere. But the minute they have to put money on the table for that process, it's incredible how action oriented they get and how well they work together."

Carrillo also administers another consortium that has formed in BBDCA's wake, the North Employers Dependent Care Association, which collaborates with the BBDCA and the YMCA in the summer camp program. She's unabashed about her own role in the consortiums' functioning: "There are dependent-care task forces all over the country, but it's very difficult to get a task force to create a program and implement it, because first, they usually don't put any cash on the table so the motivation to achieve is usually very low. They usually gather information but it rarely goes beyond that. Second, unless there is somebody directed to make it happen on their behalf, it usually doesn't. They all have full-time jobs, so the role of an outside administrator really is key."

With the BBDCA on its feet and running smoothly, the nine founding members that control the board are now admitting as members employers with fewer than 100 employees. Carrillo doesn't feel companies of this size should be involved in a consortium's formative stages because they don't offer much in terms of per-employee resources and don't have much experience with formal policies and structures. But they can certainly benefit from a membership once the consortium is in place.

In fact, neither Carrillo nor Shinton can imagine what small or medium-sized employer couldn't benefit. Says Shinton, "It's absolutely the right way for small and middle-sized companies to assist their employees with dependent care. And it's been a good recruiting tool for us, too. It creates a lot of goodwill for us among our employees whether they have kids or not."

WORKSTYLE

COMPANY: MARQUETTE ELECTRONICS

Policy/Practice: Helping employees feel at home while at work.

Bottom Line: At Marquette, a casual work-style is serious business.

Elite athletes know that to perform well under pressure, they need to somehow stay focused and relaxed at the same time. The folks at Milwaukee-based Marquette Electronics, a medical electronics manufacturer, feel that winning in today's high-pressure business climate requires pretty much the same paradoxical combination. Explains director of personnel Gordon Petersen, a technology-based business like Marquette's has to beat the competition on the drawing board before it can lead in sales and earnings, "so we try to have an environment that allows for new ideas, the crazier the better because the crazy ones are usually good ideas."

The imperative for creativity and innovation doesn't stop with Marquette's engineers. Says Petersen, "Just having a good pair of hands is unfortunately becoming an obsolete commodity. If the job just requires putting Part A to Part B, we can do it 100 percent faster and more accurately with robotics. What we want is the person with something between the ears. Even our assemblers out there are working on computer terminals all day long, because that controls the machine, that controls the information they need. So we try to create the kind of environment where our employees are using their heads to worry about company matters instead of about being bored or disgruntled or all the other things that might go on."

There's nothing particularly innovative about the Marquette formula. Mostly, it's just good sense — understanding that a company is only as good as the people who do its work and then doing what works for those people. So the Marquette workstyle starts with sensible rules — the most sensible one being as few rules as possible. The only weighty code here is the honor code. That may not be so unusual for salaried employees, but as much as possible, Marquette unbridles its hourly workers, too. A normal shift for production workers begins at 7:00 A.M. and ends at 3:30 P.M., but if you want to start an hour earlier or later, that's fine. There's no time clock to punch, no tardiness records to sweat; just let the company know when to expect you. Says Petersen, "We basically have the philosophy that you're paid for forty hours, so give us forty hours, and you figure out how to get there. Even our manufacturing areas aren't like an assembly line in Detroit — you know, if the person isn't there, the wheel doesn't get put on. So people in the company can vary their schedules somewhat and it's not going to affect operations at all.

"The number of hours you work isn't important, it's what you accomplish in that time. We prefer to have an environment where they want to be here, they want to be creative, they want to do their job."

The honor code also applies at the pay window. Says Petersen, "We pay them the forty hours and leave it up to the employee to tell us if it should be different than that: 'Hey, I worked overtime; hey, I was on vacation two days, adjust for that; I was sick one day, adjust for that; I goofed off so that should be a no-pay day.' We trust them to accurately tell us how much they should be paid, and they do."

The relaxed atmosphere extends to the dress code as well. The basic idea is to use good judgment. Dress appropriately if you're interacting with the public; if you aren't, don't dress so casually that you'll get arrested. Petersen says that cofounder and chairman Michael J. Cudahy often shows up in Bermuda shorts during the summers: "We feel that since you spend maybe half your waking hours at work, why not let the job be an extension of what you are, what makes you comfortable." It's not unheard of for male engineers in Milwaukee to quit their job across town and join Marquette just to work where they don't have to wear a tie.

Cudahy built this company from what was a little "skunk works" when it was founded in 1965, says Petersen, and although the domestic workforce has grown to 2,200 employees, he's tried to preserve whatever he could of the original informality. That means, among other things, making people feel at home while on the job. So besides relaxed dress norms, employees are allowed to make their workspaces as homey as possible. Some things — such as nudie calendars, because of sexual harassment considerations — are of course off limits. Others, such as the caged gerbils that inhabit one employee's desk, are not. And if you like a beer with your lunch, you don't have to go off-site to get it because the company sells beer in the lunchroom.

Marquette worries a lot less about wringing every minute out of employees' time than freeing their minds to focus on the job. If you need to make a personal call for an outside necessity such as making a doctor's appointment or contacting a plumber for the plugged-up sink at home, fine. Use the phone on your desk — there aren't any pay phones on-site — and then get right back to work. And if you want to make sure your kids got home safe from school, have them call you at work — please! Petersen says the switchboard lights up like a Christmas tree every day at about three o'clock.

In addition to "tweaking" its workstyle in the above ways, Marquette has also undertaken more ambitions initiatives to relax employees at work. One example is on-site day care. And beyond just keeping employees content, management keeps them motivated with profit sharing and employee stock ownership (the company funnels 5 percent of pretax profits to employees' 401(k) accounts). The potent brew may go a long way toward explaining why Marquette has grown in sales and earnings every year it has been in business.

The gain sharing also helps keep abuses of the honor system to a minimum. Petersen admits to employees' occasionally taking advantage, but when they do "it's surprising how their co-workers fink on them. 'You might want to check that, he put in for overtime and he's not working overtime' and so on. So I don't think too many people are getting away with it." He explains that Cudahy has always treated the workforce like a family, and that's how they act: "If you come from a big family, you know how brothers and sisters always fink on each other, and I think that's the way it is around here."

Petersen acknowledges that the Marquette style complicates the manager's role: "It's much easier for someone to quote the rule book and say 'Do it or else.' Here you have to look at each person as an individual. We in human resources spend a lot of time being devil's advocates for managers and being the mirror to reflect back on them and say, 'Look how you're coming across.' But I think this approach is necessary to get these very bright, creative people that we need for the future.

"By not having rules, you don't go through this matrix of 'I can't, I can't.' Here, you start out with the premise of a clean white piece of paper and you say, 'Anything is possible as long as it's not against the law or totally immoral.'"

Company: Steelcase

Policy/Practice: Job sharing.

Bottom Line: The company loses nothing to the process. Besides, sometimes two heads *are* better than one.

Steelcase, the world's leading designer and manufacturer of office furniture, is a big-time employer, with 17,700 employees worldwide. But it takes a decidedly small-company, we-can-work-it-out approach when employees request more flexible work arrangements. So it was perfectly willing in 1982 to accommodate two similarly skilled employees at headquarters in Grand Rapids, Michigan, who wanted to share the same full-time position. Human resources and the employees' manager hashed out the details and that was that. The transition was smooth, other employees noticed and thought a similar arrangement made sense for their own lives, and human resources formalized a job-sharing policy so it could process the requests in orderly fashion.

As it stands now, any Steelcase job can be shared so long as the department manager approves and the arrangement doesn't compromise performance or costs. Human resources inserted the latter proviso just to mollify worriers. But in fact, performance in shared positions has generally been excellent — in part, suggests employee relations manager Jo Pierce, because those that need this adjustment in their jobs are highly motivated to make it work for the company as well.

As for costs, the effect is negligible — a little extra administration per position, primarily for benefits. (Steelcase allows employees to choose their benefits cafeteria-style, pro-rating the dollar amount of benefits available to job-sharers and other part-timers based on percentage of full-time hours worked.) Pierce adds, "Managers may say there's a little more administration in doing performance appraisals and coaching and performance development for two people versus one, but we built into the policy the fact that the manager can limit the number of job-share positions in their department if they feel that the administration is too heavy for them. It's never been a problem."

Besides, Steelcase management seems to feel that the company gains far more overall than whatever it loses in supervisory or administrative time. Job sharing reduces absenteeism and improves morale for employees who were having a difficult time balancing work and their outside lives. Those employees also tend to be "fresher" and more productive as a result. And the company retains loyal, experienced employees it might have otherwise lost to personal or family demands.

Steelcase has also found that job sharing has increased its flexibility in covering work during peak periods, and even increased the skill spread in its jobs. Explains Pierce, "One person may be very skilled in the computer reports, the other may bring in some good written communication skills. They may not be there the same day you need them — that's the downside to it. But you're still getting an additional skill set that you didn't have before." Not bad for a program that was initiated more for employees' needs than the company's.

Those needs are increasing, by the way, with fewer and fewer parents, single or not, financially able to stay home full-time with their pre-school-age children. But although most of the early job-sharers were working parents, the program has also helped employees continue their education, work with limiting health conditions, and ease into retirement.

The very nature of job sharing tends to attact self-starters. Still, Pierce's department offers sharers support in a variety of ways. For example, while job-sharers negotiate the work coverage with each other, the department is available to solve problems that arise. Someone who wanted to job-share used to have to find her/his own partner. Now the company, which internally posts available jobs, permits a job-sharing applicant to post for a partner and let administration make the match. Pierce says that practice has gone more smoothly since her department arranged for the original job-sharing applicant to participate in the interview for her/his buddy.

Posting also opens up new opportunities for sharers. Pierce recalls getting a call from a preplexed employment department staffer wondering what to do about a job-sharing team that had just applied for a posted full-time position: "I said, 'Sounds good to me,' and they got the job."

Despite Steelcase's success with the program, Pierce acknowledges that partnering employees for a single job can't be done casually: "In my mind, it all boils down to communication. We require that job-shares be a seamless operation, in that if something was given to Betty on Monday and Jan is there on Tuesday, Jan better know what needs to be finished up and when. It's helpful when they both have similar work habits. The job-sharers themselves have also told me that it's helpful if they both have similar backgrounds as far as why they want to job-share. For instance, if they're both working mothers with young children, they're both going to be willing to fill in for the other one when there's an emergency at home."

Pierce's department retains the option to terminate job-shares that aren't working for the company, but she says she's never had to take that step. There have been a few "divorces" of job-share teams since the program began, but those situations have worked themselves out with, say, one partner taking another part-time position in the company and the other reverting to full-time in the original position.

As of 1994, 86 employees at headquarters were sharing 43 positions, including 11 exempt-level professional and 6 hourly posts (the program was expanded to include hourly employees in 1988). That's out of about 8,000 employees there. Says Pierce, "When we first introduced this in the manufacturing area, fear of the unknown took over and managers expected that 80 percent of their workforce was going to be job-sharing. But in actuality, eleven people came forward when we first implemented it. It sounds good to everyone, but not everyone is willing to take a cut in pay and benefits."

Not that more employees' job-sharing in the future would necessarily create a problem. Pierce advises managers from other companies who inquire about Steelcase's program to start small so that they can work out the bugs, but "we haven't found any issues with job sharing that there aren't some fairly easy solutions for."

DIVERSITY

COMPANY: PITNEY BOWES

Policy/Practice: Diverse hiring and promotion.

Bottom Line: The business future belongs to the fairest of the fair.

The down economic years of the early 1980s dragged down revenues at Pitney Bowes, the Stamford, Connecticut–based business-machine manufacturer, much as they did across the corporate landscape. So how was it that some women in the company's sales force kept producing as if nothing had happened? Chairman/president George Harvey resolved to find out, but after interviewing his star performers, realized the secret wasn't so much theirs as Bowes's.

According to Johnna Torsone, the company's executive director of human resources, "He found that many of them had been in other professions where they were not able to make significant amounts of money. They came to us and found that through working hard they really had the ability to achieve. For him, it was like a light bulb went on. The message essentially was that if you open up opportunities to people who haven't had them, they'll really work hard and that will raise the bar of performance for everybody in the organization."

Pitney Bowes had long been an equitable employer, at least by the standards of that time. But never before had the business benefits of its approach made themselves so clear. Under Harvey's direction, a massive diversity initiative soon dominated human resources' attention, with even affirmative action taking a backseat. Just getting women and minorities past the hiring gauntlet was no longer enough. Harvey was just as concerned with how many were climbing the company's career ladder.

Bowes defined diversity, says Torsone, as "building an environment which says to people that they can come to our workplace and not have to fit into some particular mold to be successful." It wasn't hard to measure how the company was doing in that regard. Hypothetically, the diversity percentages in mid- and upper-level management should reflect the percentages in the workforce overall. And they didn't, of course. Minorities and women were doing far better at this company than at most, but "better" wasn't the goal.

So the company undertook a cultural overhaul, first creating a Minorities Resource Group (MRG) and Women's Resource Group (WRG) to help it identify and eliminate cultural barriers to rising through Bowes's ranks. In 1990, Bowes established a Work/Life Task Force to examine conflicts between employees' work life and demands on them from their outside life, which led to expanded work/family benefits and more flexible work arrangements. Then, following a recommendation by the MRG and WRG, the company formed another task force to confront diversity issues head-on. That group developed in 1992 an overall strategic model for the company to meet its diversity goals. With the model as a guide, each of Bowes's ten business units wrote its own comprehensive diversity plans and began submitting monthly progress reports to headquarters as well as undergoing an annual diversity review.

Today, the numbers document the success of this all-out

assault on the old-boy syndrome. They also portray a company that, while short of its own lofty objective, far exceeds the American corporate averages. As of late 1994, the company's U.S. workforce is 36 percent female, and 31 percent minorities (the latter percentage surpasses the 28 percent of the overall U.S. population that is minorities). As you move up the ladder, the numbers diminish, but not all that much, particularly when you consider the time it takes to climb to the top in a company of Pitney Bowes's magnitude (nearly $3.5 billion in 1993 sales). Women hold 31.8 percent of the first-level management positions, 23.5 percent of mid-level management posts, and 19 percent of executive jobs; for minorities, the figures are 24.6, 10.5, and 10.8 percent, respectively. Clearly, like nearly every company in the country that isn't owned by women or minorities, Pitney Bowes has its glass ceilings. But the panes appear to be remarkably thin.

Still, there are those who accuse Bowes of just playing a glorified numbers game, so Torsone suggests looking behind the numbers as well: "We certainly have goals. But the focus really has been on removing the environmental barriers which may have prevented people from moving up and making sure that we are taking aggressive actions to have appropriate pools [for promotions] and things like that."

Given the overall design of its strategy, Bowes's diversity plans vary from unit to unit. However, mentoring of some sort plays a part in most. Torsone: "We don't automatically match up women with women and minorities with minorities [the way many other companies do]. We really try to match people up more with their career interests, and there is also much more informal mentoring here than formal mentoring programs." Other common elements include active career planning and development, and exit interviews, which are analyzed to monitor progress. Like many large employers, Bowes utilizes outside recruiters to fill some executive positions, and in those cases, says Torsone, "we've specifically said to every recruiter that we expect them to demonstrate the ability to produce a diverse candidate. Those who ignore that get knocked off our list. We've also had some minority recruiters on retainer to make sure that we're reaching into appropriate networks."

Management has worked hard to ensure that diversity isn't just an "add-on" program at Bowes. The initiative permeates the work environment from the diversity component in employment orientation to ongoing diversity awareness training for all employees (supported by an employee publication and corporate video) to special managers' sessions on diversity considerations. As you would expect, Pitney Bowes is a leading purchaser from minority- and women-owned businesses, but diversity concerns have also been incorporated into the company's philanthropy, which management views as an investment in its future. For instance, says Torsone, the company regularly contributes to African-American and Hispanic MBA support programs as well as to the NAACP. That said, Torsone emphasizes that the company considers far more than just the usual ethnicity and gender barriers in its initiative. Company documents acknowledge the multitude of factors that "comprise the uniqueness of the individual — cultural background, religion, generational differences, lifestyle, gender, and sexual orientation."

Of course, it helps that Bowes's employees know from the get-go that the company's diversity programs aren't just a human resources project but a directive straight off the CEO's desk. The diversity educational materials prepared for employees make it clear that Harvey's appreciation of the diversity project's business rationales go far beyond his original insight about female salespeople. Explains Torsone: "We recognized that our customer base is becoming increasingly diverse and some of our initiatives stem from the realities that the workforce available to us is increasingly more diverse. In our factory, we've had at one point nineteen different languages spoken. Plus, much of our work is organized by self-directed teams, so a lot of the ability to be effective in teamwork is dealing with people with differences."

In fact, a question-answer section in a company diversity document gets right to the nut of Bowes's strategy. "Should businesses be worried about the impact of a changing workforce?" it asks. Answer: "The only businesses that should be worried are the ones which refuse to recognize the advantages that a diverse workforce can give to a company competing in a technologically sophisticated, global market."

COMPANY: RED LOBSTER RESTAURANTS

Policy/Practice: Hiring the developmentally disabled.

Bottom Line: A perfect fit between work and worker.

The fortunate alchemy of conscientious business often transforms an endeavor that begins as charity into a fount of opportunity. Exhibit A: Red Lobster Restaurant's longtime support of the International Summer Special Olympic Games. On the return flight from the 1987 Games in South Bend, Indiana, Dick Monore, vice president in charge of public relations, and president Jeff O'Hara were swapping stories about what they'd seen and experienced. Monroe noted how Eunice Kennedy Shriver [with husband Sargent, the driving force behind the event] had told him that the games were years old before its organizers realized that the developmentally disabled could play team sports such as baseball, basketball, and hockey.

The conversation suddenly took a pragmatic turn. As Monroe recalls, "We realized that if these folks can work together as a team on the basketball court, they could certainly work together in a restaurant like Red Lobster." On the surface, the situation offered an intriguing match of needs — the developmentally disabled had trouble finding employment, and Red Lobster's restaurants had a number of low-skilled, repetitive jobs that they had trouble keeping filled. O'Hara challenged Monroe to explore the possibilities.

Before long, Monroe was back in South Bend talking to staff at an established rehabilitation agency called the Logan Center. Monore recalls, "I sat down with the folks there and said, 'We know how to run restaurants but we're not good at hiring people with disabilities and making it work.' We had hired people with disabilities over the years but didn't have a particularly good track record."

With the center's help in debugging the process, Red Lobster formalized a program that now successfully employs over 1,000 persons considered unhirable by most other employers. Suddenly, jobs that had ridiculous turnover rates — certain food-preparation tasks, dishwashing, table busing, and silver rolling — were being filled by people who, frankly, appreciated the mundanity.

"In the dishwashing area," says plain-speaking southerner Monroe, "turnover in almost any restaurant is probably four or five hundred percent a year — just a pain in the butt!" But Monroe points out, the developmentally disabled crave simplicity and repetition; it's change that drives them batty. "Once they understand the job, performance is like clockwork. You get a great employee who is happy as a clam with the job because they can do it and feel good about it and you don't have to worry about hiring a new dish guy every couple of weeks."

Red Lobster, a near-700 store chain owned by General Mills' restaurant division, isn't alone in uncovering the special talents of the mentally disabled. McDonald's and Target Stores are among major employers hiring these workers. But Monroe and other experts warn managers to expect a few challenges sprinkled in with the obvious advantages.

Monroe's first caveat to those who would follow Red Lobster: Don't go it alone. The Logan Center's guidance was crucial to the success of Red Lobster's program. Logan developed a manual and video that explained to restaurant managers the differences in hiring and training developmentally disabled workers. They also provided the company with a resource directory of agencies and other contacts in each of their markets. Many of these offer their services for free and all are dedicated to making this a satisfying employment experience. Also, many mentally retarded persons come to work with agency-paid job coaches, who learn the job first and then teach it to the employee. Job coaches will accompany the worker for as long as needed — in some cases, permanently.

Monroe also cautions managers to expect a drawn-out learning curve: "The time up front you invest in training mentally retarded people can be somewhat traumatic if you aren't prepared for it, but once they learn the job, they do it the right way all the time, so the output is what you want. In fact, typically they show up early and treat this like a career." Of course, job coaches help mitigate the initial training investment.

Monroe adds his voice to others who advice employers to not give developmentally disabled employees special treatment. Ethan Loney, who oversees equal-opportunity programs for Aetna Life & Casualty in Hartford, Connecticut, told *Training* magazine, "Individuals with disabilities run the gamut from deadbeats to exceptional workers. . . . Don't [be afraid to discipline them]. It's unfair to do anything else. Kick them in the butt when they need it and pat them on the back when they do well." Monroe concurs: "You don't hire somebody because you feel sorry for them. You hire them if they can meet your particular job need." The better-than-average reputation that mentally retarded workers enjoy owes a great deal to the pre-qualifying done by the rehabilitation agencies. Red Lobster has done its share of firing developmentally disabled workers, too — in concert with the rehab agency, of course.

Monroe doesn't shrink from acknowledging the hurdles inherent in the program, but Red Lobster does this because it works, period: "Restaurants in general typically hire younger people who don't have a lot of experience in life. But once they get over the initial awkwardness of working with people that are a little different and get to know them, it makes for an esprit de corps that is kind of remarkable. We have a hugely successful restaurant up in Pennsylvania that hired four or five disabled folks, and the manager called me and said, 'The damnedest thing is happening in this store. We had a lot of pride before because of records we set, but everybody has rallied around out mentally retarded employees. Now we're more like a family, helping everybody more, because people are learning that there's more to life than just perfect people everywhere.'"

COMPANY: TABRA

Policy/Practice: Creating an immigrant-friendly workplace.

Bottom Line: It's a small world after all.

Newcomers to this country weren't feeling very welcome in the mid-1990s. As job security and living standards continued to slide in a harsh global economy, many Americans took out their wrath on the country's most recent arrivals, voting in anti-immigrant politicians and ballot measures. Nowhere was the rage hotter than in California, where Governor Pete Wilson won reelection by exploiting the nastiness, and where the infamous Proposition 187, which denies basic social services to illegal aliens, won overwhelming approval.

A port in the storm, one small northern California factory continues to open its arms to immigrants (yes, legal ones), not to exploit them but to hold good jobs for people who desperately need them. Tabra, a jewelry maker in Marin County's Novato, employs non-natives almost exclusively, pays them well, gives them solid benefits, promotes them to management whenever possible, and beyond just tolerating their cultural differences, celebrates them.

Founder/CEO/designer Tabra Tunoa says she's always been fascinated by other cultures. For years, the former art major traveled around the world teaching. She married, although later divorced, a Samoan. Like many of her employees, she's also lived a vagabond's life, spending seven years as a street vendor on Telegraph Avenue near the University of California campus in Berkeley, then touring the circuit of Renaissance fairs and wholesale shows.

When Tunoa first started hiring for her growing business, many of her first employees were not just immigrants but political refugees, for whom she had a special feeling. Their practical advantages soon superseded the emotional ones. Says Tunoa, "Gradually in the production area, I stopped hiring Americans altogether because they didn't seem to take it very seriously. If it was sunny, they'd rather go to the beach. The refugees knew how important the job was to them so they worked hard." Some 70 percent of her workforce — between 75 and 120 employees, depending upon season — fled their countries because of war or oppression.

Entry-level employees at Tabra were starting at $5.75 per hour as of late 1994, but the average hourly production wage is about $7.80, with many in the more skilled area of soldering making $9 to $10. The company also provides its hourly employees what operations manager Bob Evans says is a standard benefits package for the north San Francisco Bay Area, including paid vacation and sick leave, nine paid holidays, and medical and dental care, for which the company pays 72 percent of the premium. After a break-even 1993, Tabra anticipated a solid profit for 1994 and was planning to distribute a chunk of that to employees through a profit-sharing plan or a year-end bonus, whichever employees wanted.

The company also holds on-site English classes for its immigrant employees, even though the production work is organized so that English skills aren't necessary. Unlike many employers that employ non–English speakers, the company doesn't discourage their use of their native language. By the same token, it had employees from ten different countries as of this writing, and as Tunoa explains, "I want it to be like a mini–United Nations here and everyone has to learn to get along. If you can't communicate in some common language, it's very difficult."

You also can't advance in the company without knowing English. Says Tunoa, "We have one Vietnamese man who's working in upper management and we have two Laotian women who are supervisors. They've been with me eight years and have been given extensive English classes — private ones as well — in order for them to be able to move up. If you're, say, Vietnamese, you can't tell a Laotian how to do something unless you can both speak English."

Despite Tunoa's efforts to promote her foreign-born employees, cultural problems sometimes get in the way. For example, it has been difficult to train women for soldering, the best-paying production job. Explains a frustrated Tunoa: "The women say, 'Women don't do soldering in our country.' They seem to think their husbands won't like it."

But barriers do fall. Tunoa takes one of her Laotian supervisors with her to an annual trade show in Tucson: "The first year, it was her first time to be away from her husband. Now she does it every year and her daughter wants to do this when she grows up. It's a good example for their children to see that a woman can leave town and do business."

Tunoa's not comfortable with the apparent class split in the workforce — all Americans in the company work in administration — but that too has its rationale: "These jobs are perfect for people who can't get jobs elsewhere because they don't need English skills here. So if I give a job to an American, it's taking away from a refugee."

With so many cultures on board, you might imagine that cultural clashes could disrupt orderly business. In the past, you would have been right. A group of Vietnamese men fought tooth and nail against taking direction from female Laotian supervisors and had to be let go. That cost the company its main soldering contingent, because the men had conspired to keep soldering an exclusively Vietnamese clique. Then the supervisors turned around and started handing out preferential assignments and training to other Laotians, although after the company brought in a consultant to address the issue, the problem dissipated.

At other times, employees of various nationalities made known their unhappiness over Latinos or African-Americans joining the workforce. As Tunoa hoped, working side by side has broken down prejudice. She also learned that "it's not wise to keep one area to all one nationality or culture. As far as I know, we haven't had any conflicts between cultures for a long time now. It's been going very well."

Despite the inevitable lumps in the batter, Tabra is in most ways the rich cultural exchange that its founder always wanted it to be. On their own initiative, cultural groups of employees take turns entertaining the staff with their native foods and festivities, and the company schedules frequent potluck luncheons that keep up the parade of international home cookin'. The cross-cultural sharing takes a more poignant form when at some luncheons, staff breaks up into small, ethnically diverse groups to trade stories of their backgrounds. Tunoa says, "We have quite a few torture victims, and they've talked some about it at these gatherings. I think that's very good for them and very good for Americans to hear that these refugees are not necessarily here just for money but because it was impossible for them to live where they were."

Tabra doesn't restrict its cultural celebrations to special occasions. The company hangs flags in the production area from every country represented by an employee. When an employee from a new country joins the company, their nationality is announced, everyone claps, and a new flag is raised. It's no surprise that the company has a long waiting list of applicants wanting to edge their way in. Says Tunoa, "Everyone has a cousin or friend who wants to come work for us, so we never have problems getting production workers. That's unusual in the Bay Area."

But there's far more to Tunoa's plan than securing a supply of able workers: "What I'm really looking for is something to help me get through life without feeling so upset by what I see going on in the rest of the world. Here in this corner, we all get along and learn to appreciate and celebrate each other's diversity. I may not be able to do anything about what goes on elsewhere, but here in my area I'm doing something. I think each one of us here feels that way."

COMPANY: LOTUS DEVELOPMENT

Policy/Practice: Offering health and other benefits to employees' same-sex partners.

Bottom Line: Fair is fair — it's also more competitive.

Since its founding in 1982, Lotus Development had maintained a non-discriminatory policy that included sexual preference, attracting a large number of talented employees from the gay and lesbian communities. It was also the first Boston-area corporation to sponsor that city's AIDS Walk. So human resources head Russ Campanello was a little taken aback when in 1990 a trio of gay and lesbian employees marched into his office and complained that homosexuals at Lotus were getting short shrift. But after listening to their complaint, he had to agree:

"They were pointing out to me that by not providing benefits for gay and lesbian employees' partners we were in fact compensating the heterosexual employees at a higher rate than we were them. Here I am sitting at a table with three folks all of whom were in committed relationships longer than my first marriage lasted, so it dawned on me that [extending the benefits to same-sex partners] was just right to do."

Campanello began researching the matter, and while the company's health insurance carrier didn't love the plan, management — including CEO Jim Manzi, a former writer for William F. Buckley's conservative political magazine, the *Na-*

tional Review — was all for it. Recalls Campanello, "By the time we rolled it out at a management meeting six months before we adopted it publicly, management thought of it as a no-brainer. I very rarely get applause for anything I do, but I did for this."

It soon became apparent why. Not only had Lotus just brought its culture more in line with its original pledge, it had also created a competitive advantage. Lotus was the first major American company other than Ben & Jerry's to extend benefits to homosexual "spouse equivalents." Before long, it seemed that nearly every company in the nation was calling to see what Lotus was up to. Says Campanello, "We were contacted by close to 500 or 600 companies looking for information. It was a full-time job for a year for a person to follow up on all the requests." He notes that a number of organizations have since written similar policies for their own workforces, including big-league players in Lotus's own industry, such as Borland, Microsoft, and Apple.

Despite the intensity of anti-gay sentiment in some parts of the country, Campanello says that Lotus hasn't suffered protests from any community groups. Nor is he aware of any loss of business from consumer boycotts. He does note that, after following Lotus's lead with its benefit policy, Apple had a go-around with some anti-gay city council members in Austin, Texas, over its plans to site a facility there. Curiously, Lotus had already been operating in Austin for some time without incident. In fact, Campanello thinks the city council's eventual acquiescence in the Apple situation had something to do with Lotus's long-running presence there.

Inside Lotus, Campanello acknowledges, the policy — which applies, he says, to "vision, hearing, dental benefits, access to family leave, to parenting leave, to bereavement, every place in our policy manual where it now says 'spouse and/or spouse equivalent'" — initially raised a few employee eyebrows: "For a short period of time, people obviously wanted to know why we decided to make this decision around benefits as opposed to different, greater benefits for other groups, but I can say with great confidence that it's one of the better running policies in the company and I think it's had a significant cultural impact."

The policy has also made a point with Lotus's health insurance carrier, because, notes Campanello, "the fears that our health-care costs would be driven through the roof by AIDS is unfounded." That didn't surprise him: "There are as many committed relationships in the gay and lesbian communities as with heterosexuals, and some would argue there are more."

Good businesspeople, however motivated by values, are never blind to the practical payoffs of benevolent management policies. Admits Campanello, "The company is not just trying to make diversity a rich cultural experience. We believe that diversity in our workforce and in our business practices is going to give us a competitive edge. So for us, being able to attract and retain the best talent means attracting and retaining the talent from whatever community they come from. We were already attracting gays before the policy. But it has helped us make people feel OK about being gay and working at Lotus, and feel that it's OK to put a picture of your partner on your desk, that it's just a safer place all-around."

COMPANY: CO-OP AMERICA

Policy/Practice: Creating a deaf-friendly workplace.

Bottom Line: Co-op discovered that it was the pre-initiative organization that was disabled.

When the staff of Co-op America made a commitment to hire deaf employees, the motivation was entirely altruistic. Co-op

America is a nonprofit organization that promotes socially responsible business, consuming, and investing: internally, it strives to remain true to the values it encourages in the outside world. Reaching out to the deaf seemed especially appropriate since Washington, D.C., where Co-op America is based, also is the home of Gallaudet University, the nation's only liberal arts college for the hearing-impaired.

As the initiative has worked out, altruism is almost beside the point. The act of integrating deaf employees into Co-op's culture has yielded so many pluses for the organization that executive director Alisa Gravitz can hardly imagine how the organization got along without them.

Start with reliability and longevity. When Alisa and I spoke in late 1994, one deaf employee had been part of the twenty-two person staff for ten years and the other for seven. A third worked at Co-op America for six years — with Co-op's full encouragement, she had completed her master's degree while on staff and then landed a job utilizing it. For an organization that was itself only twelve years old in 1994, that loyalty has been a godsend. Gravitz notes that the department where the deaf employees work, Systems and Operations, is an area fraught with turnover and dissatisfaction in other organizations, since it doesn't tie directly into program activities: "We have a group of people there [deaf and non-] who self-manage that area, who care enormously about it, and who have made a very deep commitment to it."

Meetings have also grown much more fruitful since deaf employees joined the staff. Having deaf people on board meant hiring sign-language interpreters for Co-op's staff-wide and department meetings. Suddenly, for the interpreters' benefit, only one person could speak at a time and the entire decision-making process had to become more orderly. Says Gravitz, "We can now have a productive decision-making meeting with a large number of people, which most organizational development people will tell you is impossible. Between the device of having an interpreter and the commitment that everybody has made to making sure that communication can happen, the whole discipline of working together in a group has improved immeasurably."

"Our experience with the deaf has also given us a much deeper understanding of what makes effective communication, and what makes it go wrong," she adds. "We've learned from the different assumptions that people who hear and people who are deaf make about communication, and that's been enormously important for the organization. All the organizational theories say that bringing in different points of view brings different perspectives that make the organization richer. This is a very on-the-ground demonstration of that."

One potential hitch with the deaf employees also turned out to more than compensate for itself in its organization-wide effect. For most deaf persons, English is a second language because they grow up in an American Sign Language environment. To involve its deaf employees in Co-op's highly participative work culture, management found it necessary to take special steps: simplifying written materials, holding special learning sessions to make sure the materials were understood, and so on. But the extra effort also ended up benefiting other support staff who didn't share the program staff's verbal skills. Says an obviously pleased Gravitz, "Now we've developed processes to make sure that all people here can participate in the essential aspects of the organization."

Obviously, Co-op America has had to reach into its pocket some for its deaf employees, but Gravitz hardly views the expenses as extra: "The TDDs [telecommunications devices for the deaf] are inconsequential, no more than $200 or $300. The sign-language interpreters are a more significant commitment — they probably run $1,000 or $2,000 per deaf employee per year. But we consider that a benefit, not a cost, because of the enormous productivity it brings to our meetings."

In fact, Gravitz adds, "If I were ever to work for an organization that didn't have a commitment to the deaf community, I would start it immediately just for the organizational benefits. They're amazing!"

COMPANY: HERMAN MILLER

Policy/Practice: Returning disabled employees to work as soon as possible.

Bottom Line: More value from the payroll, quicker recoveries, and — usually — grateful employees.

Jim Wilson [name and circumstances altered to protect privacy of employee] used to work as an assembler at furniture manufacturer Herman Miller, Inc. But then degeneration from Parkinson's disease caused his hands to tremble, and tremors ultimately spread throughout his body. He's no longer able to do his former work, but he's still a valuable member of the Miller team. Reassigned and retrained, he now functions as an order specialist in the customer service department.

When machine operator Roberto Mena [identity also altered] developed colon cancer, he faced even fewer options than Wilson. Cuban-born, he spoke little English, a necessary skill for reassignment to an office job. Still, after several surgeries, he too completed his recovery while working. At first, he would put in only an hour or so, gradually building up his time as his strength allowed. Today, he's fully recovered and working eight-hour days at his old post.

Few employees who become disabled on or off the job at Herman Miller get to feel useless for long. In consultation with the workers' physicians, the company returns its rehabilitating employees to work as soon as feasible, accommodating them by purchasing or designing special equipment to help them continue at their original jobs or, if need be, transferring them to new assignments. And if medical restrictions force a demotion, pay stays the same.

Herman Miller has a long history as a sensitive and generous employer, but as Dave Cotter, who heads rehabilitation services, and corporate safety manager Greg Staskiewicz tell it, the program began in the early 1980s with largely pragmatic concerns. Says Cotter: "We were finding that as a rather family-oriented-type company, we were losing contact with our employees who were away from work and they were losing contact with the job, and we didn't feel that was appropriate. Secondly, there was the money issue. If people have been here for a while, they generally receive either all or most of their base salary while they're out ill. We felt that we could put that money to use by having them come into work and do a modified job until they heal. At the same time, we were reading research that indicated that people get better faster when they're connected with work as opposed to sitting at home."

He adds: "Our disability management philosophy is that we'll do and provide just about anything to help the person back to work. With that thinking, it's not very difficult to bring people back."

Some Millerites haven't been as eager to return as was their employer to have them there. Admits Cotter, "Occasionally, some people have said 'I can't do it' and all the medical opinions and documentation that we've gathered say 'yes, you can' and that's sometimes led to a parting of the ways." But he says that the vast majority of employees prefer the speedy transition back to work:

"The key to being successful in a program like this is talking to the people immediately and continually. Greg talks to them if they've been injured on the job or the workers-comp person does. The supervisors are automatically staying in contact with people. So does our health service. When you let that person know that they continue to be a valuable part of our employment force, they generally want to return as fast as they can or faster. It's when they've been out for a longer time that you start to run into some of those problems."

Besides the planned gains, the program has produced its share of unintended benefits. For one thing, the company found that when the Americans with Disabilities Act went into effect, it was already meeting most of ADA's requirements. For another, some of the equipment designed to assist injured employees in performing their tasks has also helped prevent injuries to healthy employees. Staskiewicz notes that after the company engineered and built a device to assist employees with upper-extremity injuries manipulate upholstered office panels, those sorts of injuries stopped occurring at that station.

He also allays employers' fears about the costs of such accommodations: "Most of the stuff that we deal with costs $500 or less — retrofitting workstations and stuff like that. We try to get with the engineer and the work team prior to any type of process change and make sure that they've thought things through so we don't have to go back and incur additional expenses."

Cotter and Staskiewicz don't see any reason to wax philosophical about the social implications of their employer's policies for the disabled. As Cotter summarizes: "It just makes good sense for us to do it this way. And, yes, it seems to work well for our people."

COMPANY: HOME SHOPPING NETWORK

Policy/Practice: Hiring older workers.

Bottom Line: The so-called golden years have shone pretty brightly for HSN, too.

When Mount Burns's employer offered him full pay and benefits to retire thirty months early, he jumped on the deal. But just a short time at home in St. Petersburg, Florida, taught him that the grass on that side of the fence wasn't as sweet as it had looked. Suddenly the career salesman was home around the clock "and telling my wife how to run the house, which she had done fantastic for thirty-nine years, so she was ready to throw me out after thirty days."

Unbeknownst to Burns, his days of idle angst would soon end, because his county's largest private employer, Home Shopping Network (HSN), had fixed its gaze squarely on his demographic. Having researched the success that another employer, Days Inn of America, was having using older workers to take reservations, HSN had decided to start a similar program hiring age fifty-five-and-older workers part-time to take telephone orders and enter them into their computers. An HSN representative thrust an employment application at a then somewhat ambivalent Burns after he wandered down to a seniors job fair his wife had told him about; he graduated from HSN's first "Prime Timer Program" training class in 1990 and went to work in the call center. Two years later, the company invited him to head the program. By then, says Burns, "I was having a ball and I said yes."

Of course, HSN hadn't undertaken Prime Timer to just entertain Burns and his fellow St. Petersburg seniors. The fast-growing company was experiencing a crying need for a trained reserve staff to fill in during peak sales periods, and seniors seemed the perfect population for it. And not just because they had nothing better to do or needed some pin money to supplement their Social Security. As HSN had seen at Days Inn, older workers tend to have superior relationship skills for customer service, better work habits and attitude than younger workers, and usually stay on the job longer as well.

Older workers as a group also don't have the same need for benefits as younger employees, because most are retirees with health and pension plans. Burns says the benefits issue wasn't a consideration for HSN, although it might be for other employers. However, HSN did cherish the flexibility of the older workforce — without children at home to consider, they were free to work most of HSN's around-the-clock shifts.

Finally, HSN's pre–Prime Timer study of older workers convinced it that, contrary to stereotype, its new employees would have no trouble learning the basic computer skills needed for the telephone order work. Burns says he had never touched a computer before gliding through HSN's training class, which had been developed in conjunction with a local junior college. In fact, not only have the Prime Timers kept up with the computer-nerd generation in this area, but several Prime Timers have successfully transitioned into the customer-service department, where the computer skills required are far greater than are those for taking orders.

Prime Timers have fully met HSN's other expectations. For instance, the percentage of HSN's 1992 hires still on the job as of August 1994 was three times higher in the fifty-and-older age bracket than with younger employees. As a group, the older workers have exceeded HSN's standards on script performance as well.

In fact, so impressed have they been with the quality of employee attracted to the Prime Timer program that several HSN departments besides customer service have recruited from the Prime Timer workforce to fill their own needs; following their lead, the company plans to expand the program corporation-wide. Burns estimates that about 25 percent of the Prime Timers — over 400 strong and growing — have gone on to full-time work with the company, including a seventy-one-year-old ex-stockbroker who now works in marketing. Of course, many of the older workers prefer to stay with the original Prime Timer job, which through "Social Security leaves" permits them to adjust their earnings to the maximums allowed by the government without losing Social Security benefits.

While solving some of HSN's problems, the Prime Timer program, like similar efforts in other corporations, has addressed a not inconsiderable social issue as well. Roughly one out of every four retirees ends up returning to work, generally because of financial need. Although the practice is illegal, many downsizing employers target older workers first because of their high-priced salaries and benefits. Widows and older divorcees applying to work for the first time swell the pool further. Added to all their other advantages, older workers' availability makes them an ideal reserve force to fill in during labor shortages. Burns notes that HSN was struggling to find enough qualified workers in St. Petersburg until it began drawing from the abundant older labor force there: "It's kind of a misnomer today but St. Petersburg used to be known as God's waiting room."

For many Prime Timers, their HSN job has transformed from just a way to supplement their Social Security checks to a brand-new way of life. Prime Timers have even formed their own social club that arranges day trips, dinner dances, and so on. Burns thinks that's great but he's happy just to be a valued member of a company's team again. The sun outside continues to shine and the golf courses beckon, but he won't be retiring any time soon. He's already tried that once.

PROMOTION *from* WITHIN

COMPANY: NORDSTROM

Policy/Practice: Hiring all mid- and upper-level positions from within the existing workforce.

Bottom Line: There's pressure at the bottom, but it can push you to the top.

Joe Demarte began work with Nordstrom, the fashion special retailer, in an entry-level accounting position nineteen years ago. Today he's vice president of personnel for a company that sells $3.89 billion worth of merchandise annually. It's a nice story but Joe tells a better one: John Whitacre started as a salesperson in the shoe department in 1976. By mid-1992, he was company co-president.

Promoting from within is the Nordstrom way. You come in at the bottom, but you can go about as far as your energy, talent, and desire will take you. Demarte rattles off the examples: "The top person in our restaurant division, Joleen Davis, started as a busperson in the downtown Seattle restaurant. Mary Amundsen, our benefits director, started out as a cashier in a Tacoma store twenty-two years ago and now oversees a huge benefits plan. Our merchandise people all started on the sales floor or in stock and worked into their very high-level jobs — general managers, vice presidents."

Probably no other American company of comparable size offers so much opportunity to entry-level people. But Demarte makes clear that promotion from within isn't so much Nordstrom policy as it is culture and heritage: "It's more important to us that someone understands our company and our culture than the technical area of the job. Take my area. Anybody can learn personnel but not everybody can learn Nordstrom."

Inseparable from Nordstrom's opportunity culture is its bottom-up, self-starter modus operandi. Demarte: "We're a large company in sales but we're very decentralized. Corporate doesn't exercise any control or issue edicts. We're a support structure and each division does its own thing. Each store manager oversees their own store and each department manager oversees their own department, does their own hiring, reviewing, scheduling, and firing. It's their operation and that's how we keep that entrepreneurial spirit."

Nordstrom employee policies say it all about empowerment here. The employee "handbook" is a single card that states: "Rule #1: Use your good judgment in all situations. There will be no additional rules." Explains Demarte: "The whole point of this part of our culture is to get people to come up with new ways of doing things. There are no prescribed ways of doing things. We're looking for people to come up with stuff and rise to the top."

How they rise is different from most other companies known for hiring from within but consistent with the Nordstrom style. The company doesn't post job offerings. Instead, says Demarte, "we feel that if somebody has those talents and wants it bad enough, they're going to come forward and say, 'I want to go into management' or 'I want to be a buyer someday.' We expect people to make their interests known." In their employee reviews, managers also probe employees for their ambitions and interests and keep lists of "comers." Thus, says Demarte, "we rarely interview for these management jobs because we already know our people and their performance. If they're the right person, we'll offer them the job."

Because Nordstrom never hires non-entry-level folks from the outside, the opening of a new store is likely to occasion a mass pilgrimage of Nordstrom employees from around the country, hungry for new opportunity. In 1988, the company built its first East Coast store in Tysons Corner, Virginia, and a few hundred employees moved cross-country — most on their own dime — to staff it, knowing they were positioning themselves for a rapid rise through the ranks.

The flip side of opportunity at Nordstrom is pressure to succeed. Turnover, in fact, is quite high for new hires, although the opposite is true for managers. This isn't civil service; those who don't perform don't do well here. About the pressure, Demarte says: "Nordstrom isn't for everybody. We have high expectations for our people and they generally have high expectations of themselves. We pressure people to sell. Our business is to sell more merchandise. It happens to be a win-win situation because as people sell more, they make more in commission. We have people who make over $100,000 a year selling. And we don't have limits on how much they can make.

"The negative side is that some people don't deal well with that kind of pressure, and if they aren't cutting it they're moved down the schedule. We don't schedule based on seniority. Going back to the entrepreneurial thing, we want our best people out there taking care of our customers, so we schedule the best people for the best hours." However, people who don't make it in Nordstrom's sales environment can move laterally in the company and upward from there.

In the late 1980s, Nordstrom suffered through a major controversy over its labor practices, including placing undue pressure on salespeople. Former employees testified for CBS's "60 Minutes," the *Wall Street Journal,* and *Los Angeles Times* that managers had insisted they make personal deliveries and write thank-you notes to customers (the latter a trademark Nordstrom touch), and also attend after-hours meetings without pay. Raising the charges and catalyzing the press coverage was the United Food and Commercial Workers union, which had represented Nordstrom employees in Seattle since 1931.

Milton Moskowitz and Robert Levering broached the

subject with ten Seattle employees while reviewing the company for their book *The 100 Best Companies to Work for in America*. Few sympathized with the union's position, but veteran salesperson Caryman Komm told the authors that she had seen people work overtime without pay and that the company had recently begun paying employees to attend after-work gatherings. Salesmen John Rockwood and David Ackerman said that they felt empowered to complain about such pressures — to co-chair John Nordstrom himself, if need be, said Ackerman. Rockwood said he and his co-workers had refused a manager's request for uncompensated customer service; they suffered no repercussions. Satisfied and otherwise impressed with the company, Moskowitz and Levering included Nordstrom in the book's 1993 edition.

For his part, Demarte acknowledges that salespeople often go the extra mile — literally, when making home deliveries — and otherwise work unclocked hours to ensure future business with customers, but only because they're ambitious, not because they're pressed by management. He also notes that the Seattle employees ultimately decertified the union, by a vote of well over three to one.

Opportunity at Nordstrom is also *equal* opportunity. Moskowitz and Levering noted at the time of their writing that fifty-three of seventy-four store managers were women. The company prioritizes purchasing from women- and minority-owned businesses. It also pays better than most of its competition, from the sales floor on up. And up, apparently, is as high as you can imagine.

FUN

COMPANY: SOUTHWEST AIRLINES

Policy/Practice: Creating a spirited, entertaining environment for employees and customers.

Bottom Line: The airline that yuks it up for fun and profit.

"Sorry you have to wait," Southwest Airlines' phone message apologized, "but you know how it is with big families — everybody talks at the same time."

A couple of minutes — and comic numbers — later, I was still waiting for a live human to take my flight reservation when I heard a man's voice on the recording say: "Ever wonder why Southwest doesn't serve meals? Well, when was the last time you said yourself, 'Gee, I sure would like a hot, delicious meal. I think I'll get on an airplane.'"

Apparently, Southwest was flooded that night, because I was on hold yet several minutes more when a woman's voice cooed, "If you've been waiting for more than ten seconds, try pushing the number eight on your Touch-Tone phone." I was in mid-push when she continued, "It won't speed up your call, but it might just make you feel better. Seriously, at Southwest

Airlines we appreciate your call. Someone will be with you just as soon as possible. Please hang on. Oh, and feel free to punch the number eight as often as you like." Moments thereafter, the recording cut off in mid-routine and a reservations agent answered. I was sorely disappointed. I wanted to hear the next bit.

Okay, Southwest's isn't always David Letterman– or even Jay Leno–quality material (adjust the order of the names to your personal taste). But how often do you encounter this kind of frivolity from a major corporation? And the best part is that the employees can often outdo the scripted stuff. Some of the flight staff, pilots especially, work the onboard intercom as if they were rehearsing for a second career on the comedy club circuit. Says Ann Rhoades, who as "vice president of people" oversees Southwest's personnel, training, benefits, recruiting, and employee relations functions: "They announced the other day when I got on a flight — they knew who I was — that the author of *The Happy Hooker* was on the flight and you could go get her autograph in seat 17A. It was so embarrassing but it was a riot. Are they bad or what?"

Southwest utilizes peer hiring — that is, flight attendants interview flight attendants and so on. In 1992, pilots began interviewing their own and, recalls Rhoades, "the very first class that we hired called Herb [CEO/chairman/president Herb Kelleher] and said they wanted to meet him in the boardroom to show him how effective pilot hiring was. The group of pilots walked in with white canes and dark glasses. They started it and now every single pilot class tries to outdo them."

That anecdote tells you all you need to know about the tone Kelleher sets for his workforce. One of the most colorful figures in American business, this Irishman loves his Wild Turkey, and neither Rhoades nor anyone else at Southwest hides the fact from the public. Then again, how could they? Kelleher, who has decorated his office with little turkey figurines, may be a louder advocate of the legendary bourbon than he is for his own airline. In 1994, he told a *Fortune* reporter, on the record: "I met the president of the company that makes the stuff down in Louisville not long ago, and I told him that he may be just a man to most people, but to me he is a god."

Kelleher is also walking — er, stumbling — proof of the power of humor to diffuse a volatile situation. In 1992, Stevens Aviation sued Southwest for using a slogan — "Plane smart" — it claimed it published first. Kelleher suggested settling the issue in a nontraditional manner that must have sent chills through the litigation departments of law firms throughout the country. The two rival chairman rented Dallas's downtown sports arena and arm-wrestled for the rights to the slogan before a roaring crowd. Admission was free, but significant donated proceeds were sent to charity. Oh yeah, Kelleher lost two of three matches but by prior agreement, both companies continued using the slogan.

You don't fake spirit like this, but Kelleher's style serves a larger purpose, too. Says Rhoades, "Herb tells stories about himself and he sets the stage to laugh at himself. You have a CEO doing that and it becomes contagious. Our people show it to the customers and I think that's real important."

Of course, none of this would wash with employees if Southwest wasn't otherwise a great place to work. By virtually all accounts, it is. Generous profit sharing has made some early employees millionaires. You can go far position-wise as well — Southwest fills most high-level jobs from within. And labor relations are something else Southwest takes seriously. About 90 percent of the employees are unionized; as of mid-1994, the company had never had a layoff and had only suffered one strike, a six-day walkout by machinists a decade earlier.

Opportunity and good times at Southwest do come at a price. People work exceptionally hard here. It takes more than good punch lines to build the most profitable airline in the country. Dirt-cheap fares explain much of the success, but Southwest partially finances those through lean-if-not-mean staffing. At headquarters at Love Field in Dallas, "we rarely work less than twelve hours," says Rhoades. "We often work on weekends and through the week. People have fun but they're working their tails off."

Of course, casual dress on the job helps mitigate the otherwise hard-driving environment. And "casual" sometimes just begins to describe the attire. On the afternoon I spoke to Rhoades, her department was having "Mismatch Day." In hot weather, flight attendants and ticket agents often wear Bermuda shorts, golf shirts, and sneakers. A recruiting ad underscores the dress code's appeal. "Work at a place where wearing pants is optional," it pitches. "Not to mention high-heeled shoes, ties, and panty hose."

Then there's Southwest's empowerment culture, which extends far beyond peer hiring. This is a company that literally interviews applicants for creativity and a sense of humor because it places a premium on innovative, on-the-spot problem solving, and lighthearted but ultra-attentive customer service. Of course, the word is out about the desirability of showing your interviewer not just your best but your funniest face. Rhoades remembers one applicant who copied a Wild Turkey label onto her résumé. Another showed up for the interview in a gorilla costume. As the above-mentioned recruiting ad continues, "We're always looking for people who take their jobs seriously. But not necessarily themselves."

Training, Education *and* Personal Growth

Company: Chaparral Steel

Policy/Practice: Developing employees' abilities through on-site training and subsidized education.

Bottom Line: Golden apples for the teacher.

In 1984, management at minimill Chaparral Steel decided to challenge the gospel: that mills its size can produce only low-grade commodity steel, leaving the higher-grade stuff to the big guys. All minimills at that time used vertical casting, which limited product quality, because no one had ever figured out how to cast steel horizontally. Then again, no steelmaker had a workforce like Chaparral's which is why executives there felt ready to attempt the impossible.

Chaparral's edge was between its employees' ears. Top to bottom, the Midlothian, Texas–based company's workers were highly educated and inquisitive, and trained both from within and, with management's active support, from without. No rival could match their knowledge of the industry's technology, so management confidently assembled a project team, including line operators.

By mid-1985, the team had developed a radical new concept for horizontal casting, an engineering company had executed it, and line operators had monkeyed with it sufficiently to produce occasional successful billets. They had the process perfected and in full production by mid-1988. In 1990, as reported in a *Harvard Business Review* study, Chaparral turned out 300,000 tons of steel "whose quality was even higher than the company had hoped at the project's outset. It was an amazing feat for any steelmaker, let alone a minimill with fewer than 1,000 employees."

Impressive as it was, the casting feat was just the latest validation of the Chaparral management concept. This is a company that empowers its workforce in not only the usual ways — decision-making power and a share of company profits — but also with knowledge, and lots of it. "Roughly 10 percent of an employee's time is spent in some form of on-site continuing education," says Dennis Beach, vice president of administration. Plus, many employees supplement that training by taking outside courses in universities, subsidized — sometimes in total — by their employer. Many companies pay premium prices to recruit employees with glossy résumés. Chaparral takes the opposite tack, developing its human potential from within.

Explains Beach, "We rely heavily on face-to-face interviews and we judge people more on personality traits than anything else. If you're going to have a team, you need team players. We're more concerned that people are internally motivated and fit together in a group and are able to go through our continuing-education process than that they know algebra. We can teach them the technical stuff." Only when the company hires engineers and accountants does it check educational backgrounds, Beach adds.

The Chaparral style developed accidentally in the mid-1970s during the company's delayed birth. Texas Industries, a Dallas-based cement and concrete producer, and another large company had started Chaparral as part of a vertical integration scheme to produce reinforcing bar for their regional market. With production scheduled to begin in March 1975, they hired roughly 235 production people in February to give them a few weeks' worth of job orientation. It was largely a green bunch — no experienced steelworkers lived in the immediate area.

Before long, it became apparent that snags would delay the start-up until May. After considering whether to delay the new employees' starting date as well, management decided to take advantage of the opportunity to create a more elaborate training program. They had a few experienced steelmaking surpervisors on hand, whom they asked to develop a thirteen-week training program covering safety, equipment operation, company organization, and so on. When May rolled around, Beach recalls, "the start-up was one of the easiest and quickest in the world at that time. We ran very new equipment with very few hitches, hitches that were corrected on the fly. We were off and running and making quality steel from the very beginning. Our shareholders were both surprised and pleased."

Today, Chaparral operates a continuing-education center on-site in which production, maintenance, engineering, and administrative personnel alike go through a forty-two-month program. The company also encourages outside education, Beach says, "any way you can think of."

Indeed. When management identifies production employees with management potential, it pulls them off the job and sends them to college at company expense. Employees who approach management about furthering their education also receive 100 percent tuition and book reimbursement for courses directly work-relevant and partial subsidy for courses less directly applicable. Beach tells of one production employee who wanted to study to be a dietician, in effect preparing himself for another career. Chaparral didn't pay for his nutrition courses, but it did foot the bill for the math and business classes that were part of the program.

Chaparral acknowledges employees' continuing education in their pay envelopes as well. Employees earn increases by completing training and by learning new tasks related to their work area. Beach explains that the lines between jobs are more blurred at Chaparral than at other steel plants, and not just in steelmaking areas: "Even our janitors have full responsibility for their tasks. They have to have the supplies and equipment and materials ready and schedule their own time and all the rest of those things that have to happen, so there are a lot of administrative details involved. I wouldn't call that unskilled labor by any means."

The empowering of even entry-level people through training and broad job responsibilities also carries through to other aspects of the Chaparral culture. Teams not only do the work at Chaparral, they organize it. No one punches a time clock and teams schedule their own shifts. Says Beach, "We take a project approach to things in that we sit down in a production area and line out what we would hope to accomplish, assign responsibilities, and away they go. It's not a traditional supervised workforce. All employees are salaried [unlike other minimills where pay by piece is common]. The people who are doing the job are the ones to decide how best to do it. As my boss says, 'You hire good people and get the hell out of their way.'"

On-site continuing-education courses take place before and after shifts and the company pays modest amounts for employees to attend them, but the main monetary incentives are the pay increases that accompany course completion. Although most employees participate, Beach acknowledges that "not everybody here agrees that continuing education is the role of an employer. Some feel like you're infringing upon their privacy and that to reward that or to even insist on it as a condition of employment is unfair." Most Chaparral employees seem to feel otherwise. Turnover here is about 5 percent, about a third, Beach estimates, of the industry average.

What's working for employees is also working for the company, big-time. Chaparral continues to astound its industry with its ability to compete with large, vertically integrated steelmakers. From the humble 1975 start-up, it has become the nation's thirteenth-largest steelmaker. The primary reason, according to a *Harvard Business Review* analysis, is management's belief that the company's ability to improve production and tolerances is without limit. Nobody makes steel faster and few make it be̶tter. And key to those results, note the *HBR* study's authors, is "its exceptional ability to train and broaden the knowledge of people at every level of the company." Chaparral Steel may lack its full-size competitors' capital resources, but the way it mines its human resources considerably narrows the gap.

COMPANY: RHINO FOODS

Policy/Practice: The "Want Program," a peer-counseling initiative that assists employees in attaining personal goals.

Bottom Line: A growing company built on growing people.

Jim Careau, who supervises the third production shift at Rhino Foods, is the kind of employee every company wants, an employee who thinks like an owner. Then again, Careau is an owner — of his own mail-order business, which he and his fiancée run on the side with Rhino's active support. Before he joined Rhino, Careau had been out of work for about six months. "I knew what it was like to go in a store and not be able to afford something," he remembers. He hoped to someday start a company that could make available to low-income people everyday goods — "anything from stuffed animals for children to TVs and VCRs" — at wholesale prices. Thanks to Rhino's Wants Program, Careau's "someday" is now.

The Wants Program pairs Rhino-ites with other employees who have attended a special training to become volunteer Wants coordinators. Coordinators help their "wantees" identify goals that they're willing to actively pursue and the skills and/or necessary resources to make their wants happen. The goals need not be as concrete as Careau's. Although many wantees target such tangible ambitions as buying a house or learning to skydive, others aim at becoming a better communicator or parent, or better at controlling their anger. Once the goal is clarified, the coordinator then helps the wantee design an action plan, including timelines for achieving each step. Wantees and their facilitators meet regularly to check progress and adjust the plan if need be. Says Toni Cook, who oversees the Wants Program, as well as being one of its coordinators, "Wants coordinators don't counsel or help people do the things on their list. The role of the coordinator is to be a great question-asker."

The Wants Program sprang, paradoxically, from a party conversation of which founder/president Ted Castle wanted no part. Feeling trapped as another businessman bent his ear about employees who never work as hard or smartly as their employer, Castle tried to take something positive from the diatribe. He realized his own dedication to his work grew directly from the freedom it afforded him to achieve other things he wanted. Creating Rhino Foods had enabled him to attain financial independence, flexibility in his work life, and a laboratory, Rhino, in which the former hockey coach could test his ideas about building a winning team in a business setting. He left the party imagining a Rhino Foods in which everyone shared the experience that they could create whatever they went after, for themselves and their company.

Today, the Wants process has become so integral to Rhino's culture that management now requires all employees to attend a few trial sessions. After that, they can choose to opt out, but few do. Says Cook, summarizing a 1994 company survey, "Basically about 92 percent of the people that responded were consistently giving answers that were in support of the program, so it seems to be highly regarded in the company, and the feedback that we get in the Wants meetings is that people are getting what they want — not all of them, but there's a good record of that."

Commercial dishwasher Joe Rayta is part of that record. When he joined Rhino in 1991, he had been separated from his wife and two children for two and half years, largely because of his problem drinking. His first want was to stay sober and rejoin his family. Six months later, the Rayta family was whole again and Joe began discussing with his Wants coordinator his desire to buy a house. After two years of Wants meetings and macaroni-and-cheese dinners, the Raytas were homeowners. As of this writing, with several DWI arrests on his record, Joe has jumped through nearly all the requisite hoops to reobtain his driver's license, Want number three.

A few caveats: Although Rhino's intimate, empowered culture and hiring process tends to weed out applicants not conducive to the Rhino workstyle, some Rhino employees find the Wants program either too time-consuming, too intrusive, or simply not interesting to them. Cook also notes that the original program, although conceived by Castle, was requested by, and developed with the participation of, Rhino employees. She's skeptical it would work out if imposed from on high in a more autocratic environment. Cost-wise, human resources director Marlene Dailey estimates that the company invests about 500 hours of annual employee time (for a sixty-five person workforce) in Wants. Then again, Rhino turnover is near zero, and revenues and the workforce have grown impressively since the program was implemented in 1990. But Castle thinks the very fact that the program has persisted is the best testimony to its success: "It's so easy to think up ideas that sound good but just die away. This program has really held in there through thick and thin."

And that was his Want from the start.

Support *for* Retirees

Company: H. B. Fuller

Policy/Practice: Compassionate treatment of older workers, including a pre-retirement program that pays employees in demanding jobs to do volunteer community service in their final year at Fuller.

Bottom Line: A statement to the entire workforce that Fuller means what it says about putting people before profits.

Specialty-chemical company H. B. Fuller is a far-flung multinational with scores of operations worldwide. It does not, however, maintain an office at the Nature Conservancy in Tucson, Arizona, where Fuller employee Harry Heimann spent his final year of active service with the company assisting the conservancy with its field monitoring and research. Nor does Fuller have ties to the Oregon Museum of Science and Technology in Portland, where employee Don DeBord served his pre-retirement year helping to manage science fests and maintain classrooms and equipment. But the St. Paul, Minnesota–based company did pay Heimann and DeBord their full pay and benefits for their volunteer service as it does several other Fuller participants in a unique program called Bridge to Retirement.

Jim Metts, Fuller's vice president of human resources, re-members vividly the case that precipitated the Bridge initiative: "In 1990, we had an employee in an adhesive plant who was sixty-three, sixty-four years old and had been with the company something like thirty-five years and he was really having trouble keeping up. He came to [chairman/CEO] Tony Andersen and asked if there was some way that he could get a reduced-work situation to get out of this hard production work. He said, 'It's killing me but it's all I really know how to do.' Tony called me and said, 'Look, I betcha we have some others like this in the company. What could we work out to help the guy?'"

That discussion led to Metts developing, with another Fuller human resources manager, the Bridge to Retirement, which offers employees the opportunity to wind down their Fuller career by working as a volunteer for a year at an ap-proved community-service organization, with full pay and benefits maintained by the company. Metts had been with Fuller about six years at that point, having worked previously for a major electronics corporation. "At the other place," he says, "very few people worked to age sixty-five in production because it's grinding work, and if you don't perform, you fall by the wayside. People don't fall by the wayside at Fuller, whether they take part in the Bridge program or not."

"Believe me, we have performance standards," he adds, "and they have to be met. But a lot of companies start to force people out with performance evaluations as they get older. Here, we have a tolerance scale. If you can do what we call 'good,' which is the middle rating, you don't have to worry about it. If a long-service well-intentioned employee can no longer handle a physical requirement of his or her job, we'll address that in a thoughtful way."

"Thoughtful" means moving the employee to a lighter-duty assignment until he or she is ready to retire. The Bridge is also designed to be light duty because employees are required to volunteer only thirty-two hours per week. But the program allows employees more control over their situation than in a company reassignment. Application to the program is strictly voluntary. Employees also choose, contingent on Metts's department's approval, their community assignment, which Metts says is designed to match participants' interests, needs, and abilities with an appropriate community organization. The best-case scenario, of course, is that besides both financially and emotionally easing the employee's shift into a retirement lifestyle, the assignment will serve as a good forum for continued service in the retired years. In that way, the Bridge continues to benefit both the employee and the community long after the ties to the company have been cut.

Because of cost, which Metts estimates to be about 170 percent of the employee's salary (including the cost of a younger replacement in the employee's former job), Fuller limits the number of Bridge participants at any one time to eight. Although other staff besides production workers can apply, the latter receive first priority because the program's primary intent is to relieve older workers of work that has become too physically demanding for them. Eight may sound like a tiny number for a large company like Fuller, but Metts says the company has never received as many as eight Bridge applications from production employees in any one year, so it has filled out the program with applicants from midlevel management.

In fact, the paucity of applications from those Bridge was designed to serve most led human resources to make a major adjustment to the program. It turned out that many potential applicants were waiting to apply to Bridge until one year before Social Security eligibility because they didn't want to suffer an income gap, even though they had long since passed the time they could comfortably do their job. Fuller addresses that issue now by paying any employees who have completed their Bridge year monthly checks equal to their estimated Social Security payments. The checks continue until their sixty-second birthday or for twenty-four months, whichever period is shorter.

Although Bridge to Retirement was developed initially to help a few overwhelmed employees out of a jam, it has come to mean much more to the company than that. The program has also enabled Fuller, an exceptionally community-minded corporation, to provide community organizations with full-time volunteers. And Metts is just as pleased with the powerful statement it makes to the workforce. "Our jobs in the plants are tough," he admits. "In the summertime, it gets really hot in those places. So we're relieving that for older employees and we know that's appreciated. And not just by the employee, by the way, but by other employees who've had to work with that guy and see him struggle and who may see themselves in his situation someday. There's tremendous commitment back toward the company when they see that sort of concern being shown to our people."

HEALTH CARE

COMPANY: SAS INSTITUTE

Policy/Practice: An on-site recreation and fitness center and health-care center plus a subsidized healthy lunch program.

Bottom Line: Investing in employees' health returns millions to SAS in tangible benefits, plus low absenteeism, high productivity, and enviable morale.

To watch the government struggle to rein in health-care costs, you'd think the task was impossibly complex. You get an entirely different picture when you examine health care at SAS Institute, a major software firm based in Cary, North Carolina. The SAS formula is simple and direct: Encourage prevention and early intervention, and pay ordinary claims out-of-pocket. But the result is spectacular: costs that are $1,000 less than the U.S. corporate average per employee, even though SAS figures in the price of operating an on-site health-care center and picks up 100 percent of the employees' health-insurance tab.

Besides the health-care center, the SAS corporate campus features lavish fitness and recreation facilities, tied into the center through comprehensive wellness programs. The 26,000-square-foot fitness building includes two basketball courts, three racquetball courts, a training room with weight and other exercise machines, an aerobics room, a fitness testing lab, steam rooms, pool tables, and a juice bar. Outside, employees can avail themselves of three lighted tennis courts, a multipurpose athletic field, a two-mile running trail, walking trails in the surrounding woods, and a recreational lake. Many companies with facilities like this charge employees for their use. Not SAS — the facilities are part of the health strategy, and about two-thirds of the 2,000-person workforce take advantage, says Dave Russo, director of human resources.

Also key to the strategy is a two-level on-site cafeteria, appropriately named Pennies because it serves company-subsidized healthy lunches. SAS charges employee diners only for the cost of ingredients; the company eats the cost of the building, staff, and food prep, which discounts the lunches 60 percent, Russo estimates. In support of the exercise and wellness programs, the meals are low-fat, low-protein, and high-carbohydrate — and they're apparently tasty, because Pennies serves between 1,700 and 2,000 of them per day.

The elegance with which these programs work together belies the fact, says Russo, that "they weren't planned in a co-ordinated effort but came together from working the same issue from serveral sides." In 1982, Russo was just completing his first year with the company when CEO/co-founder Dr. James Goodnight called him into his office to discuss the company's health-insurance premiums. Goodnight, whom Russo calls a true visionary, was perplexed that the company's health insurance, then carried by Blue Cross/Blue Shield, cost far more than SAS's claims and youngish workforce seemed to justify. "He said, 'We've got to break this cycle. When we're large enough to stand on our own, I want to do that.'"

Sure enough, when SAS reached the 500-employee level in 1985, the risk numbers made sense and they purchased a self-funded insurance plan — that is, they pay everyday claims out-of-pocket and the insurer protects their assets against catastrophic claims. Recalls Russo: "At the same time, we were talking about the idea of preventive medicine, because [Goodnight] said, 'If we keep our folks healthy, then our self-funding is less likely to get hard hit, right?' and I said, 'right.'" That was the genesis of the health-care center, a primary-care practice run by family nurse practitioners and supported by consulting physicians. Says Russo, "The intent was to take care of the cold before someone has pneumonia, take care of the ingrown toenail before someone has to have foot surgery, et cetera. It's worked out famously."

The fitness center and recreation facilities originated in a different insight — that exercise helps relieve both physical and mental stress and is a good company socialization tool besides. After both the fitness and health-care centers had been operating for some time, the nurse practitioners and fitness specialists got together and created wellness classes and seminars to bridge their respective domains. Now classes promoting healthy lifestyle, along with rewards for meeting certain fitness challenges, keep participation in the various programs high and health costs low.

The company also offers a full plate of complements to the health and fitness mix. Those include classes for expectant mothers and new parents; ergonomic training and healthy back classes; and support groups for employees who've suffered a catastrophic illness personally or in their family, among numerous others. The capper is a stress reducer supreme — low-cost Montessori child care at on-site centers regarded as among America's best. (Most of SAS's regional centers across the country employ only ten or fifteen people, but they too take part in the wellness programs and fitness initiative because SAS subsidizes employees' membership in local health clubs. The one requirement: the club must offer comprehensive exercise, not just, say, racquetball or bodybuilding.)

It may be hard to imagine a company doing more for its employees' health but that's exactly what SAS is imagining. On the drawing board as of late 1994: hiring the two consulting physicians as full-time staff of the health-care center; adding preliminary X-ray capability, which Russo thinks may save the company $150,000 to $200,000 annually after the first years's expense; operating a pharmacy in-house, which could save an annual $300,000 after the first year; and building a physical-therapy room and contracting with a professional to staff it part-time, a projected $100,000 savings yearly.

SAS's innovations haven't gone unnoticed. In gatherings of human-resource professionals, Russo amazes when he tells his colleagues that SAS's biggest health claims are always for premature births, a factor beyond the reach of their programs. He blows what's left of their minds with the next sentence: The company's health-care costs inflate only 3 to 4 percent annually. In some years, that amounts to several times less than the national rate.

"We've been consulted by companies time and again who want to know what we're doing and how do we do it," Russo says. "For the most part, they look at our benefits and throw their hands up and say, 'We can't afford to do that without a total revamping.'" But a few organizations are starting to lean their way, he adds, because their health-care costs are way out of hand. "We tell everybody who wants to listen," Russo adds, "you can get control of this but you have to be willing to invest the seed money to do the preventative stuff, the stuff you may never see, smell, or touch."

COMPANIES: THE LYME TIMBER COMPANY
AND BABSON BROTHERS

> *Policy/Practice:* Subsidizing employees' aerobic exercise (Lyme); encouraging wellness self-care (Babson).

> *Bottom Line:* Big-company savings and better employee health at small-company prices.

The Lyme Timber Company, with its fourteen employees and $2 million in annual revenues, doesn't have near the resources of SAS Institute but its leaders have reached a similar conclusion: investing in employees' health is well worth the cash outlay. Lyme, based in Lyme, New Hampshire, is an environment-minded real estate investment partnership. It specializes in buying large-scale timberland tracts in cooperation with regional and national conservation organizations such as the Nature Conservancy or Trust for Public Land. Its health program for employees reflects the company's outdoor orientation: the company will pay up to half the cost of employees' purchases of rowing shells, canoes, mountain bikes, kayaks, and cross-country ski equipment (company contribution limit: $250 per employee per year).

The policy also covers health and athletic club memberships — some employees utilize the subsidy at the athletic facilities at nearby Dartmouth College — and "any other aerobic-oriented exercise program or apparatus," but general partner Peter Stein admits a preference for heavy breathing of the outdoor kind: "There's a fair amount of activity for some parts of the organization in doing outside work — looking at property and what have you. So, particularly for the office staff, the program has provided incentive for them to be outside as well, and I think that's helpful."

What's also helpful is the policy's effect on employees. "We don't have a significant sick-day problem," says Stein, noting that half of Lyme's staff takes advantage of the exercise program.

One thing Lyme's program didn't accomplish was lowering the company's health-insurance premiums for its employees. Lyme's carrier, Blue Cross/Blue Shield of New Hampshire, wasn't open to the idea. But don't make up your mind about employee health programs based on Lyme's insurance experience. Several major insurers, Travelers being a prime example, court employers that have a wellness program in place and will assist corporate clients without programs in installing one. Many insurers, including Metropolitan Life, Prudential, John Hancock, Travelers, and Aetna, also reduce group-life premiums for companies that offer wellness programs to their employees.

Nor does a company have to build a state-of-the-art gymnasium like SAS's to qualify for premium reductions. Babson Brothers, a dairy-farm equipment maker with 400 employees, saved 5 percent — $5,000 — on its group-life premiums in 1993 simply by initiating a no-smoking policy and a fitness program based on incentives for self-care. The Naperville, Illinois–based company, which like SAS Institute (see page 120) is self-insured for health care, has also dropped its health-care costs per employee to about $2,500, compared to a national average of about $4,000, says Dale Termunde, who has spearheaded Babson's health initiative.

There's no rocket science to Babson Brothers' success here, just some strategically applied behavioral science. As Termunde, the company's legal director, points out, "Our program is very positive. We make it fun and we make it worthwhile for employees financially." For instance, since 1990, the company has sponsored a voluntary mini-physical for employees that covers weight, blood screening, and blood pressure. The company compiles the participants' data and then reduces the health-insurance deductible by half for employees who are within the norms or better. Those that aren't can earn the same discount by demonstrating substantial progress in two out of three categories — weight, blood pressure, and cholesterol — by the time of their next physical. About 85 percent of the workforce take part in the program.

Participation in fitness programs isn't quite on the same level, but is still substantial, thanks again to Babson's positive reinforcement. The company picks up half the tab for employees' health-club memberships. It also holds monthly Get Fit days on which participating employees can wear exercise clothes to work, are given a healthy bag lunch and a health-related speaker or video at lunchtime, and get to leave work half an hour early to compete for prizes in company-administered runs and walks.

To be sure, a few Babson health programs rely more on sticks than carrots. Take for example the way the company en-

courages seat belts and motorcyle helmet use: it radically reduces the insurance payout for an employee's injuries in a
motor vehicle accident if the police report shows that the employee wasn't wearing the appropriate precautionary device.
The company also makes clear to expectant parents and their
spouses that it will cover only half the birth costs for those
who don't attend the in-house prenatal program. By the same
token, participants get gifts, including a child car seat.

The Centers for Disease Control and Prevention notes
that, on average, companies with wellness programs report
seven dollars in ultimate savings for every one dollar invested
in an exercise program. Those numbers don't surprise Termunde at all: "Obviously, the things we pay for also pay back
to us."

SAFETY

COMPANY: DuPont

Policy/Practice: Operational safety and health.

Bottom Line: Number one may not be quite good enough.

Note: What started out as a laudatory piece on DuPont's safety practices ended up as something of a cautionary tale after I interviewed a veteran frontline employee, an individual selected for me by the company's external affairs department. I decided to stay with the DuPont example because I believe the company's relatively modest failings as pointed out by John Hall are instructive, and because DuPont's safety record is still one of America's best.

Forgive the folks at DuPont if they seem obsessed about safe operations in their plants: the company began life as a gunpowder maker in 1802. Hypothetically, the potential for accidents at what is now the nation's largest maker of chemical products is still explosive. But you're actually far less likely to hurt yourself working for DuPont than you are in most other companies, regardless of their business. For instance, employees at the company's Chattanooga, Tennessee, plant hold the National Safety Council record for most consecutive injury-free workdays: 2,490. That's nearly seven years! Overall, the company shows an injury record ten times better than the chemical industry average, and forty times better in lost-work cases.

You also learn something about a company's safety performance by its status with its peers, both in its own industry and in the corporate world at large. Numerous major corporations benchmark their safety programs on DuPont's. The company also does a nice little side business providing comprehensive safety training to other companies, yet more evidence of its credibility in this area. Clients in recent years have included such diverse operations as Digital Equipment Corporation's semiconductor facility in Hudson, Massachusetts; a flooring coating plant for Armstrong World Industries; and Burlington Northern Railroad.

Behind the reputation, rhetoric, and statistics lies a solid core of principles and practices, one of which is involvement of top management in injury prevention. For instance, CEO Edgar Woolard — as have several company CEOs before him — requires that any lost-time injury at any company facility worldwide be reported to him in writing within twenty-four hours. DuPont employees suffer from fifty to seventy lost-time injuries annually, says Michael Deak, the corporate safety and health officer. That's not a bad record for an outfit that employs over 71,000 people in the United States alone.

As vital as top management's role is, you need to have sufficient on-site staff on the case if you're going to monitor operations as complex as DuPont's. Homer Turner, a thirty-two-year DuPont veteran who oversees safety, health, and emergency response at DuPont's Chambers Works site in Deepwater, New Jersey, notes that out of about 2,400 employees, "we have thirteen or fourteen people who spend full-time in safety, probably an equivalent number on the environment, and about half that number spend most of their time on occupational health and wellness."

DuPont gets high marks too for both the way it investigates what Deak calls "every deviation from expectation" and what it does with the information. The company explores every incident — that is, every potentially dangerous situation that might lead to an accident — as well as the management process that allowed it to happen. It then not only integrates what it learns into its own operations worldwide but shares the information throughout the industry via both informal contacts and membership in such organizations as the Chemical Manufacturers Association (CMA). Business reasons, of course, explain the generosity because first, notes Deak, "There's no room for error and we also believe that our performance is judged by the performance of our competitors. We get lumped into the same box, if you will."

None of these efforts would count for much if employees took the rules casually, but management makes it abundantly clear to them — through repeated trainings and otherwise — that safety is a condition of employment. You best follow procedures to the letter if you expect to keep your job here, and you won't go anywhere as a manager if inordinate injuries occur on your watch.

DuPont was highly bureaucratized and hierarchical before Woolard came on board, generally bad news for a safety program because line employees have few if any avenues for communicating their safety concerns to somebody who can act on them — besides supervisors, that is — who could be the source of the problem. Woolard has worked hard to break down the layers of crust, and has been at least partially successful. Turner notes that one of the big changes at DuPont since his days as a line employee is the involvement of frontline people in safety discussions and planning as well as facility design.

But John Hall, a mechanical technician at Chambers Works with twenty-seven years' experience at DuPont, suggests that the company has yet to fully liberate frontline folks to speak up on safety issues, and could be doing much more in a number of other safety areas as well. When we spoke in early 1995, Hall — former head of his union's health and safety committee — didn't dispute that the company deserves its reputation relative to most of its competitors, but did suggest that the reputation may be threatened in a number of areas. Among his points:

- Downsizing has increased the workload on survivors, which could cause safety lapses in the future: "Some people tend to be really overloaded and how people work through that, I don't know." (Company spokesperson Lori Fenimore asserts that the company recognizes the potential impact of downsizing on safety, and has considered that in its safety planning for years. She notes that "DuPont didn't have an increase in recordable injury rates through 1993. We had a slight increase in 1994, but we're off to a good start in 1995.")

- The company sometimes overstresses safe behavior because it doesn't want to spend the money to improve equipment and facilities, a misplaced priority he compares to the early 1990s controversy over General Motors trucks with sidesaddle gas tanks: "Naturally, if you weren't speeding you maybe wouldn't have an accident, but does that mitigate the gas tank that blew up?" (Fenimore contends that equipment, facilities, and behavior get equal attention from the company, and says that Hall's Chamber Works facility, for example, spent "well over $1 million in 1994 on facility improvements that impacted safety.")

- Too many midlevel managers have no long-term commitment to the company, because, says Hall, "they're shuffled in and out too fast" and therefore look more to temporary than permanent solutions to safety problems.

- In times of high demand, productivity concerns sometimes override caution, especially in occupational health areas that don't show up in the stats, such as low-level emissions inside the plant.

You can't knock results, and DuPont's have been superior. But Hall's comments, in the light of expert occupational safety and health advice, make one wonder if the company will be able to maintain its superiority in the future. Psychologist George Everly, Jr., who has written and researched widely on occupational health, stresses that research in the field shows that in low-injury plants, management/employee contacts were frequent, informal, and positive, which in turn created opportunities for employees to communicate about safety issues and suggest improvements. At DuPont, contacts do seem to be frequent, at least as regards safety, but as even Fenimore admits, the company is still working on the formality and positivity factors.

With regards to the latter, it seems that DuPont dangles safety rules more as sticks than carrots; in fact, Deak admits that the system could conceivably encourage employees to hide injuries to avoid a dressing-down or worse, although he's convinced that the DuPont approach prevents far more problems than it creates. Fenimore says the company is trying to increase the rewards for safe behavior to bring more positive reinforcement into the mix.

Everly also notes that low-injury plants tend to have more stable workforces — that is, less absenteeism and turnover. As downsizers go, DuPont is known as one of the most sensitive; in 1992, the company slimmed down by 6,500 employees without a single involuntary separation. But that's not to say that those who remained didn't suffer; Hall suggests they did. Low-injury plants were also more likely to use senior employees rather than supervisors to train workers, something that Hall counsels as well.

Hall's suggestion that the company sometimes prioritizes productivity over safety must be tempered in light of the company's clear message to employees that safe performance is a condition of employment. However, some of his other comments deserve close attention from DuPont's senior management for there's scant margin for error in an industry like theirs. When it comes to safety, DuPont may indeed be number one, but as even its executives will admit, number one isn't necessarily as good as it gets.

EVALUATION

COMPANY: NATIONAL GEOGRAPHIC TV

Policy/Practice: A feedback process designed to align leaders' actions with company values.

Bottom Line: How to make platitudes into certitudes.

Pam Meyer always felt that one of her strengths as a manager at National Geographic TV was her ability to share information with others. In a media production outfit like hers, that skill is lifeblood. So imagine her surprise when she discovered, through an organizational development tool called "360 Degree Feedback," that her co-workers saw her as an information hoarder.

How did she take it? Jump out the nearest window? Put letter bombs in her critics' mail slots? Resign and take a cashier job at Newberry? "I ended up doing these regular books and handing them out to people," she says cheerily. "I would never have done that if I hadn't had that feedback."

That's exactly the kind of personal and organizational growth that "360 Degree Feedback" was designed to spur, says Dr. Anthony Smith, a managing director of a consulting firm called Keilty Goldsmith and Company (KGC), which originated the process and brought it to National Geographic TV. The new development tool turns the old employee evaluation model on its head, so that managers are getting feedback on their leadership. Explains Smith, "If you really want to know how to lead people more effectively, you don't talk to your boss — you talk to the people you're attempting to lead."

But there's more to it than that, he says: "We try to help organizations think about very specific behaviors that correlate with their espoused values. So teamwork means that when you are in a team meeting you feel comfortable enough to challenge people. That when you are in meetings you contribute, and you also share information freely."

KGC, based in La Jolla, California, called the tool "upward feedback" at first. The new name better reflects the fact that feedback comes from other directions besides bottom up. At minimum, managers get the goods both from those who report to them and from management peers. In fact, KGC even solicits feedback from customers when relevant.

Here's how it works: The consultant — in National Geographic TV's case, Smith — helps company leadership articulate the organization's core values and the specific behaviors that support those values being realized. With that information in hand, the consultant composes a survey designed to measure how closely managers walk the company's talk, as perceived by their closest associates in the company. The survey asks respondents to rate the manager in a number of specific areas related to the company's core values. Following the ratings come several open questions where the respondent comments at length on the manager's general strengths and weaknesses and recommends specific behavior changes the manager could make to become more effective in the organization.

Once the surveys are completed, the consultant aggregates both the ratings and comments into a single report on each manager to protect the identity of those giving the feedback. The consultant then reviews each report with the individual it concerns. For example, in the case of a hypothetical manager named Bill, Smith says "I would have studied his report before he and I had a session, and then say something like, 'I've read your report and here are the two or three things are clearly strengths: people think you're very community minded and they think you're a really honest person and there's zero question about your integrity and ethics and so forth,' so I certainly want to recognize the good news because positive reinforcement enforces the desired behavior.

"The other thing I want to do is to try to identify just one or two things Bill can do differently. People are not going to be able to change fifteen things. Behavioral change is very difficult. Bill will be lucky if he can change one or two. So part of our expertise is to identify the one or two things that are going to have the most significant impact on his credibility as a leader. When we come back in either six months or a year, whatever the time frame is, Bill will get feedback again and we'll track it to see if indeed he's made improvements, particularly in those areas that were identified as weaknesses. You're only getting feedback on the things the company has said are a core value and so therefore it becomes pretty hard to argue with."

KGC prepares a second level of feedback that can be even more powerful for the organization. Typically, says Smith, the head of the company will receive a summary report aggregated from all the individual managers' reports: "Usually we make sure it's a pretty large sample, so the leader knows, 'My God, all of my managers are terrible at this, that, and the other behavior. I need to think of some things to do organizationally to make the environment more conducive to those behaviors.'"

Like any value-related process, 360 Degree Feedback only works to the extent that it's supported at the top of the company. At National Geographic TV, head man Tim Kelly proved his commitment to the process from the beginning. "Before he had anybody else get feedback, he was the first person to go through the process and he got a lot of feedback because he manages a lot of people," says an admiring Smith. Of course, commitment also means showing staff that feedback will play an ongoing role at the company and is not just the flavor-of-the-month. At National Geographic TV, 360 Degree Feedback has been in place since 1991.

The drawback to the process, obviously, is that not everybody takes correction gracefully. Some managers, in fact, will try to guess who made the most critical comments and seek revenge. "We have to constantly remind people and warn them that this is a developmental process, not an evaluative process," says Smith. "It's based on perceptions, and perceptions aren't always accurate, but they are useful for leaders to know."

Meyer, obviously, is one of those who takes the feedback well. "It's great," she says, "because there will be commonalities in what people say. They can perceive you as behaving in a certain way that you had no idea that you behaved in. So if someone sits down and they say look, eight people scored you very high in this area, or very low in this area, there is a certain kind of weight that it carries that you wouldn't necessarily respond to otherwise."

SECTION II

Customers &
Suppliers

EXCEPTIONAL CUSTOMER SERVICE

COMPANY: A. G. EDWARDS

Policy/Practice: Structuring the business for total customer service.

Bottom Line: Profits that have only grown stronger the less the company focuses on them.

Without question, film director Oliver Stone pandered to popular prejudice about the investment business when he created "greed is good" trader Gordon Gecko. But he didn't invent the character from thin air, either. Even away from the exaggerations of the silver screen, this is an industry more than a little tainted by allegations of "churning and burning" (overtrading in customers' accounts to generate more commissions), charging high fees for dubious services, luring investors of modest means down imprudently risky paths, and pushing the brokerage's own mutual funds at customers instead of better-performing outside products. Reinforcing the stereotype is the fact that, as reported in *Smart Money* magazine, such major firms as Dean Witter Discover, Smith Barney Shearson, Paine Webber, Kemper Securities, and Prudential

Securities have been shaken by scandals in recent years over various abuses of clients' interests.

The most notable exception is A. G. Edwards, Inc., a $1.2 billion company headquartered not on Gecko's high-flying Wall Street but in the more stolid environs of St. Louis, Missouri. Under the direction of Ben Edwards III, great-grandson of the firm's founder, A. G. Edwards demonstrates daily that there's another way to achieve success in financial services — by building an unmatched reputation for putting customers first and by structuring its business to keep it that way.

A. G. Edwards, in business for more than a century, was just another player in a crowded field when Ben Edwards assumed management of the company from his ailing father in 1965. Meeting regularly over a two-year period, he and the company's top managers hashed over a new operating philosophy that would separate the company from the competition for the long haul. When the process ended, they had defined the A. G. Edwards of today — a company that delivers "financial services of value" ("not the hula hoops but the solid stuff," according to Edwards) to mass and upper-income investors through "a network of retail branches acting as agent for the customer."

To Edwards, those last six words were the key. "If we were in truth to be acting on behalf of our client," he recalls from his St. Louis office, "then we would have to make some real changes" — in short, overhauling the entire incentive structure from what was the industry norm.

"First, we'd have to tell our investment brokers that their first allegiance was to their client, not us. Secondly, it meant that we had to get rid of any override compensation in our headquarters. That changed the whole concept of headquarters. Instead of being a profit center, it became a giant service center. We couldn't really represent to a client that we were acting as his or her agent if we had a trader trying to skim an eighth or a quarter off of a trade. We changed the compensation in headquarters to where everyone was on salary and the only bonus they got was on overall firm profit. They could not get a bonus from the activity in their area."

The third change meant perhaps the biggest break of all from industry status quo — a virtual prohibition against manufacturing their own products. Explains Edwards, "If we had our own financial products, we would be pushing them instead of working for the client. Some of our competitors have come up with excellent products and we use them if they let us. But they can't always be the right product for the customer. The head of one big firm, whom I won't name, told me once that he knew his brokers hated to be pushed to use their products but that was 85 percent of the company's profit and he'd get fired if he didn't follow that course." A. G. Edwards did collaborate with two other firms to create a money fund at a time when the only such funds available were those offered by big brokerages. Consistent with its pledge to not make products where quality alternatives exist, it has created no others.

Ultimately, even the bottom line, which in pre–Ben III days had been company objective number one, took a backseat to serving the customer because, Edwards explains, "we didn't want to go shooting off in a different direction just because it looked profitable. Our goal was to run our business as well as we could. Of course, we knew we had to do whatever we had to do profitably or we would forfeit our ability to do it at all. So profit became the how, not the what. We don't have any budgets or any size goals at all. We just try to stay alert to opportunity and be concerned with the quality of what we do. It was curious to me that when we removed profit as a goal of the company, almost overnight our profit margins widened."

SVN member David Hills, who specializes in socially responsible investing in an A. G. Edwards office in Portsmouth, New Hampshire, noticed the difference as soon as he joined the firm: "When I do go to St. Louis for meetings, there is little or no talk about the profitability of the firm. All the focus is on what it is that clients want for service that we can improve upon. That really struck me, having been in the business for years. No one ever says anything to me about the level of business that I do with my clients."

More validation pours in from the industry's media organs. In 1991, *Kiplinger's Personal Finance Magazine* rated

Edwards best broker for small investors, awarding the company its only five-star rating. In 1993, *Smart Money* ranked Edwards first among a group of seven bellwether firms, with highest possible scores in the vital ethical categories of commissions and fees, arbitration awards, freedom from pressure, and staying out of trouble. That same year, *Registered Representative,* the trade journal for retail stockbrokers, underscored Hills's impressions by grading Edwards tops in overall ethics, image, and, again, freedom from pressure to sell certain products, among other top marks.

The unassuming Ben Edwards mostly lets the company's reputation speak for itself, but he has railed against his competition — in A. G. Edwards's 1993 annual report and in press interviews — for being fee-happy: "Policies that are solely to benefit the company tend to use the customer," he asserts. "I don't deny that brokerages have real costs behind their fees, but who asked them to provide the services in the first place? They're jamming services down clients' throats that in many cases they don't want. It's making it harder for the customer to come out ahead, and that will eventually hurt all of us in this business. Our approach has been to try in every way we can to keep our costs down so that we don't feel that we have to charge our customers more."

Compared to its fast-track rivals, A. G. Edwards appears . . . all right, boring. But there's a place for "boring," especially in investment. Under Ben's grandfather Albert N. Edwards, the firm's greatest client loss on 1929's Black Thursday was only $5,000 on an over–$1 million account, largely because the firm disallowed the highly leveraged stock purchases typical of the day. The company still deemphasizes margin buying along with other cliffhanger strategies, such as options and commodities. So A. G. Edwards hasn't fully capitalized on fads like the junk-bond-run craze of the 1980s. Then again, it hasn't paid for them later.

A. G. Edwards's business approach makes for a more even performance in other ways as well. Because it has no proprietary products, it doesn't pay the fixed management costs that its rivals do when sales of their mutual funds slip. In fact, many of its costs — for example, sales commissions and distributions from its generous profit-sharing plans — automatically drop when business slows.

Ben, though, prefers to diffuse the talk about management genius: "I think that when we begin taking ourselves too seriously, we lose sight of the fact that it's our clients' money that's making all this happen. We should be doggone grateful for that and knock ourselves out to deserve it. If we can keep that attitude, we're going to be here a long time." They're already working on their second hundred years.

Company: Vitas Healthcare

Policy/Practice: Advocating 100 percent for patients, and letting profits take care of themselves.

Bottom Line: Putting customers first made Vitas number one.

In 1978, Hugh Westbrook and Esther Colliflower founded Vitas Healthcare to provide terminally ill people the chance to die with dignity and peace instead of in futile, debilitating treatment or desperate neglect. It was a job Westbrook, an ordained United Methodist minister, and Colliflower, a registered nurse, thought they had fully prepared for through their respective professional training and a course they had researched and taught for Miami-Dade Community College. But as they faced their first patient, they realized they hardly had a clue about how to serve her.

Emmy Philhour, a feisty cancer patient, had refused further radiation or chemotherapy treatments. She knew she was dying and that the therapy would only make her more miserable, not save her life. Her physicain referred her to West-brook and Colliflower, who had once discussed their hospice concept with him. As Westbrook recalls, "Emmy said 'Look, I know you don't really know what you're trying to invent here. If you guys will help me die at home, I'll teach you how to do it.'"

Apparently, Westbrook and Colliflower were excellent students. Today, Vitas is the nation's largest provider of hospice care, a modality that emphasizes keeping dying patients at home, alleviating pain and their other symptoms as much as possible, and inviting them and their families to participate in the planning and delivery of care. Philhour and subsequent patients taught the company that most terminally ill persons first want to reestablish power over their lives. Typically, that power has been handed over to professional caregivers trained only to attack disease, even after intervention has become hopeless and can only cause further harm or discomfort. In contrast, explains Westbrook, "we try to make the patient central to the circle of decision making so that the physician, the nurse, the social worker, the chaplain, the home health aide — whoever it is that is going to be a part of the team caring for this patient — ask the patient, 'What is it you would like to have happen?'"

As the above indicates, the decision sharing automatically puts Vitas in the business of providing multidisciplinary care. Its care teams typically include medical, psychosocial, and spiritual professionals, since at any time the patient could request one or all of those approaches. "It's not that we had this great idea that a business ought to be customer driven or any of the catchphrases that you hear today," Westbrook adds. "It's simply that we wanted to respond to the needs that were presented by patients and have those patients participate in making the choices about how they would spend their last time on earth."

The politically savvy Westbrook knew early on that there would be more to this patient-centered model than simply improving quality at the patients' bedside: "If your fundamental mission is to provide an alternative for terminally ill patients and their families, that means more than just putting together a business and getting people to go out to patients' homes and provide care. It means that you take on the insurance industry, Medicare and Medicaid, regulatory people in the government bureaucracy, and all the people who have an economic interest in seeing you fail."

In 1979, Westbrook authored and helped gain passage of a bill licensing hospices in Florida. That legislation established standards of quality for care of the terminally ill that became embedded in a federal law that Westbrook helped draft and lobby for as well. Fewer than two dozen hospices existed then; now the movement numbers over 2,000, about three-quarters of which are certified under the law. His leadership in the National Hospice Education Project, a national grassroots organization established to promote awareness of the hospice option, helped convince Congress to pass in 1982 Medicare reimbursement for hospice care, a crucial step in expanding the reach of the movement. Vitas has also fought court battles both for patients and against other health-care organizations that, Westbrook says, "were trying to illegally and unfairly throw roadblocks in our way."

On patients' behalf, Westbrook has even vied with Vitas's own investors. Vitas won't turn away any patient who wants its services. Overall, Westbrook estimates that the company gives away more than $3 million worth of care a year, including an extensive program that subsidizes AIDS patients, who cost far more to provide for than most other hospice candidates. Vitas's charity didn't sit well with the company's original investors, particularly in 1984, after President Reagan's Office of Management and Budget slashed Medicare reimbursement for hospice care by 25 percent. Nor were the investors crazy about the company's efforts to set up an employee stock-ownership plan.

But Westbrook was determined to run Vitas his way, not maximize profits for stockholders. Vitas bought back most of the investors' equity, and after several tough years, turned its first profit in 1987. After another losing year in 1988, it has been profitable every year since. Says Westbrook, "The former investors that I've talked to very much wish they were investors today. But they are not."

Far from crippling the company, the free care that Vitas provides has helped spur the company's rapid growth. As Westbrook explains, you can't get away in this business with only accepting physician referrals who can pay or who have reimbursement available: "If you do something like that, you'll never get a referral from that physician again and rightly so. And so we've discovered over time that by helping the doctor solve some of his or her problems, we've developed good, long-lasting relationships with physicians and have found that they're learning to use us more and more.

"We recently did a study in Broward County, Florida, which includes Fort Lauderdale, where we've operated the second longest period of time. Well over one-third of the people who die in Broward County die in our hospice. That was a shocking statistic to us, but that says something about the impact that a hospice can have if it gets in and is trying to be responsive to the medical community and the other helping professionals and is trying to do this right."

Vitas has also led the way in bringing hospice care to the inner city. With no other hospice addressing those needs, the company hired security guards to accompany its care teams into dangerous housing projects. Says Westbrook, "That costs a lot of money and we had caregivers who put themselves at risk, but we think it's part of the mission of what we're about. When you look at it from a business perspective, however, it's also great marketing, because you're going where patients are, where you can sell your service. So we think that our mission orientation is also good business."

In a nation anxious to control runaway health costs, the future for Vitas glows brighter still. Much of the health-care crisis stems from the vastly expensive treatments lavished on patients with no chance of survival. Westbrook believes that many of those patients might choose the far less expensive hospice care if that choice was offered them, so he's optimistic that continued promotion of the hospice alternative will inspire the health-care establishment to more widely promote it to patients. "[Westbrook] has been on the right side of the issues for years in terms of health care and life with dignity," notes Ruth Shack, president of the Dade Community Foundation, recipient of a seven-figure Vitas donation in 1992. It appears he and Vitas may be on the right side of the marketplace as well.

COMPANY: TRAVELHOST

Policy/Practice: Relentless efforts to save its customers money.

Bottom Line: The more money and energy the company expends on behalf of its clients, the faster it grows.

For all the focus these days on customer service, few companies do much about the service many customers prize most — looking out for their wallets. In southern Oregon, Travelhost in Medford takes better care of its customers' finances than many of those customers do for themselves. Since she opened the business in mid-1991 with husband and silent partner Tom, Marilyn Walendy has cued her staff to notify customers when airfares go down — but not just so Travelhost can sell them new tickets. Through a program called Fair Fare Review, the company also contacts customers who have already paid for future flights, offering to tear up the old tickets, issue new ones at the reduced price, and refund the difference in cash or credit.

Walendy brought the business — a franchise converted to an individually owned enterprise — with the thought that by defining unique services and marketing them throughout the Rogue Valley, she could distinguish Travelhost from its competition. Her customers effectively discovered the first service for her: "People were calling us to ask when the fares were going down, so I thought it would be neat to advertise that 'Hey, we'll call *you* when the fares drop.' In other places where I'd worked in travel, people had kept an informal list to notify regular clients but they never advertised the service because they didn't want it to get big. And it does become a real time-consumer."

Of course, the time and money involved in what Travelhost calls Fare Watch was nothing compared to the next program she initiated, Fair Fare Review. Says Walendy, "There's not only the overhead involved in the physical issuing of the refund, but also issuing a new ticket and itinerary, plus the time it takes to fill out the volumes of paperwork for the airlines." And when Travelhost exchanges the old tickets for newer, cheaper ones, it also sacrifices a big chunk of its commission from the airlines.

But Walendy isn't complaining, because the seemingly perverse mathematics of her strategy has paid off exactly as hoped. As of the end of her third year in business, Travelhost was doing over $2 million in gross sales, and "that's a sizable travel agency in this community, especially considering that we started with nothing."

Customer service at Travelhost may start with Fare Watch and Fair Fare Review, but that's far from where it ends.

"I'll ask the airlines to do anything," Walendy admits. "All they can do is say no." She recalls one instance when someone referred by a Travelhost customer called her at home on a weekend, panicked because she had just received word that her mother, who lived in the Midwest, was critically ill. Could Marilyn get the airline to waive its seven-day advance notice for a discount fare? she pleaded. Walendy knew it was the policy of the major carrier to waive the notice for a family member's death, but not for a final bedside visit. It took three calls to three separate reservation agents, but "I finally got an agent who would do what I wanted, so we got her off to see her mother before she died. I'll always keep asking the airlines until they run out of excuses or I run out of energy."

Walendy does place limits as to how far she'll go to please customers, but those are based on principle, not convenience, as her stand against a statewide ballot measure that would have mandated discrimination against gays demonstrated. A similar countywide measure had passed in conservative Jackson County just months before Walendy put the "No on Measure 9" poster in Travelhost's window. She also spoke out before the Medford City Council, the local chamber of commerce, and at rallies against the measure, and made Travelhost's office and phones available to the local activist organizations battling for the measure's defeat.

"Of course, I felt that taking this stand would possibly have a negative impact on my business, and I did have some people on the religious right tell me I should remain neutral. But I decided that people who would stop doing business with me over this were people with whom I didn't really care to do business anyway. I probably also picked up some clients out of this who I really treasure and that's great, but I certainly didn't do it to impact the business. I did it because I felt the measure was wrong and we can only be silent so long."

Walendy can point to far more direct evidence than her impressive revenue growth that caring about customers pays off for Travelhost: "I don't think a day goes by that somebody doesn't call and say I heard that you refund or I heard that you have a fare watch or I heard you'll help me because I have such-and-such a situation." But Walendy is also convinced that her way will soon be the only way for travel agencies: "More people are going to be using CompuServe for just cut-and-dried air tickets and not particularly needing all the attention an agency gives. So I think that the clientele that my service brings in are people who appreciate when you go the extra mile." No doubt — in just the short time that Travelhost has been going the extra mile, it has shot a mile ahead of the pack.

RESPONSIBLE MARKETING *to* DIVERSE POPULATIONS

COMPANY: FINAST

Policy/Practice: Operating supermarkets in distressed urban areas.

Bottom Line: Social and economic benefits for previously neglected communities and profits for Finast from serving a previously neglected market.

On July 26, 1968, pent-up racial tensions in downtown Cleveland exploded into a firestorm of violence and wanton destruction. As in Los Angeles, Detroit, Newark, and other cities in preceding summers, citizens frustrated with rampant crime, unemployment, overcrowding, and civic neglect in their neighborhoods struck blindly at their own fragile community. Ten people were killed that night and forty-seven shops destroyed before the National Guard took control of the streets.

From that night forward, even the basic ability to buy decent food at reasonable prices disappeared from downtown. Following a national trend, supermarket chains, along with most other retail businesses, began shutting down operations in urban Cleveland and pursuing the affluence — and placidity — of the suburbs. If downtowners wanted to buy their groceries locally, they now had to pick their way through the narrow aisles of tiny corner food marts with their dismal selection, wilted produce, and through-the-roof pricing. In yet one more way, urban existence grew more miserable and more money drained out of the meager downtown economy.

Today life still is no picnic in central Cleveland but the shopping situation has turned around. That's because since 1986, a company called Finast has opened eleven gleaming stores in the inner city, providing not only much-needed service but also economic promise in the form of jobs, fair prices, and neighborhood revitalization. It's working for Finast, too. As of 1993, the stores were yielding $200 million in annual sales and were profitable as a group.

Even socially motivated retailers confront some nasty objective barriers to earning acceptable returns in distressed urban areas. A short list includes high real estate costs in some downtowns, high rates of vandalism and shoplifting that increase insurance and security costs, indigent shoppers with limited spending ability, increased training costs due to low levels of education and previous work experience in the local labor force, high interest rates demanded by lenders for those neighborhoods, and sometimes their unwillingness to lend at all.

So how did Finast succeed where others feared to tread? The story begins when Julius Kravitz and his investment group bought the Pick-N-Pay grocery chain, which had operated for decades in downtown Cleveland, and merged it with a northeast chain to create the new public company, Finast. Kravitz ran Finast as chairman with fellow Clevelander Richard Bogomolny serving as president/CEO. Bogomolny later explained to writer Jonathan Eisenberg of the Business Enterprise Trust why Finast stayed downtown as its rivals fled: "It was partly because we had so many stores there and there was no good financial way to get out, but it was also because we saw an obligation and an opportunity — the obligation to serve the people of the city of Cleveland, and the opportunity to do that profitably."

Indeed, if Finast could find a way over the usual hurdles, its only remaining competition was the corner stores. In the first years, finances forced the company to shutter some urban stores but the dream of returning remained. The dream became more real after Bogomolny recruited a man named John Shields, who had run Jewel supermarkets in urban Chicago and who believed that good business and good public policy could be married. Hired as Finast's Ohio Division president, Shields networked with local leaders and found $50,000 in interest-free community development loans from the city for the refurbishing of an inner-city store. A drop in the bucket, it was still enough to convince a wary Finast board to approve a test of the urban concept.

After two rival supermarket chains attempted hostile takeovers in 1984, Bogolmolny, Shields, and other managers (Kravitz had died in 1979) mounted a leveraged buyout of their company. That removed the board from the picture but left Finast bereft of investment capital. Three years later, the owner/managers sold the company to a $10 billion Holland-based conglomerate in exchange for an agreement that would leave Finast's management in place and provide $100 million for development. Suitably capitalized, Finast moved on its downtown reentry scheme under full sail. The count thus far: six state-of-the-art "superstores" — high-volume, discount operations in the Wal-Mart mold — and five impressive smaller stores.

It's taken a different kind of investment — of desire, creativity, and sheer tenacity — to make the stores work. The community was conditioned to see urban retailers as garbage merchandisers charging rip-off prices. That's not the kind of atmosphere that most companies would jump into with expensive new stores, but regional vice president Henry Edwards was undaunted. Edwards, an African-American, had been hired in part to show Finast how to win community trust. Under his guidance, management learned how to court — and gain counsel from — church leaders, civic activists, and other leading neighborhood citizens. Properly schooled, Finast began recruiting employees through churches and local citizen groups and hiring store managers with the same ethnic backgrounds as local consumers. As Edwards predicted, downtown burst forth with eager shoppers. Ernie Burnley recalled to Eisenberg the opening of the Glenville neighborhood store, which he then co-managed: "Customers were coming from everywhere. The community was ecstatic."

Once it began opening stores, Finast had to resolve security issues, another delicate matter requiring community input. Management heard from its community contacts that many potential customers were still likely to travel to suburban stores to shop unless Finast could provide a safe environment. By the same token, going overboard would turn off the neighborhood. With the help of its new downtown friends, Finast learned to provide the proper balance, and word of mouth about the increased safety brought in more shoppers.

Finast vaulted over other hurdles on the strength of its own ingenuity. Take for instance the problem of indigent customers bringing more to the checkout counters than they could afford, which burdened store staff with the task of putting the groceries back. Finast's solution: install calculators on the shopping carts so customers could subtotal as they shopped. That maneuver has saved the company hundreds of work-hours per month since. In a related move, Finast began providing sensitivity training for cashiers so they could more compassionately deal with customers embarrassed by paying with food stamps.

Finast fought through rookie mistakes to learn other on-the-job lessons, as well. For instance, foodstuffs at its super-store in the heavily Puerto Rican neighborhood of Westown didn't turn over the way they had in other locations until staff surveyed customers for their preferences. Once fresh yucca and plantains and twenty-pound bags of rice started appearing on the shelves, sales shot up and the store became profitable. Now Finast analyzes register receipts *and* queries customers. It also continues to hire managers who understand the tastes of Finast's urban shoppers.

For all its battles with the learning curve, Finast has also discovered that urban stores offer some distinct advantages. For one thing, it turns out that ethnic populations in the inner city tend to buy a higher percentage of high-margin grocery items — such as fresh meats, produce, and prepared foods — than do suburban shoppers. That fact and higher overall sales volume have compensated for inevitably higher operating costs, such as security, which Finast continues to learn to reduce as well. Financial assistance from Cleveland and the federal government in the form of tax abatements and interest-free development loans hasn't hurt, either.

Says Edwards, "We don't claim that we know it all relative to the urban market, and we're still learning. We've been successful because we've been willing to pay the price to learn what those [lessons] are."

Social Criteria Purchasing

Company: J. C. Penney

Policy/Practice: Purchasing from minority- and women-owned businesses.

Bottom Line: Let others quibble about quotas. Penney's just getting closer to its customer.

When J. C. Penney began its minority-supplier purchasing initiative in 1972, company executives were chasing more of a social bottom-line result than a financial one. Not anymore, says Lucy Berroteran, Penney's manager of minority- and women-owned business development: "We started to do it because it was the right thing. We felt we needed to help build the minority economic community, but it turned out to be a good business decision all the way around."

Penney is not the only retailer to understand that minorities are the growing edge of purchasing power in the nation. But it's better positioned than most to take advantage of an increasingly diverse marketplace. Its network of minority- and woman-owned suppliers accounts for more than half a billion dollars of purchases annually as of this writing, and "a lot of times, these suppliers understand the ethnic consumer better and can provide you the right product at the right time. And with the right pricing and same quality," notes Berroteran.

Of course, as Penney's purchasing from disadvantaged suppliers has grown more strategic in a business sense, it has never lost its ethical drive and that's enabled the company to hurdle most of the obstacles that trip up similar initiatives in other companies. At a Social Venture Network conference on minority purchasing held in Atlanta in 1993, National Minority Supplier Development Council (NMSDC) president Harriet Michel noted that minority purchasing efforts often bog down for the same reason that minority businesses were cut out of the loop before the initiative — old-boy relationships between purchasers and vendors. Berroteran serves as the intermediary between Penney's purchasers and top management, and when she wants a purchaser to consider a new minority-owned vendor, she doesn't get much resistance:

"The way to address a lot of the issues that come up is to get commitment and involvement from the top. That's how Penney has done that. Look at our management committee, which is our top fifteen people and our CEO, and you'll find that every one of those folks is 100 percent behind this program." In other words, Penney's buyers know who Berroteran speaks for and they're only too happy to comply.

Berroteran herself exemplifies something else that Penney does right — having an advocate inside the company for its minority vendors. Minority suppliers are generally smaller, relatively inexperienced companies, at least in terms of dealing with giant corporations like Penney; without help, that can be a crippling disadvantage. Berroteran: "As I like to tell the suppliers, my office gives you a place to go if you don't know what you're doing or if you have a question or you're having a problem that you don't want to take up with the buyer at this point because you don't want to sever that relationship. On the other hand, it also gives the buyer an area to call into. Either the buyer or the supplier can come in and say, 'We need you to intervene.' That's part of the developmental relationship we form with these vendors."

In fact, says Berroteran, no minority purchasing initiative

can succeed without some degree of "coddling." It's part of purchasing tradition and a prime reason that old-boy networks persist. Berroteran has worked hard with many a buyer to get them to order from a new minority vendor only to have the relationship flounder because the buyer doesn't give the vendor enough support afterward: "In those cases, I tell the buyer, 'I don't want you to do anything more for this supplier than you did to bring the big guys on ten years ago. You had to hold their hand, and I'm not asking for more than that.' With the culture here at Penney, that works."

Through Berroteran's office, Penney takes minority vendors under its massive wing in other ways as well. If, for instance, a buyer gives the vendor a larger order than it has ever filled, Berroteran may intervene in the small company's relationship with the cutting or sewing factory, or even ask a large supplier like a Levi Strauss to help the vendor ramp up its production to the new scale. Penney will even partner with competitors on a minority vendor's behalf: "I'll say 'Look, I want you guys to meet somebody because he's really good and we may not be able to give him enough business. Maybe you and Nordstrom and Federated and whoever else has a purchasing program can get together to help build this company.' And it's good for the supplier, too, because they aren't relying on one company as a customer."

For all the developmental help, purchasing relationships with Penney are ultimately business relationships, pure and simple, which is all that advocates like Harriet Michel ask. Says Berroteran: "Those suppliers who believe that just because they have the first order, they'll get the next one are misled. Whether you're minority or majority owned, you have to be able to compete price-wise, quality-wise, and product-wise with everybody else out there. But for minority suppliers, the hardest part is getting in the door, so we get them in the door. After that, they have to perform just like everyone else."

Penney has done a terrific job of providing opportunities for minority businesses beyond its purchase of store merchandise. In addition to looking for minority suppliers for such needs as store fixtures, lighting, janitorial, landscaping, and so on, it tries to support minority businesses outside its direct purchasing influence. For instance, Penney requires all of its vendors to utilize Electronic Data Interchange (EDI), a computerized billing operation that saves Penney time and labor. Few minority vendors can afford the investment for their own system, so Penney will refer them to third-party services, including minority-owned services.

Penney doesn't contract with many minority-owned professional services because it does most of its accounting, legal, and other such work in-house. But it still finds creative ways to support minority firms. For instance, Penney maintains an agreement with its insurance carrier to seek minority counsel when it hires attorneys for a case involving the corporation. Penney also does considerable banking with minority-owned institutions. In addition, Penney has maintained about a $1 million investment in NMSDC's Business Consortium Fund, which helps bridge the capital gap for minority companies needing to meet unusually large orders.

Berroteran notes candidly that Penney has received some pretty sweet publicity about its purchasing from minority- and woman-owned companies (it added woman-owned businesses to its initiative in 1992), another reason other corporations might want to follow its lead: "Penney has won a lot of awards for this [for instance, NMSDC's Leadership Award in 1992], and gotten a lot of other recognition. That lets people know that Penney cares, and that's good practice if you're in the customer business. And I don't know anybody who isn't."

But the best reasons to start a purchasing initiative are the core business reasons, she adds: "I can't say this enough. These vendors aren't social concerns, they're good quality suppliers and if you take that approach, you're going to have a successful program."

SOCIAL MISSION PURCHASING

COMPANY: DEJA SHOE

Policy/Practice: Social mission purchasing.

Bottom Line: Buying latex fabric from Amazonian rubber tappers and Indians helps the rain forest bounce back.

Julie Lewis wouldn't have described it in such terms back then, but the idea of entrepreneurially solving social problems took root in her while she was still a high school student in Palo Alto, California, in the early 1970s. Already a passionate environmentalist, she drove out to the local landfill, thinking it would be swell to volunteer to reclaim recyclable materials. The dump's managers thought otherwise, turning her down because of the liability risks.

Clearly, Lewis takes her no's personally. Two decades later, she founded a Portland, Oregon–based company, Deja Shoe, which makes outdoor casual shoes out of pretty much the kind of stuff she wanted to haul from the dump — old tires, polystyrene coffee cups, polyester soda pop bottles, seat cushion foam, grocery bags, and cardboard boxes — plus such industrial scrap as trim waste from disposable diaper and wet suit manufacturers and reject coffee filters and file folders.

With the company's original mission — expanding markets for recycled materials — set in motion, she and her Deja cohorts began hunting down other ways to use the company's purchasing power to further social goals.

Meanwhile, across the country, anthropologist and rain forest advocate Jason Clay had experienced an entrepreneurial brainstorm of his own. Clay, currently a Social Venture Network member, was then working with Cultural Survival, an organization dedicated to the rights and welfare of indigenous peoples. He came to the realization, as rain forest dwellers had known all along, that standing forest could generate far more income than clearing it for pasture or agriculture. So he began dreaming up businesses based on forest dwellers' harvesting non-timber rain forest products, a concept he knew could preserve native peoples' homes and livelihoods at the same time.

Serendipity soon joined Clay as a full partner. Clay's chance meeting with two members of the Grateful Dead led to the band doing a 1988 rain forest benefit at Madison Square Garden, with his project at Cultural Survival a direct beneficiary. A chance meeting with Ben & Jerry's Ben Cohen at an after-concert reception with the band led to the idea for Rainforest Crunch ice cream, using brazil nuts harvested by forest dwellers. The profuse pre-concert publicity had also magnetized tremendous public focus on the rain forest issue and helped create a market for Rainforest Crunch and hundreds of other products that would soon follow.

And, yes, Deja now offers one of those products, its Seringero "street hiker," made from a material called Treetap Vegetal Leather, a cotton-backed latex fabric made by rubber tappers and Indians in the Brazilian Amazon. The rubber tappers had lost most of their business to Indonesian plantations that could supply rubber at less cost, but some had been making waterproof sacks from this fabric for their own use for generations. Recalls Lewis, "I'd heard about this material being used in backpacks and accessory items from a friend of mine who had gone down there and said, 'You guys should use this.' So I contacted Cultural Survival to ask where I might get ahold of it."

In 1994, Deja made about 20,000 pairs of shoes with the material, which Lewis describes as looking and feeling like bomber jacket leather. At the other end of the supply line, a number of forest dwellers are now working in the trees again, which means they're not moving to the city for jobs and abandoning their land to forest-leveling ranchers and farmers. In the program's first year, Deja helped its Brazilian supplier, Couro Veyetal da Amazonia (CVA), establish thirty-six Amazonian production sites in three extractive reserves.

Deja's doing more for its rain forest partners than just putting them back to work, however. The company has chosen not to reserve exclusive rights to the material but rather develop it to the point that other manufacturers will become interested, broadening the market for the producers. Explains Bob Farentinos, Deja's vice president of environmental affairs who played a major role in building the program, "Do you play proprietary games with people's health and with the environment if you're a socially responsible company? The answer is obvious. The main reason for this program is to be true to our commitment to sustainable development, because without developing markets for recycled materials and sustainably harvested plant materials, it won't work. We've been acknowledged in the marketplace as the leaders in our industry for environmental footwear, and we're never going to lose that."

Besides, it's not as if Deja has completely ignored its own interests. The company crafted a royalty agreement with supplier CVA that gave Deja exclusive rights to use the material until the product and production processes were developed to commercial-quality levels. Deja has reached that point, but it has retained the right to identify and qualify other footwear manufacturers to use the material. Those manufacturers will pay a royalty in exchange for both permission to use the material and instruction on how. A portion of that royalty will go to Deja for its developmental efforts and technology transfer. On its own initiative, Deja also pays a royalty to the tappers and Indians for both intellectual property rights and what Far-entinos calls cultural property rights: "They need to be compensated for their images and their lifestyle because we use that in the marketing of our product."

The above implies that Deja had some problems with the original material, and it did. That's part of what distinguishes "social mission purchasing" from, say, minority-owned vendor programs. The latter are usually based on conventional products and services and an expectation of market-level quality. But partnerships undertaken for less established social/business purposes sometimes take a little work to bring the supplier up to snuff. Deja had some quality problems with the first generation of Treetap, as it did with some of its early recycled fabrics. The second generation is far superior, says Lewis, and "we're really excited about it."

But the missteps cost the company in both returned product and additional quality-control research. Many of Deja's customers are mission driven, just like the company they patronize, but Lewis knows that even conscientious consumers have limits to their patience. Unfortunately, so do Deja's venture capitalists, who sometimes push the company to market products before it's entirely comfortable with them. Says Lewis, "That's the hard part about being this kind of company. Hopefully, people will understand and hang in there with us long enough so we can get to a place that we need to be." Scores of Brazilian forest dwellers — not to mention a multitude of rain forest flora and fauna — are counting on that goodwill, too.

OVERSEAS SUPPLIERS

COMPANY: LEVI STRAUSS

Policy/Practice: Ethical guidelines for global business dealings — large company example.

Bottom Line: Levi's contracting standards are fast becoming as classic as its 501s.

In March 1992, Levi Strauss became American business's standard-bearer in something besides blue jeans. With its competitors tripping over each other as they rushed to low-wage labor markets overseas, the company announced a two-part set of ethical policies to govern its choice of contractors and countries in which it would do business. As if to underline its seriousness, the company's board later that year voted unanimously to begin withdrawing its $40 million of Levi commerce from China because of that nation's continuing human-rights violations. Soon thereafter, the company withdrew from Burma, too, stating that it was impossible to operate there without directly supporting the country's brutal military dictatorship.

This impressive series of events is just the latest in a history of social-minded management almost as old as blue denim. During the Great Depression the market for jeans nearly disappeared, but Walter Haas, Sr., who married into the Levi Strauss family, and his brother-in-law Daniel Koshland gave their employees work laying hardwood floors in a company plant so they could support their families. Haas's sons Walter, Jr., and Peter, who together ran Levi between the 1940s and 1970s, led most American companies in integrating factories in the South.

The policies regarding overseas contracting bear a genetic link to those earlier initiatives, for they stem from the regime of current CEO Robert D. Haas, a former Peace Corps volunteer and son of Walter, Jr. Handed the reins of the company in 1984, Haas then tightened his control when he engineered a leveraged buyout in 1985 that put 94 percent of the company's stock in Haas family hands. The buyout itself was ethically compromised — Levi closed twenty-six factories and slashed 6,000 jobs to help offset the $1.6 billion in new debt. However, the irony of the job cuts aside — and it's a huge aside — Haas used his newly won freedom to implement his high-ideals vision in a company he'd watched grow bloated and bureaucratic.

During the latter half of the 1980s, Haas led management through an exhaustive reexamination of Levi's core values. The effort culminated in a document articulating Levi's business and social mission. In addition to stating several specific business goals, the document commits the company to high standards in management openness, trust of employees, diversity, employee empowerment, corporate communication, and overall ethical behavior. "We pretty much view that document as our Bible," says vice president of community affairs Judy Belk.

So it didn't take long before some managers, good "Bible" students that they were, were suggesting that the company require similar behavior from its business partners. "Externally during that time," recalls Belk, "labor unions, activists, socially conscious investors, and the press were beginning to ask tough questions about U.S.-based businesses operating in Third World countries, and some companies were replying, 'We aren't accountable for our business partners. Our commitment ends when we pay our contractors for the products.' We didn't think the ethics were that clear-cut.

"The external pressure," Belk continues, "is that we're a consumer-driven company. Outside of our values, our brand and reputation are our most valued possessions. We were hearing from consumers that they were beginning to be much more concerned about where their products were being manufactured and under what circumstances. We wanted to be responsive and we wanted to do the right thing."

Thus, the Levi Strauss sourcing statement. The first part of the document "Business Partner Terms of Engagement" declares the company's intention to work with contractors enforcing high ideals in such areas as environmental standards; safe and healthy work environments; compliance with applicable laws; and employment practices including wages and benefits, working hours, child labor, prison and other forced labor, discrimination, and disciplinary practices. One plank in the terms states "we will not use contractors who . . . require in excess of a sixty-hour week," a shocking number to most Westerners, including several Levi managers. However, Belk says: "The norm in these countries is more like seventy-five to eighty hours."

The associated "Guidelines for Country Selection" delineates both business and social considerations. Among the latter, the guidelines declare the company's intention not to initiate or renew operations in countries where health and safety conditions put company representatives at serious risk or where pervasive human-rights violations occur. Primary among the business concerns, of course, is protecting the Levi Strauss brand's good name.

Statements are nice, but where Levi has really broken ground is backing them up. In addition to the China and Burma decisions, the company initiated audits of its contractors' facilities and operations, a daunting task considering that Levi works with roughly 600 contractors in fifty countries. Given the uneven reputation of Third World factories contracting with foreign corporations, Levi was pleasantly surprised on its tour. Says Belk, who has personally visited several of Levi's contractor facilities, "We found that 70 percent of our contractors were in compliance. About 25 percent we found were lacking in terms of needing to improve standards such as bathrooms, emergency exits, and wastewater treatment. The remaining 5 percent we felt either had conditions that were too deplorable or we were not at all encouraged that the conditions would change." The company terminated those relationships.

Belk says the standards have helped change behavior. "We've been told by our auditors that work standards have dramatically increased as a result of us being very clear about what our guidelines and expectations are. Reactions have been positive from our contractors as well.

But Belk adds that the company doesn't have the kind of clout in contractor relationships that some might expect. For one thing, a factory doing business with Levi often performs work for several other companies as well, none of which are asking for more than quality work. For another, factory owners often want long-term deals before they'll consent to upgrade conditions, and Levi isn't always willing to make that commitment. Explains Belk, "Another side of our ethical business practices is not to play games with our business partners. Plus, you have to understand that one of the benefits of having contractors as part of your sourcing strategy is the very flexibility that it offers you."

Despite widespread acknowledgment for Levi's leadership in overseas sourcing ethics, the company's reasons for exporting jobs in the first place don't wash with some social activists. The company endured a firestorm of criticism, two class-action lawsuits, and an employee-sponsored boycott when it closed a San Antonio Dockers plant that employed more than 1,100 people and moved the production to Costa Rica. Levi Strauss had no choice but to move to a low-wage country, president Thomas Tusher told *Business Week,* because its competition in the casual cotton pants market was doing the same thing.

The company ultimately received acclaim for how it handled the closing — giving workers ninety days' notice (sixty is required), extending health benefits for three months beyond the notice period, and providing severance pay, outplacement assistance (for fifteen months after plant closure), child-care assistance, educational services, and so on. Belk says that some 770 of the former employees found other work, including 270 placed at other Levi facilities. Courts dismissed the two lawsuits as without merit. And notably, *Hispanic Business* magazine in 1993 named the company one of the 100 best companies for Latino workers, with *Vista* magazine rating it one of the 50 best for Latina women in 1994.

"It's interesting that since that plant has closed, our U.S. workforce has increased from about 19,000 to 24,000," says Belk, "so I bristle when people allege that we're shipping jobs offshore. Actually the reverse is happening." In fact, company documents show that 85 percent of its jeans sold in the United States are made there, where the company still operates thirty-seven factories.

Still, the Dockers dilemma illustrates how difficult it is to maintain any kind of social profile in a business where the competition will kill you on price if you don't compromise yourself somewhere. Belk acknowledges that the Terms of Engagement or Guidelines for Country Selection can't always be perfectly applied and enforced in every instance. What she doesn't say is that if Levi isn't perfect, nobody's doing it better.

COMPANY: DEJA SHOE

Policy/Practice: Ethical guidelines for global business dealings — small company example.

Bottom Line: Social credibility and commitment have increased this company's impact on vendors far beyond its modest buying power.

Environmentalist Julie Lewis founded Portland, Oregon—based Deja Shoe in 1991 to make shoes from recycled materials. So it figured that when the values-driven start-up drew up its guidelines for global sourcing, the ideas would be recycled as well. For inspiration and benchmarking — and ultimately consultation — the company looked to Levi Strauss, the undisputed ethical pathfinder among companies contracting with offshore manufacturers.

Why was the supposedly socially responsible company sending its manufacturing offshore in the first place? Lewis doesn't equivocate: "People who say they'll only buy things that are 'made in America' don't realize that it's a global economy out there and that doesn't always work."

"Over the years, we've had many doors slammed loudly in our faces," adds Bob Farentinos, vice president of environmental affairs, explaining that most American factories don't want to work with product runs as small as Deja's nor are they set up for Deja's unique materials and processes. Those that have offered to work with the company will process Deja's orders only as custom shoes, which Farentinos says would triple or quadruple the shoes' retail price. And if Deja can't compete on price, it can't accomplish its mission — expanding markets for recycled and sustainable plant-based commodities.

By contrast, many overseas factories welcome start-ups. Besides, says Lewis, "Most of the factories that subcontract work to non-leather footwear companies are offshore. Basically, it's become an industry there and is more evolved there." Then toss in the fact that several Deja executives, including CEO/president Bruce MacGregor, came to Deja from Reebok's Avia subsidiary equipped with ready-made contacts with Taiwanese manufacturers. Going offshore was a no-brainer.

But the strategic advantages didn't erase the human-rights and environmental concerns, even though both Lewis and Farentinos maintain that their Taiwanese partners, who have relocated their factories to mainland China, run much cleaner operations from all standpoints than their competition in the area. So Deja went to Levi and, to a lesser extent, fellow green clothier Patagonia and Human Rights Watch, for guidance. Not surprisingly, the "Deja Shoe Global Sourcing Guidelines" cover pretty much the same territory as Levi's in pretty much the same way (see page 165).

Deja emulates Levi's attitude in its sourcing relationships as well. All factories being considered for Deja production must undergo a thorough audit, a two-part process consisting of a detailed questionnaire for the factory owner to complete followed by an interview with a Deja official. Like Levi, Deja isn't looking for perfection, just a commitment to improve up to Deja standards. "Constructive engagement" they call it here as they do in Washington, D.C., but Deja seems a little more intent on the "constructive" part than do the folks on the Beltway.

Deja also trumps Washington in knowing where to draw the line. So the company had no qualms about telling a monolithic Japanese holding company from which it had been buying a synthetic shoe fabric that it wasn't sure it could continue their relationship. Why? Deja had learned from friend Rainforest Action Network (RAN) that one of the holding company's subsidiaries was, in Lewis's words, "raping Indonesian rain forests." "Now if you can imagine the scale here," adds Farentinos, "it's a David-and-Goliath situation — a company probably in the hundred-billion-dollar-a-year range listening to a company about these issues that's new on the block and first year has gross sales of a couple million. And we're Americans on top of that.

"We said, 'Look, we can't be working in the Amazon trying to save the rain forest [Deja's purchase of a sustainably harvested rubber fabric — see page 160] on the one hand and have a business associate who's accused by the environmental community and others of trading with these wood chippers in Southeast Asia.' But two days after we broached this issue, the president of the company in North America came here to Portland and sat down with us." As of this writing in early 1995, the dialogue was continuing after discussions moved to New York and then Tokyo. But it appears the company may soon modify some of its environmental practices to keep Deja, which has won a United Nations environmental award among other public acknowledgment, as a client. "Sometimes I wonder why these huge corporations and factories listen to us," says Farentinos, "and I think the answer is that everybody wants to do the right thing but they're not aware of what that is or how to do it."

Deja has also staked out important social middle ground with its assembly contractors. For example, to address the toxic work conditions under which many shoe assemblers work, Deja developed a water-based adhesive for some of its styles and has trained its contractors to use it. Says Lewis, "We're excited about that because the workers aren't inhaling volatile chemicals, and the contractors are excited about it because they can now use this technology with their other vendors."

Lewis doesn't deny that Deja's lack of monetary clout sometimes makes life difficult. It's not always easy to get a contractor to adapt to Deja's idiosyncratic materials and methods, and Deja comes up with one of those after another. But the company's credibility in the environmental community, and relationships with powerful groups like RAN, expand its aura considerably, enabling David to deal with Goliath even without benefit of slingshot. Says Lewis, "We aren't going to say 'No, we won't deal with companies that are supposedly doing bad things with the environment or their people.' We're going to go in there and say, 'How can we help you do better?' I think that's the way that businesses are going to effect change."

Community &
Society-at-Large

CASH PHILANTHROPY

COMPANIES: BEN & JERRY'S AND WORKING ASSETS FUNDING SERVICE

Policy/Practice: Social change philanthropy.

Bottom Line: Checkbook activism.

If you think the economy is squeezing your lifestyle, consider the plight of the Gwich'in Indians on the coastal plain of the Arctic National Wildlife Refuge. The soil of the plain never thaws, so little grows there but tundra and, in the summer, vast clouds of mosquitoes. With jobs even scarcer than people and arctic grocery prices stratospheric, many of the highly traditional Gwich'in support their families as their ancestors did — following the 200,000 caribou that roam the plain, which supply them not only meat but also bones for toolmaking and skins for clothing.

In recent years, the oil industry has forced on the Gwich'in a nontraditional ordeal as well: lobbying Congress through an advocacy organization called the Gwich'in Steering Committee to permanently protect the refuge as wilderness. Oil companies have long pursued access to what they maintain are rich pools of oil beneath the plain, and their sorry environmental track record threatens the caribou herds and thus the Gwich'in's very existence. Unfortunately, battling big oil takes big bucks — consistent bucks, too, because the industry will gladly concede its opponents a battle or two if it can exhaust their resources in the process.

Until a few years ago, the Gwich'in might have scanned the entire universe of corporate philanthropy without finding a sympathetic ear. Corporate philanthropy does plenty of good in the world, but it does not traditionally fund constituencies as far out of the mainstream as the Gwich'in, particularly when corporate brethren glare from the other side of the issue. In the last decade or so, however, a number of smaller progressive companies have funneled generous chunks of their revenues to exactly the type of desperate — and to the mainstream, obscure — social causes that the Gwich'in represent. A $10,000 1993 grant from the Ben & Jerry's Foundation (plus $15,000 from the Threshold Foundation, a group of progressive philanthropists first gathered by Social Venture Network co-founder Josh Mailman) "allowed us to keep our doors open under extreme fiscal stress," longtime Gwich'in advocate and Gwich'in Steering Committee consultant Bob Childers told me from the committee's Anchorage, Alaska, office.

In the overall corporate landscape, Ben & Jerry's Foundation is still a small funder (about $800,000 distributed in 1993), but its thoughtfully selected grants make all the difference in the world to stressed, bare-bones organizations like the Gwich'in Steering Committee. In 1991, the committee attracted substantial foundation support to help it rout a Senate bill that would have permitted oil exploration in the refuge. However, once that fragile victory was bagged, the committee's funding dried up even though big oil immediately began planning its next massive assault on Capitol hill. "The progressive funds like Ben & Jerry's and Threshold were the only ones who stuck with us when it wasn't flashy," Childers said, sighing, aware that the insolvent committee still faced a scary future, particularly with the Republican majority elected to Congress in 1994.

The story of Ben & Jerry's Foundation may not be as gripping as the Gwich'in's, but it helps illustrate the new direction in business philanthropy pioneered by progressive companies. Ben Cohen and Jerry Greenfield didn't plan on having much extra to give away when in 1978 they started a little ice-cream operation in an abandoned gas station in Burlington, Vermont. But everything they did in those early days worked, and suddenly Ben & Jerry's began ascending with the thrust of an Atlas missile. The two founders were so startled to find themselves members of what they regarded as the exploiter class that they contemplated selling the company.

Luckily for both ice-cream lovers and others with more basic needs, Cohen and Greenfield decided to stick it out and keep growing the company "into something we could respect ourselves for," Cohen recalls. The new idea was to create a business that used its wealth-creating capacity to further progressive social goals, a model that would demonstrate to the mainstream business community that profits on the one hand and the needs of people and planet on the other need not be opposed. Fundamental to that model was a foundation that would donate 7.5 percent of pretax profits to community organizations, scooping the competition several times over. (The average corporation gives under 2 percent of pretax profits.) What's more, the foundation would address causes that were starkly underserved by traditional grant making, such as poverty, bigotry, peace, and human rights.

Cohen made the Ben & Jerry's Foundation a reality in 1985 by donating $500,000 of stock for an operating endowment. Over the years, the foundation has come to focus not only on neglected causes but also on social change. Explains director Ellen Furnari, "We were flooded with human and social service kinds of proposals, all of which sounded wonderful, but we felt that being a small foundation, we wanted to concentrate on addressing the underlying causes for these problems." This too sets the company apart from most other corporate givers. In many companies, somebody upstairs simply writes disinterested checks to traditional umbrella organizations like the United Way, which rarely if ever distributes funds to grassroots groups or considers emerging issues. Nor will you find many Fortune 500 corporate foundations supporting a redistribution of power and wealth.

In a similar reflective vein, the foundation has moved to walk its talk internally by democratically involving employees in both review of grant proposals and the actual grant making — after all, Furnari points out, employees contribute funds in the sense that money fed to the foundation isn't feeding their compensation. If fact, 35 percent of the foundation's funds now go directly to employee community action teams in five company sites. The teams then choose projects that meet community needs in Vermont and supply the requisite bucks and volunteer labor. For example, in 1994 one team challenged other teams to match its assistance to Vermont Cares, the main AIDS service organization in Vermont whose building was destroyed by arson.

For the moneys that the foundation distributes on its own, says Furnari, "we have a guideline — and we're very clear that guidelines aren't rules so we certainly make exceptions — that we fund organizations that have budgets of about $300,000 or less. So I'd say that a significant part of our funding goes to very small, very much frontline organizations, community-based — you know, a couple of staff people plugging away."

It's likely that Working Assets Funding Service, which offers a baldly progressive cause-oriented credit card, long-distance telephone service, and travel agency, consults the biggest grant-review committee in philanthropy, because its customers nominate, and then vote on, recipients for the company's grants. Of course, as with any corporate philanthropy, the customers are the ultimate source of the funds. But the circuit from customer wallet to grantee follows a more direct route in Working Assets' case — each time a customer uses one of its services, the company donates a fixed percentage to the grant pool.

Company co-founder/CEO Laura Scher exults that this formula yielded over $1 million in grants off $35 million in revenue in 1993. That percentage far exceeds even the profound generosity of Ben & Jerry's, a $154 million business that year. With the company one of the fastest-growing in the country, the grants pot is growing commensurately.

Like many progressive philanthropists, says Scher, "we like to fund small organizations," and she acknowledges several issue preferences as well. So the company takes several steps to make the grant making more than a popularity contest. Customers must confine their nominations to four categories — peace, human rights, economic justice, and environment — and groups of at least national scope. Adds Scher, "We like to create a balance of organizations that focus on the issues we've identified. Like in the human-rights category, we're going to find a group that works on a woman's rights of choice, and a group that works on gay and lesbian rights, and children's rights." So what customers ultimately vote on is actually a company-selected ballot of thirty-six finalists. Working Assets then allocates funds by percentage of votes.

As with Ben & Jerry's, the social savvy behind Working Assets' grant making helps mitigate the limitations of its far-less-than Fortune 500 pocketbook. Scher takes obvious pleasure in noting that "when we started our phone service, AT&T that same year caved in to right-wing pressure and stopped granting to Planned Parenthood. We had this dream of replacing that. AT&T had given Planned Parenthood $50,000, and this year [1993] Planned Parenthood got $55,000 from Working Assets."

In-Kind Philanthropy

Company: Merck

Policy/Practice: Donating or otherwise facilitating the distribution of critical drugs to needy populations.

Bottom Line: Probably the greatest in-kind giving program in U.S. corporate history.

The reason they call the disease onchocerciasis "river blindness" is simple and hellish. Transmitted by the blackfly, which breeds in fast-flowing rivers in Africa and Central and South America, onchocerciasis has left sightless millions of people in those countries. The blackfly carries larvae of the *Onchocerca volvulus* worm. When the fly bites a human, the larvae infect the body, quickly growing into threadlike adult worms that live under the skin for up to twelve years. The prodigious offspring, called microfilariae, migrate through the skin, causing severe itching, skin eruptions, and weight loss. When they colonize the eyes, they create lesions that can cause total, permanent blindness. Flies biting infected humans ingest the microfilariae, and then carry them as infective larvae to new victims.

In some areas of West Africa, roughly 15 percent of the population are without sight. Overall, the World Health Organization (WHO) estimates that 18 million people are infected throughout the world, and some 85 million threatened. The disease devastates whole economies and social structures, not just individual lives. Entire communities sometimes abandon their riverside homes to escape the blackfly infestations, leaving behind their best croplands, the source of their food, cotton, and livestock feed. Then there is the problem of providing for the helpless victims.

In the last few years, a happier and hopeful side to this story has emerged, thanks to the efforts of pharmaceutical giant Merck, developer of a remarkably effective treatment for river blindness. The drug, called ivermectin, doesn't kill the adult worms, but it does destroy the microfilariae, eliminating serious symptoms and hampering the adult worm's ability to reproduce. Annual dosages, which have no substantial side effects, keep the disease under control until the adult worms die of old age. In 1994 alone, Merck, a leader in an industry not always thought of in humanitarian terms, provided free ivermectin, trademarked in human formulation as Mectizan, to 11 million people. As of mid-1994, Merck had donated more than 29 million Mectizan tablets. And the project is ramping up to reach 23 million people by 1996, helped by a World Bank grant program expected to attract $120 million over twelve years to aid the distribution endeavor.

The Mectizan story began in the mid-1970s with the serendipity that is the lifeblood of the drug industry. Merck researchers had been looking for a drug that could attack stubborn worm parasites in livestock. In 1975, they hit pay dirt, literally. A bacterium in a soil sample dug up at a golf course near Ito, Japan, not only wiped out the worms in infested mice but did so in tiny amounts with no adverse effects.

After isolating the key compound and synthesizing a still more active analogue, Merck scientists were developing the drug for the animal health market when in 1978, they tripped upon a more urgent application. In tests, ivermectin demonstrated its effectiveness against a filarial worm in horses; Merck's William Campbell realized the worm resembled the river blindness parasite and alerted management. His boss,

Dr. Roy Vagelos, encouraged him to follow up on the river blindness application. By 1981, clinical research reached the stage of the first tests on human patients; as with mice, a single dose decimated microfilariae counts with no serious reactions.

As ivermectin continued to prove out in the lab, Merck's management began to focus on the problem of distributing the drug. By mid-1986, the company had already invested millions in researching ivermectin's use for river blindness, with millions more likely before the clinical trial phase ended. Yet it was clear that neither the victim populations nor their governments could pay for the drug. And outright donation of the drug presented its own problems. If Merck gave away Mectizan, would the costly program discourage rivals from researching drugs for other tropical diseases? Besides, would patients value a free drug? And would they trust it?

Meanwhile, ivermectin was passing through the final stages of the test gauntlet with no signs of problems. In October 1987, aware that French authorities were about to approve the drug (many of the river blindness victims were in French Africa) and his company would be asked for its decision, Vagelos — now Merck chairman — announced that the company would provide ivermectin without charge to as many people as needed it for as long as necessary. Recalling the decision today, Vagelos says simply, "It was something the company could not step away from once we recognized the potential of the drug."

Working with WHO, Merck sought third-party support for a distribution program, fraught with its own daunting challenges. River blindness plagues mainly remote regions of nations with scant resources and infrastructure to supply even their citizens' most basic health needs. But Vagelos's October 1987 announcement stated, "distribution to the people in need was the final responsibility of our company."

To help with the massive effort, Merck sponsored an expert committee headed by international public health expert Dr. William Foege, head of the Carter Center in Atlanta. Former president Carter himself has since played a key role in coordinating the cooperation of foreign governments in treating their citizens, and numerous voluntary non-governmental organizations have pitched in with dollars and labor to deliver Mectizan into the bush. While the helping organizations have been crucial, Merck's participation remains massive. Several full-time positions, including physicians and marketing people, are devoted to the project. Then there's the ever-increasing production of Mectizan itself, says Vagelos.

In their 1993 book, *The One Hundred Best Companies to Work for in America,* authors Milton Moskowitz and Robert Levering said of the Mectizan project, ". . . cynics might say that Merck, as one of the most profitable companies on the face of the earth, could easily afford this kind of largesse. But that misses the point. Other companies make a lot of money and don't act the way Merck does. The culture here is steeped in acts of benevolence."

Indeed. In the 1940s, a Rutgers University scientist working on a Merck grant discovered streptomycin, a key antibiotic in the treatment of tuberculosis, then a major killer internationally. Under George W. Merck, the company relinquished patent rights and helped companies around the world learn to produce it. In 1987, the company made available to the Chinese, without profit, the vaccine-making technology to help prevent liver cancer, a leading cause of death in that nation. Partially inspired by Merck's Mectizan program, DuPont and American Cyanamid have sponsored a water filter distribution program to eradicate Guinea worm disease.

Despite the river blindness initiative's considerable and continuing cost, Vagelos says that shareholders have been completely supportive. "I've received more mail based on this decision than on anything else we've done as a company. Not one wasn't positive." He adds, "More important than our shareholders, I thought, was the effect on the people at Merck, who wrote to me — literally by the hundreds — about what a fantastic move this was for our company."

In September 1994, Vagelos journeyed with Jimmy and Rosalynn Carter to the village of Nia in Chad. Nearly every one of the 500 residents has contracted river blindness, which until the trip physician Vagelos had never observed firsthand: "We saw a twenty-five-year-old woman with an infant who is less than a year old. The woman was completely blind. We heard from another woman that she has a son at home, age fifteen, already blind." Vagelos saw as well the suspicion with which victims tend to eye free pills. But he stayed long enough to also see the fear change to overwhelming gratitude: "The Mectizan stops the itching, which they notice within a few days. Then they defecate these dead worms. So for the first time in their lives they have rid many of these intestinal parasites and they know they are not going to be blind."

COMPANY: MORRISON & FOERSTER

Policy/Practice: Donating tens of thousands of hours of legal services annually to needy persons and parties acting in the public interest.

Bottom Line: Don't worry about "MoFo" — it's benefiting nearly as much as its pro bono clients.

In 1992, northern California's San Jose Unified School District, operating under court supervision because of a 1984 Ninth Circuit ruling that it was intentionally segregating its Latino students, went back to court to try and get the supervision lifted because, it argued, it had eliminated the problem. But most Latino parents in the district felt otherwise, and they too had counsel — a crack team from one of the most prestigious law firms in the country, San Francisco–based

Morrison & Foerster, who represented 13,000 Latino students in the case.

As co-counsel with the Mexican American Legal Defense Fund and two other public-interest law organizations, the "MoFo" team litigated the case for over a year, ultimately negotiating a consent decree that obligated the district, under continuing supervision, to boost Latino participation in gifted programs, eliminate discriminatory ability-grouping practices, improve bilingual education programs, and increase parents' involvement. The case, considered a landmark in school desegregation law, won an award from the California State Bar. MoFo's charge for team services: *nada*.

And that was hardly a onetime gesture by the firm. MoFo, in fact, does more pro bono work for the public interest and disadvantaged persons than any law outfit in the country — over 84,000 hours in 1993 alone, including 67,000 hours by partners and full-time associates. If you'e counting, that's the equivalent of a firm of forty full-time attorneys plus ten non-lawyer professionals doing purely public-interest work. MoFo, however, is *not* a public-interest law firm. It is one of the most successful law corporations in the country, with much of its revenues generated by high-priced business litigation.

By the same token, says Jack Londen, who led the team that litigated the San Jose case and chairs MoFo's pro bono committee, pro bono work is central to the Morrison & Foerster culture and ethic: "People come to MoFo because they believe in pro bono and want to do it. From at least the early fifties, this has been true of people in the top levels of management all the way down."

Londen, who also heads one of MoFo's corporate litigation teams, argues that MoFo's business edge depends in part on the firm's pro bono program: "Put it this way," he says. "Suppose you were a car manufacturer and you gave your engineers who design great cars the same pay and offices and other perks as other car manufacturers, but you also gave them this added perk — that every so often they could take over the assembly line and build whatever kind of car they want. Because you offer that perk, the engineers that you would get are going to be the ones who love building cars and are devoted to their profession.

"It's my belief that people who want to do pro bono include those people who really believe in the law, and are good lawyers because they are devoted to it. It works out well for us because if we pull in one more rainmaker — an attorney who's not only very good but also perceived as such by clients — the additional work that person can bring us over the course of a career is enough to pay for the cost of the whole program. I can't prove it because I can't measure it that well, but I can point to people who came to MoFo because of our pro bono work and who turned out to be that type of rainmaker."

But the pro bono program does far more for MoFo than just give it a recruiting advantage, maintains Londen: "We spend a lot of time on important matters that involve great sums of money on corporate balance sheets. We care a great deal about our clients' matters but it's also good for balance to be able to do something that affects somebody's life in human terms."

For Londen personally, the San Jose case supremely demonstrated that sort of opportunity: "There's a generation of lawyers for whom the *Brown v. Board of Education* case that the Supreme Court issued in 1954 is a high point. It showed that the courts and the Constitution can change and that conversion improved the country. The chance to work on the legacy of that case in real life was very exciting."

In the overall scheme of corporate philanthropy and in-kind donations, MoFo's pro bono program also stands apart in its emphasis on social justice. In 1993, nearly all of its pro bono hours were spent on cases involving disadvantaged children and education; persons with disabilities and AIDS; housing and homelessness; nonprofit organizations; and a multitude of civil-rights issues. For instance, the New York office in 1993 helped protect women's access to family planning clinics by defending and enforcing judgments that the National Organization of Women (NOW) had obtained against Operation Rescue and other leaders of the anti-abortion crusade. Most companies — of MoFo's size and establishment credentials, anyway — wouldn't go near a controversy like that and would also stay clear of many other social causes with which MoFo identifies itself.

Part of that difference stems from the American legal ideal of everyone being equal before the law. But part is quintessential MoFo. Says Londen, not every MoFo attorney volunteers for pro bono service, "because that's viewed as a matter of personal choice." But those who don't still seem to find a way to contribute. "There are a lot of lawyers who themselves don't do [pro bono] but who take pride and do a little bit more billable work so that others can do it. I don't imagine there's anybody who interviews here without talking to us about our pro bono program."

VOLUNTEERISM *and* OTHER COMMUNITY INVOLVEMENT

COMPANY: WHITE DOG CAFE

Policy/Practice: Using the convening power of a retail business to raise social awareness and involvement.

Bottom Line: Total quality management carried to its logical extreme.

As Judy Wicks recounts all the social programs she runs through her business, you wonder if you've misunderstood. You've heard her say that the White Dog Cafe is a single Philadelphia restaurant, not a chain with stores strung coast to coast. How then to explain all this activity?:

- A citizen diplomacy effort called "Table for Five Billion, Please!" in which Wicks, her chef-partner Kevin von Klause, and as many customers as they can entice into joining them journey to foreign nations — Cuba, Vietnam, Nicaragua, and others on the wrong side of U.S. foreign policy — and establish sister restaurant relationships;

- An analogous program, the Philadelphia Sister Restaurant Project, that promotes understanding between ethnic groups and classes by ushering White Dog patrons to minority-owned restaurants and other establishments in neighborhoods they might otherwise avoid or neglect;

- The PUPPY (Promoting Urban Partnerships with Philadelphia Youth) Program, which engages inner-city high school students in mentoring relationships, school-to-work transition projects, and youth activism;

- Community Tours to promote customer awareness of issues and culture in distressed Philadelphia neighborhoods;

- A Table Talk lecture program, which follows White Dog meals with speakers and discussions on issues of public concern:

- Annual multicultural events at White Dog, such as Martin Luther King, Jr., memorial meals, a Native American Thanksgiving dinner, and a Latin American buffet called Noche Latina.

It doesn't stop there. White Dog also hosts political fundraisers for liberal and progressive candidates, an annual AIDs dinner, cast parties for theater openings, and benefits or at-cost events for local social-change organizations. It furthers other social goals through its purchasing. The restaurant buys produce and humanely killed animals when available from local organic family farms. The Black Cat gift store adjoining White Dog stocks community-based products (example: jewelry made from recycled Mardi Gras gowns by disabled and homeless workers in New Orleans).

It's hard to imagine that one could manage a profitable business with so much energy — and often, cash — flowing to the peripheries. But White Dog does just fine, thank you. In 1993, the restaurant and gift shop had sales of about $3.65

million with profits of about $300,000. That 8 percent profit margin beats the industry average by about three points although Wicks then plows about 10 percent of after-tax profits back into White Dog social-change projects and progressive philanthropy.

You might also expect that the mind-spinning distractions would play hell with the quality. But quality is White Dog's hallmark. In 1993, *Condé Nast Traveler* magazine named White Dog as one of the fifty top American restaurants, the only Pennsylvania establishment honored. That same year, *Inc.* magazine acknowledged White Dog for quality of a different kind, listing it as one of the best small companies to work for in the nation. (Former waitress Wicks provides long-time waiters with health insurance and paid vacations, among other unusual working conditions in this low- to no-benefit industry.) The company's all-around success comes as a bracing rejoinder to those who insist that such high ideals and profits can't be wed.

So how does Wicks do it — besides having a metabolism like Philadelphia Electric? For one thing, her several managers handle the day-to-day operation of White Dog and Black Cat while she attends to the social-change agenda. But she's still got both hands in the business as well, overseeing it as general manager in weekly meetings with senior staff:

"I used to think about getting out of business and becoming more involved with just the issues part of it," she admits. "And then I realized, what makes it work for me is using the restaurant as a vehicle. I'm convinced that business is the way to go, that if all businesses don't start getting in some way involved in social issues and making decisions that benefit communities, then nothing is going to change." Toward that end, White Dog runs a New Visions in Business program with speakers focusing on how to use a company as a catalyst for social change; Wicks solicits attendees to invite their bosses — on her dime — to future sessions.

Judy is the first to acknowledge that her activism has boosted the business as well. Wicks and White Dog have received numerous awards, some of them national, along with profuse media attention, even though White Dog doesn't aggressively promote its image as a values-driven business. Focusing that kind of public attention on an eaterie that could stand on its culinary reputation alone is a combination that cooks.

None of this is to suggest that the various pulls on Wick's attention don't cause tensions: "I think the managers feel that I neglect them a lot of the time. It's certainly not an easy thing but I don't know how else to do it. The actual mechanism of the business is just not enough to hold my attention and I find myself more and more drawn into the social-issues part of it. I feel really fortunate to have the type of business where I can link the two pretty nicely." In fact, when we spoke, she was in the process of establishing a nonprofit organization that could expand the reach of her social endeavors.

One thing that hasn't taken away from the business is her out-front progressivism. The upscale, not inexpensive fare draws as many customers from the wealthy, largely Republican suburbs as from the university neighborhood. Wicks says that Arlen Specter, the Republican senator from Philadelphia, and his wife eat there often: "I've never had anyone say that they wouldn't come here because of my politics. I've had even people who disagree with me tell me they respect what I'm doing." Besides, she adds, "You spend most of your time at work so if your work isn't somehow involved with social change, it's just not going to happen. You have to find a way to combine work and citizenship whether you own your own business or not."

COMPANY: XEROX

Policy/Practice: Social-service sabbaticals and other financially supported employee volunteerism.

Bottom Line: The community obviously benefits, but Xerox may be the biggest winner of all.

For seven years, Monica Milstead sold copiers, fax machines, and laser printers for Stamford, Connecticut–based Xerox, and she did it well, winning several company awards. But she was growing restless, for her job didn't begin to address the totality of who she was. She wanted to move people's lives, not just hardware.

Fortunately, Milstead works for a community-minded company that includes concerns like hers in the way it defines work. Milstead, who holds a master's degree in urban sociology, spent calendar year 1994 doing fund-raising, marketing, and public relations for a small Orange Country, California, public-service agency, ARK Services for Abused Children, which provides support services for abused children in foster care. The project was her idea, but Xerox supported it by paying Milstead her full paycheck, benefits, and vacation time through its social service leave program. At year's end, Milstead returned to her job, which the program guaranteed while she was away.

Many manufacturers have followed Xerox into the copier business, but none have duplicated its outstanding record of community involvement. In addition to more conventional employee volunteerism (see below), Xerox allows several highly qualified employees each year to do what Monica has done, take fully compensated time off — up to twelve months — to contribute to social-action projects. Employees initiate the process: they choose the agency with which they wish to work, enlist that agency's cooperation, and apply for the leave — with or without their manager's permission.

Yes, managers can appeal upstairs to keep their charges on board, but they've learned to think twice before trying. Says Joseph M. Cahalan, who as vice president of the Xerox Foundation oversees social service leaves, "only two managers have ever pled that the employee was too valuable and not be allowed to go." In the first case, the company asked the employee, a one-man band in his job, to delay his leave for ninety days while his manager coped with replacing him. In the second instance, recalls Cahalan with a chuckle, "the CEO wrote a letter himself that I had nothing to do with chastising the manager, saying the individual might just as well leave the company tomorrow for a whole variety of other reasons, so you should probably reconsider your succession practices."

The tone of that response goes back to the leave program's origins in the early 1970s, when, Cahalan says, the company "was doing very, very well." As he tells the story, company executives were flying back to Stamford after presenting a large donation to a California university when then-president Archie R. McCardell remarked to the human resources director "how easy it was for Xerox to have made this grant. They fell into a conversation about what really would be a sacrifice and concluded that a truly major contribution would be volunteering some of our best people to the nonprofit sector."

Xerox places few strictures on leave applicants. Primarily, they must be employees in good standing with at least three years of Xerox service, and the target project just be neither political, religious, nor sectarian. (A church-sponsored homeless shelter would be okay; recruiting members for the church would not.) Of the some 400 people who have take social service leaves, Cahalan can only remember one who abused the program by not doing what he applied to do. He was terminated. (The company does require employees to file monthly reports while on leave.)

Xerox makes no pretense that the nonprofit sector is the only beneficiary of the program, because the company usually gets back an employee who is reinvigorated, profoundly grateful, and even more able than when he or she left. Says Milstead, "Xerox has done a wonderful thing for me and I feel very loyal toward them. But I've also learned a host of new skills at ARK. I've managed public events with teams of fifteen to twenty people — that was a new, wonderful experience. And I'd never worked with the press before." She was still in the midst of her leave when she applied for a job in Stamford managing an employee communications project. "It's a long shot," she admitted at the time, "but it's an example of the kinds of things I could get into now."

In fact, Cahalan notes, the very nature of working for small nonprofits tends to broaden volunteers, who usually wear far more hats in those settings than in a mega-organization like Xerox: "As fate would have it, over the last several years we've been trying to break the company down into smaller entrepreneurial groups where you get people away from being a specialist and into being much broader based. So the program fits hand in glove with the kind of management people we're trying to develop."

If the social service leave program was Xerox's only community effort, its impact would be largely symbolic. As of this writing in mid-1994, the company employed about 56,000 employees nationally; it caps social service leaves at about twenty approved applications each year. But in 1974, the company started the Xerox Community Involvement Program (XCIP), largely in response to returning social service leave-takers who wanted to continue volunteering with their employer's support. Cahalan says that about 20,000 — well over a third — of Xerox employees annually participate in XCIP projects. In fact, Milstead began her association with ARK as a volunteer through XCIP. She has participated in the program since her first days at the company and continued to take part in meetings during her leave.

Through XCIP, Xerox channels both funds and employee volunteer teams to local projects in communities where the company operates. Although site managers can initiate XCIP committees, committees usually form because of an employee's interest in a particular community need. The manager then appoints a committee coordinator — often that same employee — who recruits a team of volunteers that represents a broad cross-section of the local company workforce. The team then selects projects, recruits additional volunteers as needed, and implements action strategies.

Those strategies often include a request for seed money from Xerox, which seems happy to comply so long as the project (1) attracts the enthusiastic participation of Xerox volunteers; (2) depends more on the creative application of their talents than whatever modest support the company provides; and (3) makes a lasting impact on the community. Project examples include renovating a teen center, tutoring children in disadvantaged neighborhoods, and holding fundraising events to support social service centers.

At the time of this writing, Xerox had been through a series of downsizings and restructurings and employee morale was not what it had been. Milstead understands the company's restraint about trumpeting its employee volunteerism to the public, but suggests it consider promoting its social efforts more widely within: "If employees are focused on using the power of the corporation to make a difference in the community, they feel so good about what they are doing every day that they feel better about their jobs overall and perform at a higher level."

COMPANY: THE BODY SHOP FRANCHISES

Policy/Practice: Paying employees to volunteer for community projects.

Bottom Line: A big reason that Body Shop employees act like more than just warm bodies.

The growth of the Body Shop from Anita Roddick's little natural cosmetics shop in Brighton, England in 1976 to a $657.3 million company in 1994 is one of progressive business's most colorful stories. But despite the prolific revenues, 1994 was not one of the Body Shop's boffo years. In September 1994, *Business Ethics,* a magazine widely read by those who track business responsibility, published a too-hot-to-touch feature — written by freelancer and former ABC "Nightline" reporter John Entine — accusing the Body Shop of unsavory business practices and unrepentant hypocrisy concerning its social posture. Amid a flurry of charges, Entine maintained that the company deceived consumers about both the naturalness and freedom from animal testing of its product ingredients; misled franchisees about the financial prospects for their stores; and oversold the public about the extent of its philanthropy.

The Body Shop described by Entine was not one that Kate Abell, an employee of the Montgomery Mall Body Shop franchise in Bethesda, Maryland, recognized. In addition to her duties as a retail clerk, she receives paid time off to deliver hot meals to homebound AIDS patients: "The community service projects were one of the things that drew me to the Body Shop. I think it's really phenomenal that I'm paid to do work whose rewards to me are much greater than money could ever match."

Kevin Spriggs has managed the store at which Abell works since 1991. The impact of the meals program, which store staff participates in as volunteers for an organization called Food & Friends, hit home for him after the name of a patient to whom he and the staff had delivered meals for several months suddenly vanished from the delivery list. "That usually means they're very sick in the hospital or they've died." Spriggs notes. In fact, the man had improved sufficiently to get an apartment and begin living independently. Says Spriggs, "He felt the meals, and the people who brought them, were really important to his recovery. Now, he goes around to schools and talks about AIDS."

Spriggs finds it almost as gratifying to watch how the volunteering affects his staff: "Typically, I see a lot of growth in them as human beings, and I think a lot of it ties in to the way they are at work. In most stores, you don't know what happens to the money after you sell the pair of gloves. But here, you know that it helps support projects like this, and I think we actually get better employees from that alone."

The Body Shop's community orientation also attracted Helen Mills and Susan Spriggs (Kevin Spriggs's mother) to the company. As partners in the Soapbox Trading Company, they own the Montgomery Mall store at which Kate Abell and Kevin Spriggs work, as well as four other Body Shop franchises in the Washington, D.C., area. Mills first heard about the company from her sister after the public relations firm where the latter worked was engaged by the Body Shop to handle its initial American publicity. Intrigued by the company's progressive philosophy, she and Spriggs inquired about buying a franchise. Mills recalls, "When they interviewed us on our interests in giving back to the community and our commitment to supporting that, we found that very exciting and honorable and it really helped bond us." After confirming their impressions of the company while guests of Anita and Gordon Roddick in their Scotland home, Mills and Spriggs became the Body Shop's first American franchisees.

As of late 1994, the Food & Friends project had run longer than any volunteer program at any American Body

Shop store. But it wasn't the only community project on the Montgomery store's docket. In summer 1994, staff there also volunteered to provide child care at a family shelter in nearby Rockville. Every other Thursday evening, two employees traveled to the shelter for a three-hour shift paid by Soapbox. The store's staff also takes on some joint projects in conjunction with employees at the other Soapbox franchises.

Soapbox permits staff at each of its stores to choose their own projects and decide how they want to use their paid volunteer time, which Soapbox limits to an average of about twelve hours per month per store to control costs and ensure proper coverage during working hours. Says Mills, "On an ongoing project, we like them to have it come from their hearts and their minds and allocate their energy toward it." But she adds that employees tend to do considerable additional volunteering on their own time and have also pitched in to help with community projects that Soapbox initiates outside its stores.

For instance, in 1993 Mills, Susan Spriggs, and two others created a company called City Works to create jobs for the economically disempowered. City Works hires clients of an organization called Jubilee Jobs, a job-placement firm for the disadvantaged, to screen-print T-shirts, which it then sells to its biggest regular account, the Body Shop, and a growing list of other customers. It then plows its profits back into job creation at either City Works or Jubilee Jobs. Says Mills, "Our [Body Shop] employees have really gotten behind City Works. We've had hundreds of hours devoted to that project."

Mills acknowledges that because her franchises are more established than many, they have an easier time sustaining projects than franchisees in their start-up years, "but every franchisee that I talk to has something going," a testimony to the values orientation of the international corporation's franchisee recruiting process. (In its company stores and corporate offices, the Body Shop encourages full-time employees to volunteer for four paid hours per month and part-time employees two hours per month, a policy Entine failed to cover; the corporation suggests that franchisees adopt a similar practice.)

Of course, because Soapbox lets staff develop their own projects, "each of these projects is in various states of building up or winding down in step with the interests of the staff and staff turnover."

The latter factor plays a much smaller role at her stores than at other retail outlets, however. In addition to the exceptionally low turnover of sales clerks, Mills says that managerial turnover "is next to nothing. We noticed at our managers' meeting recently that our shortest-term manager has been with us four years and the others have been there five and six years. You just don't keep people in the same job with those kinds of hours without a job-enrichment factor, so the community service has also been a very strategic business thing."

As an early franchisee, Mills knew the Body Shop in its formative years. She describes a well-intentioned but often naive senior management that seemed overwhelmed early on by the market response to its concepts. Plain and simple, she says, management made some hasty and ill-advised decisions, especially in the hiring area, in its frantic efforts to build an organization: "So that was really the larger issue [of the 1994 controversy]. It was not an ethics story, it was a business story and that's where [Entine] was off."

So she remains confident that the Body Shop's core ideals such as store-supported community service remain its business edge: "Our practices and our values are unparalleled in rival stores, and that gives us a hard-core employee and customer alliance that the competitors can never touch."

COMPANY: BLUE FISH CLOTHING

Policy/Practice: A paid volunteerism program aimed at schools with little or no arts funding.

Bottom Line: A niche-market company finds the perfect niche for its good works.

Blue Fish Clothing exudes a decidedly counterculture vibration in a marketplace that clearly still clamors for it. The company makes dreamy, free-flowing garments in natural fabrics. Each item that emerges from the studio is unique, block printed by hand by fabric artists who then sign their work.

There's another countercultural side to Blue Fish as well — a host of progressive social practices. The company does most of the basics: using recycled paper and soy inks in the office, donating to environmental groups, and so forth. But in the last couple of years, it has also added an initiative as distinctly Blue Fish as a block-printed T-shirt: a growing program called BlueFishgarten, which brings Blue Fish staff to share their art making with children.

BlueFishgarten took shape in late 1993 under the leadership of Fleurette Wallach, the company's "director of culture works," who had joined the company earlier that year with husband Marc, a fashion-industry veteran hired as the company's CEO. Fleurette, whose Blue Fish responsibilities include the company's community-involvement activities, had for several years previously taught in a federally funded reading-improvement program at a small Catholic school, St. Boniface, whose students were predominantly from Hispanic families in a low-income neighborhood. The financially troubled school had been without an arts program for a decade;

after coming on staff, it didn't take Fleurette long to find a match between the children's needs and what Blue Fish could supply.

"[Blue Fish founder Jennifer Barclay] built this business after starting out block-printing clothes in her parents' garage. So she has this dream and it becomes a very successful reality and now she wants to help others do the same. We wanted to share with children that art is a way to make dreams real."

Besides, the idea made so much sense in other ways as well. Blue Fish uses the kind of simple, life-affirming images in its block prints — animals, celestial bodies, acoustic musical instruments, and abstract designs — that a child would appreciate and most are drawn from multicultural sources. In addition, as Fleurette says, "the children see people who are actually making a living at their artwork — doing something and really loving it — so they understand that they can make careers out of something that gives them great joy."

In December 1993, Fleurette conducted a BlueFishgarten test run by taking twelve Blue Fish fabric artists to St. Boniface along with a collection of Blue Fish linoleum blocks and enough blank T-shirts for every child in the school. Recalls Wallach, "All of the children did their own designs and then they kept the shirts as a Christmas gift they could keep or give to someone. They were thrilled!"

Blue Fish volunteers have returned to St. Boniface every few months since, although at the principal's suggestion, they now focus the program on one fourth-grade class to establish some continuity and rapport with the students. Besides helping the kids block-print shirts, the volunteers work with them on collaborative projects such as paper and cloth quilts made from block-printed squares, and lead them in poetry, storytelling, and music sessions as well. The program has expanded within Blue Fish, too, so that not just the artists but any employees who want to go and can free themselves from their work can participate.

When Fleurette and I spoke in early 1995, she and Blue Fish were on the verge of duplicating the program in a public school in the same neighborhood as St. Boniface. The big picture includes bringing the program to other public schools in the Philadelphia and New Jersey area that have suffered cuts in arts funding, and possibly cookie-cuttering the program in other Blue Fish locations across the country. Communications coordinator and BlueFishgarten volunteer Carol Goodale, for one, thinks the success of the effort is almost preordained: "One reason I've been so fond of this program is that it seems to really grow from the center of us."

Social Entrepreneurship *and* Community Development

COMPANY: COOPERATIVE HOME CARE ASSOCIATES

Policy/Practice: A worker-owned enterprise that creates hundreds of decent jobs for disadvantaged women while providing critical services in New York City's health-care system.

Bottom Line: All of the above and consistent profits, too.

Zianna Bennett was "gainfully" employed before she found Cooperative Home Care Associates (CHCA), but she had to wonder whose gain that term referred to. Her job at a small retail store paid her five dollars an hour, not nearly enough for the single mother and her two small children, and required her to work nights, weekends, and holidays with little predictability. "It was either not paying the rent or working crazy hours and having to pay baby-sitters," she remembers. Then she saw a help-wanted ad for a job at CHCA that changed everything.

Zianna now works as a counselor in CHCA's entry-level training program, drawing on the background from her bachelor's degree in social work. She completed the degree at night over a span of several years, after the steady hours and decent income of her home health-care aide job at CHCA enabled her to stabilize her home life.

It's entirely by design that working at CHCA, located in New York's troubled South Bronx, works for Zianna. The company was founded in part to provide high-quality jobs for inner-city women. Most of CHCA's 300 employees, in fact, were worse off than Zianna before coming to CHCA, attempting to get by on public assistance. That CHCA has been able to achieve its mission while improving the quality of home health care in New York City and earning steady profits besides is one of the great stories in recent social service history.

That story begins in 1982, when New York's Community Service Society (CSS), a social service organization founded in the mid-nineteenth century, hired Rick Surpin to help create community-based enterprises that could employ people from low-income neighborhoods and thus help break the cycle of poverty. The enterprise development concept sounds noble but the challenge is intimidating because you are hiring workers with few or no job skills and experiences and little sense of their own possibilities besides.

The fiercely optimistic Surpin figured he had an answer for all that, however — the cooperative model, in which workers own voting stock and elect the board of directors on a one-person, one-vote basis. Cooperatives, he felt, had a real chance of creating jobs with decent compensation, working conditions, stability, and opportunities for advancement. In theory, stock ownership along with the democratic structure would help raise his employees' self-esteem and promote a sense of responsibility for the entire enterprise, as well as increase employees' income. That in turn would enable the people and the company to grow together. It was an inspiring idea, but it was grounded almost entirely on faith because the history of cooperatives was rife with failures. Then again, that was also true of community-based enterprises in general, so what the hell?

Surpin dug right in and started, with CSS sponsorship, a cooperative called On-Time Carpentry but he soon grew impatient with its potential. As well he should have — at its peak, it would employ only twelve disadvantaged workers. As Surpin rethought his plan, he realized he hadn't thought big enough. He set his new goal at 100 jobs minimum. Furthermore, the new company would perform a socially useful service in a growing market. That way, if all went well, the business could grow in job opportunities and the impact of its service simultaneously.

With a CSS team he had formed to help him with the project, he went hunting for the right industry to fit his big ideas. The team soon settled on the home health-care industry because it seemed to meet the twin goals of a vital service and an expanding market. At the time, revised Medicare policy was pushing thousands of infirm New Yorkers out the hospital doors. Not only were the sheer numbers of patients overwhelming the home health-care system, but many of the Medicare "ejects" had far more severe illnesses than care providers normally handled.

One huge problem: the jobs themselves were wretched. Wages, locked in place by regulatory and bureaucratic precedents, stunk; benefits were few; hours unstable and almost exclusively part-time; and career advancement nonexistent. The work — which ranged from simple companionship, cooking, and housecleaning to bathing patients, lifting them from bed to wheelchair, and helping them with toileting — could be exhausting emotionally and physically, and degrading as well.

Compounding the problems for patients and workers alike, the huge demand pushed the system to reward quantity — the ability to deliver warm bodies to bedsides, as a CHCA document puts it — over quality. Yet it was precisely here that the CSS team perceived a sliver of opportunity. They bet that if they could just improve the quality of the jobs, their aides would deliver better care. That left just one little conceptual challenge — transforming the entire New York health-care system to recognize, utilize, and reward their superior service!

All of these challenges had to be addressed alongside the two fundamental problems of a community-based enterprise start-up: (1) meager financial resources and (2) the need to find a competent, committed executive who will work for dirt wages in high-crime neighborhoods. Finally, the CSS team had to contend with its own inexperience in the health-care business, including a lack of "insider" contacts to help make things happen.

Sure enough, those problems bred others. For instance, the lack of contacts and knowledge in the health-care field at first kept CHCA from fulfilling its pledge to its employees of full-time work. That led to dissension in the ranks and high turnover. Plus, the organization was unable to find the right CEO until Surpin abandoned his other duties at CSS and took over the reins.

That was in 1987, also the year, not coincidentally, that CHCA's turnaround began. The company turned its first profit that year, helped by CSS's subsidy of its team's salaries. As it recruited more contractors and more money poured through the system, CHCA was able to deliver on more of its promises — better pay, better benefits (it had not been able to offer benefits in the beginning), and more full-time work.

From there, things started to fall in place much as Surpin had originally drawn them up. With the company beginning to make money, workers showed more interest in becoming member-owners. Once in, membership and participation in running the operation increased their self-esteem and interest in raising the quality of their service.

Finally, as CHCA became an industry insider, it was able to leverage its influence so the system would reward its greater quality. CHCA led the formation of a coalition of major stakeholders in the system. The coalition, called the New York City Home Care Work Group, became a major player in New York's health-care industry and convinced New York State to implement a more equitable reimbursement plan for home care. As of end 1994, CHCA had been profitable for six straight years.

As of this writing, CHCA employs over 300 African-American and Latina women, most of whom had previously relied on public assistance. The women earn on average about

$7.50 per hour, compared to about a $6.00 industry average, and those with three years at the company are guaranteed at least thirty hours of work per week, also bucking an industry standard. While nobody's getting rich here, workweeks average thirty-five hours a week, for a monthly paycheck of $1,100. Employees also receive one of the industry's best benefit packages, including health insurance and paid vacation and sick time. And the 70 percent of the workforce who are member-owners of the cooperative split profits as well, about $150,000 currently from $5.5 million in revenues. (Employees pay $1,000 — $50 down and about $3.50 per week — to become member-owners.)

True to Surpin's original intuition, as CHCA has been able to improve conditions for its employees, the business has also improved. Several of the cooperative's major contractors rate it as their highest-quality provider. The company is growing at a rate of about thirty employees per year, and the annual turnover rate is about 20 percent, half the industry average.

So successfully has CHCA's experiment in the South Bronx turned out that the Charles Stewart Mott Foundation, which helped finance CHCA, and Ford Foundation are funding replication efforts in other major American cities. As of this writing, two such sites — Home Care Associates of Philadelphia and Cooperative Home Care of Boston — are operating and on track to soon be self-supporting. Other communities are adopting the CHCA model on their own, including the Valley Care Cooperative in Waterbury, Connecticut.

For all of CHCA's success, however, Surpin remains disappointed in the organization's failure to deliver on one of his prime aspirations — providing a strong career ladder. He'd had high hopes for a nursing education program that CHCA established in 1989 for its home health aides. But as of late 1994, only three of the twenty employees who have enrolled in the program have graduated. Most of the students — hampered by poor educational background — were unable to pass the program's rigorous math and science requirements. By the same token, the three graduates now work as nurses for CHCA.

As a worker-owned enterprise, CHCA has made a number of business decisions that few for-profits would emulate, not the least of which is pumping so much of its initial capital and, later, earnings into wages and benefits and training programs. Says Surpin, "Even though we're financially viable and will continue to be, we certainly could have chosen a different path that would have made us viable faster. But I don't think we would have had the same quality, and I don't think we would have been as true to our social mission of creating good jobs for our people. So I guess we turn traditional business thinking on its head. But we have our own logic about what it means to do this, and that logic has paid off, in real return on investment, in both traditional and social terms."

COMPANY: BROOKLYN UNION GAS

Policy/Practice: Improving housing and job opportunities for its low- and moderate-income ratepayers.

Bottom Line: By investing it its own customers, Brooklyn Union Gas is helping to secure both its future and theirs.

The health of any company depends in part on the health of its social environment. But few experience that business reality as directly as do utilities like Brooklyn Union Gas. Brooklyn Union supplies the boroughs of Brooklyn, Staten Island, and Queens — about 65 percent of New York City — with natural gas, tying its economic fate to the fates of some terribly troubled communities. But as president Robert B. Catell told *New York Newsday* in 1994, "We can't just pick up our pipes and go somewhere else."

That's why Chris Haun, director of the company's Area Development Fund, doesn't feel the need to indulge in mushy talk about social returns when he discusses the strategy behind Brooklyn Union's community revitalization programs: "We're taking the facilities in our territory that were abandoned and reviving them into productive stock. So we get additional gas load benefit from that. Then you change one building in the neighborhood, and other buildings in the neighborhood are also going to improve."

From the perspective of the programs' total impact, however, Haun's comments seem more modest than blunt, because the programs' social returns nearly match the pragmatic ones. As of late 1994, Brooklyn Union's grants and loans have helped produce 7,167 units of affordable housing, helped numerous businesses relocate to the rebounding neighborhoods, and helped existing businesses expand. With decent homes and jobs, residents can begin building more stable, hopeful lives. Plus, many of the businesses assisted are minority owned, creating positive role models for area youth and more jobs for the disadvantaged labor force. That's the key to the Brooklyn Union program — self-serving though it is, that's not where the service stops.

Brooklyn Union kicked off its community development initiative in 1966 by establishing the Cinderella Program, which provided grants for the rehabilitation of neighborhood housing. Twenty-odd years later, the federal government created tax credits for investments in low-income housing, and Brooklyn Union recognized the opportunity to make a decent return in pure investment terms while simultaneously developing its service area.

Thus was born the Area Development Fund, a $7 million revolving loan fund created in 1989 as a companion program to Cinderella. The fund produced an almost immediate win-win-win for local entrepreneurs, residents, and Brooklyn Union. Small-time building companies, several of them minority-owned, that were unable to obtain conventional financing got the financial boost they needed from Brooklyn Union; residents got new decent housing stock; and, with the tax-credits, Brooklyn Union got solid returns on its money.

Before long, however, the utility realized that it took more than just housing to transform a neighborhood, so it began loaning money for small business development in neighborhoods that had suffered dramatic job losses. But Brooklyn Union doesn't loan to just any business — the company must be vitally tied to the community as well. For instance, in 1992 the fund extended $65,000 to a minority- and woman-owned cleaning service in Queens that was experiencing rapid growth after nine years in the neighborhood. Result: ten new jobs and a vigorous local business.

Beyond housing and businesses exists a third layer of community development, and Brooklyn Union has sent assistance in that direction, too. To date, about half of its loans have been made to community-building nonprofit groups, including the Bridge Street AME Church, which used its money to build a day-care center; the Franciscan Sisters of the Poor, which received $200,000 to transform a former orphanage into a shelter for homeless men; and St. John's Elementary School, which borrowed so it could buy energy-efficient lighting.

And then come the loans that serve multiple purposes. For example, assistance provided to Korean lightweight judo champion Suk Chon Lee to build a judo center in the Bushwick neighborhood not only added jobs to the community but also created something of a cultural resource in the mostly African-American area. The center could eventually provide a bridge between the estranged African-American and Korean populations. As a local minister told reporter Deborah Haines, "[Lee's] part of the puzzle that makes up community."

Because of the creative manner in which it's administered, the Area Development Fund has magnetized vast amounts of investment in its service area beyond its own limited ability to lend. The fund partners with other lenders and gives credibility to borrowers who in its absence would be turned down by area banks. In the housing area alone, Haun notes that the fund's loans have attracted several hundred million additional dollars in construction loans.

Of course, not every loan has worked out as planned. Haun says that some repayment schedules have had to be readjusted and a couple of borrowers have gone under: "We try to choose our partners carefully if we're doing a partner-type project but naturally, some things happen. What we're doing in most instances is kind of cutting-edge. We're taking a lot of risk by financing some start-up companies, by developing some housing projects with various developers that might not get assistance elsewhere." But overall, says Haun, "the balance of the return is probably about 8 percent right now, including the tax credits plus interest on our loans, so we're doing well by doing good."

With federal deregulation lurking around the corner for the utility industry, Brooklyn Union faces the potential loss of large commercial customers to independent power producers offering lower rates. So shoring up and expanding its customer base among residents and smaller businesses has become even more crucial to its financial future. Because they also dovetail with the company's broad community outreach efforts, the loans have also made a great marketing tool for bonding customers to the utility.

Many companies look at giving back to the community as a nice thing to do, when you can afford it; Brooklyn Union sees things differently these days: it can't afford *not* to give.

ADVERTISING *and* MARKETING

COMPANY: RYKA

Policy/Practice: Simultaneously generating revenues for a social-change organization and a company through a combined marketing campaign.

Bottom Line: This shoe company and its cause are a perfect fit.

After six hard years going head to gargantuan heads with Nike and Reebok, Ryka Inc. president/CEO Sheri Poe decided to try something radically different in the women's athletic shoe market. She created a foundation dedicated to helping end violence against women and linked her company's products to it, pledging 7 percent of the company annual pretax profits. Sales soared — in 1993, the first full year of ads promoting the initiative, the company brought in $14.4 million, up from $4.7 million in 1990. Critics, of course, dismissed the campaign's success as just another cynical case of "cause marketing," but Poe wasn't ruffled. "I defy anyone to accuse me of not being emotionally involved with this issue," she says wryly from her Norwood, Massachusetts, office.

No one who knows her story would even try. In 1971, the then-nineteen-year-old Poe was raped at gunpoint while hitching a ride from a part-time job back to the Southern Illinois University campus where she was a freshman. She reported the crime to authorities, but police, doctors, and a therapist shamed her into believing the rape was her fault because she had been hitchhiking. The police then persuaded her to not press charges because her attacker had friends in the department and there was no chance of conviction.

In the wake of the incident and all that immediately followed, Poe became bulimic, the crest of a long, downhill slide. Years of binging and purging led to chronic hepatitis and liver damage, the inability to hold a job, and, finally, a sickly subsistence on welfare. When a doctor warned her that she was killing her chances of having children and would soon kill herself, "something snapped inside me," she recalls. "I realized that being raped wasn't my fault and it was time to start living again."

Poe moved to California, married, had two children, and went to work for her husband's employer, which made fitness-related gift items. She also started a regular exercise program to assist her recovery, ultimately taking up aerobics. It was in the aerobics workouts that the idea for Ryka was born. "My back was always aching," Poe remembers, "and I knew it was the shoes. I was thinking, Imagine all those shoes being sold and nobody's really designing for the contours of a woman's foot!" She was also thinking, What an interesting idea for a business! Poe then started calling on investment bankers to see if any of them agreed with her. Only one did, but one was sufficient. She and her husband helped raise $4 million on the over-the-counter stock market, enough to get Poe started.

So Ryka was off and running, so to speak, even though Poe soon divorced her husband and first Ryka partner. (She later remarried and had two more children.) She proved early on that she understood not only women's shoes, but also how to reach her market, playing up from the beginning that hers was the only women's shoemaker also managed by women.

While Poe was finding her voice as a marketer, she continued to remain silent about her rape experience until 1992, when she read that Oprah Winfrey — to whom she had sent a pair of shoes the year before, thus triggering an invitation to a show about woman entrepreneurs — had testified before Congress that she had been sexually assaulted as a child. "I knew then that I could be doing something for women who had gone through what I had. And Ryka was the perfect vehicle."

Thus the Ryka ROSE (Regaining One's Self-Esteem) Foundation, with its dual mission of working to stop violence against women and helping survivors recover their self-respect and rebuild their lives. Poe started Ryka ROSE with 90,000 shares of her own Ryka stock, and funneled $10,000 per quarter to it from the company. The 7 percent of profits will kick in, of course, as soon as the company becomes profitable. In the meantime, Ryka houses the foundation, absorbing all of its overhead.

But even without Ryka profits, ROSE has affected victims' lives from the start. As of this writing, the foundation has distributed $250,000 in grants to direct-service agencies and educational programs nationwide; partnered with the National Victim Center to establish and maintain a national toll-free information line; and supported other educational efforts, including distributing 350,000 copies of a brochure entitled *What Every Woman Needs to Know About Violence Against Women*. The company itself also receives frequent calls from women victims looking for referrals. "It's an amazing feeling to have an impact on so many people," Poe exclaims.

Of course, thanks to today's socially attuned consumers, Poe's efforts on behalf of victims are selling a few shoes, too. And that's hardly beside the point. It would be selling Poe short as a businesswoman to say that Ryka ROSE's synergistic effect on her business never mattered to her. But it shouldn't matter to anyone else, says Poe: "I don't think you can even compare what Ryka does with ROSE to what people call cause marketing, but if you want to call it that, the difference is that here the cause part really does come first."

Company: Timberland

Policy/Practice: Using the company's advertising space to convey important social messages, and partnering with a social-change organization for combined social and business purposes.

Bottom Line: A call to action against racism and other social problems, increased brand-name recognition, low-cost organizational development — the list goes on and on.

Where the rubber hits the road in corporate social action, some rubber-soled shoe companies are tearing up the track. Reebok has embraced a cause, human rights, that few other corporations will touch (see page 224). Ryka startled the competition with its awareness campaign focused on violence against women (see page 212).

Then there's Timberland, purveyor of rugged outdoor footwear. The Hampton, New Hampshire–based company, which also makes apparel, has riveted its brand name to campaigns against racism and for citizen involvement in community action. The kicker, so to speak, came in 1992 with an ad campaign stamping such headlines as "Give Racism the Boot" in major newspapers throughout the United States and Europe and on billboards in New York City. The ads also invited readers to join the fight against intolerance by pulling their boots on and contacting an organization called City Year. Like Ryka and Reebok, this company has turned the concept of cause marketing on its head and now markets causes.

One of those causes is City Year itself, which for Timberland is not just a passive recipient of corporate support but what vice president of community enterprise Ken Freitas calls a true partner. City Year, based in Boston, recruits young adults from diverse backgrounds into what it terms an urban peace corps. Participants, aged seventeen to twenty-three, spend one year performing full-time community service in cities nationwide, doing such things as working in classrooms and after-school programs, and restoring parks and social service centers. In 1989, City Year's first program year, the organization approached Timberland about donating some of its sturdy footwear to help volunteer corps do their work. Timberland agreed and donated for the next year as well. In 1991, Timberland COO Jeffrey Swartz invited City Year co-directors Alan Khazei and Michael Brown to the company to explore a more involved sponsorship. What developed from that meeting is a relationship so unique as to transcend the notion of corporate philanthropy.

Essentially Swartz, executive of a fast-growing company doing hundreds of millions in business per year, and Khazei and Brown, ambitious social entrepreneurs, have crafted a kind of organizational symbiosis to help both entities reach their expansive goals. Explains Freitas, "City Year is fundamentally about new ways of thinking, learning, and doing. It's based on getting people together, finding common ground, and then working toward a common purpose. Those principles are exactly relevant to our business and honestly, I think, any business."

For Timberland, City Year has held workshops on team building, diversity, and visioning. Those have been invaluable for the company, says Freitas, both in its domestic operation and its transformation into a global enterprise: "One of the things we do as a company in order to grow is to get people to develop themselves and systems on their own, and that means getting diverse people to work together. City Year has taken us through some very powerful training exercises for that purpose." Timberland also draws on City Year's graduates as a valued source of new employees. Finally, City Year projects provide a perfect forum for the socially committed Timberland's employee volunteerism. The company gives employees up to four fully paid days off each year to perform community service. As many as 250 employees and their families have taken part in City Year "Serveathons," and hundreds of others annually participate in community-service programs developed in-house with City Year help.

In return, as the organization's official outfitter, Timberland has provided City Year staff and volunteers with thousands of uniform parts and other pairs of shoes and clothing annually; loaned employees, including an executive, to the organization; donated office space and a toll-free telephone number; and provided endless promotion in its stores and advertising. Plus, of course, bucks — $1 million in 1992 and beginning in 1995, $5 million spread over five years for City Year's national expansion. Swartz insists the grants are an investment, not charity. As he wrote for members of Business for Social Responsibility (BSR), to which Timberland belongs, "Many companies pay thousands of dollars for the type of team-building skills we learn through giving. So not only is Timberland furthering positive change and community betterment: we are making an investment in our infrastructure."

Since the original anti-racism ad campaign, Timberland has continued to merchandise its products through what it calls beliefs-based marketing communications. For example, each of its "model people" ad series hails the contributions of an individual activist or community volunteer who "pulls on [his/her] boots and makes a difference." Each ad promotes City Year as well, including the toll-free number, although none of the ads I've seen commands your attention like the first campaign. Of course, that series would be tough to beat. Its in-your-face social missive did similar wonders for Timberland's brand recognition. When we spoke in late 1994, Freitas called the ads "the single most powerful piece of communication that we've run in the past five years."

One message that Timberland does continue to communicate effectively is the notion of business as a social enterprise. Its Business for Social Responsibility membership identifies it with a broad slate of progressive social-change goals. Timberland is also a signee of the CERES Principles, the nation's leading code of corporate environmental ethics. The company has adopted a set of principles for overseas contracting modeled after Levi Strauss's cutting-edge guidelines (see page 165) and, like Levi, pulled business out of China to protest human-rights abuses following the Tiananmen Square massacre in 1989. Timberland also applies strict social criteria to other business partner relationships.

But much of the company's social vision will continue to be focused on City Year. As Timberland and City Year continue to develop together, more Timberland community-service teams fan out in the community "pulling their boots on to make a difference" and spreading goodwill in the process. And City Year volunteers show up to serve in more and more cities nationwide outfitted in Timberland from head to toe. As Freitas says, "They're out there as symbols to the world that young people are a resource of positive change. That image is helped along by Timberland, and that is nothing but good — good for our shareholders, good for our employees, good for our consumer, good for our community. On all accounts, that's the successful part of it."

COMPANY: NATURAL COTTON COLOURS

> *Policy/Practice:* Prohibiting the advertising of the company's product in a socially exploitive manner.

> *Bottom Line:* A complicated idea ethically and pragmatically, so the company is still tinkering with the weave.

Starting with a tiny bag of seeds in 1982, Sally Fox spent many long years selectively breeding plants to obtain her final product, naturally colored cotton in a range of greens, browns, and reddish browns (see page 233). So it doesn't surprise to hear her say, "I think of this cotton as my child." She also reacted like a parent — that is, an enraged parent — a few years ago when she first viewed an ad for a client in Amsterdam. The artwork sent by the client displayed fabric made from Fox's cotton draped over nude women in what she considered were lewd, demeaning poses. What was worse, her logo was stamped on the art right next to the manufacturer's. "I was furious," she recalls. "I just don't want the fruit of my labor used in advertising that is at all exploitive."

Fox immediately modified her trademark licensing agreement to preclude the logo's use in advertising that was "provocative," thereby ensuring a more dignified future for her baby. Or so she thought. Enforcement has been tough. So has the problem of reconciling cross-cultural differences over acceptable standards of sensuality. When we speak in early 1995, Fox sighs and says, "I've had people sign it and then still do it — mostly European customers. I just received these posters showing women with their shirts unbuttoned down the front so you can see their breasts. In the U.S., we would consider that pretty wild, but in Europe, there are really different standards. They don't see this as provocative."

Fox acknowledges that her own objections to sensual advertising may even be out of joint with American norms. Customers first purchased her product for the jeans market, and suggestive jean ads — featured erotically posed women *and* men — have been de rigueur for years. But she's disturbed by the no-holds-barred approach that many marketers take when vying for the consumer's frayed attention. She mentions one ambiguous ad for a prominent jeans maker that appears based on a theme of child molestation: "I don't think people have to stoop to these tactics to create shock value, which is what this is all about."

Fox also stresses that it is in no way her intention to censor advertising content: "If someone wants to use a suggestive ad to catch your eye, that certainly may be a viable strategy for them. I just didn't want my trademark with it. I wasn't objecting to nudity in ads. But the fiber and the cotton is so special — a gift from nature — so it's kind of my way of saying, 'If you're going to use my name in an ad, then use it in a way that has dignity.'"

Despite her initially tough stand, Fox may be modifying it in the near future. Demand for her product is increasing, as is her ability to supply it, and that's caused her to rethink the trademark provisions: "It's not that I'm getting a bunch of complaints, but I don't know if it's appropriate as this product gets larger." She points out that her cotton has some important work to do in the world. Most of it is grown organically, with vast implications for pesticide-free agriculture. Its use also eliminates dyeing and bleaching from the milling cycle, which are the most environmentally damaging stages of the milling process.

In fact, she's just as concerned that an environmentally irresponsible manufacturer could use her trademark to *greenwash* its public image as she is over other content. So, the licensing agreement may soon be changing at Natural Cotton Colours, Inc., but the reflective management style that spawned it will continue.

Social Leadership

COMPANY: STONYFIELD FARM

Policy/Practice: Building a demonstration-quality social enterprise.

Bottom Line: A model ideals-driven business, by design.

In 1993, the Council on Economic Priorities (CEP) nominated Stonyfield Farms for one of its coveted Corporate Conscience awards. Because of its promotional value, that's an honor the leaders of most American companies would give their eyeteeth for, and possibly other important body parts as well. But Stonyfield isn't most companies. Rather than pour the champagne, Stonyfield's president/CEO Gary Hirshberg withdrew the company from consideration.

"I wasn't satisfied we were anywhere near deserving of that award," he recalls. "I wrote [CEP executive director Alice Tepper Marlin] and thanked them profusely and said I hope we will be able to be reconsidered in the future."

They were, the following year. CEP named Stonyfield the winner of its 1994 award for environmental stewardship, and this time Hirshberg accepted for the company, proudly. So what had happened in the intervening twelve months? Nothing, and everything. Nothing in the sense that for some time now, Stonyfield has pledged in its mission statement "to serve as a model that environmentally and socially responsible business can also be profitable." Everything, in the sense that only after some crucial steps that the company took after 1993 was Hirshberg ready to expose the model for all the world to see.

To understand why Stonyfield played so hard-to-get, you need to know some company history. Founder/chairman Samuel Kaymen and Hirshberg originally created Stonyfield in 1983 to feed cash into their nonprofit educational endeavors in environmentalism and sustainable agriculture. But as the company matured, they realized it was a far better vehicle for taking their message to the uninitiated than their nonprofit organizations had been. Stonyfield soon became the primary focus of their social goals.

In 1989, they broadened its mission still more. At a stage when most young companies would still be pinching every penny, Stonyfield had been pouring its scarce resources into such social "distractions" as employee benefits, environmental philanthropy, and a special program with Ben & Jerry's that paid premium prices for dairy products from local family farmers practicing sustainable methods. Yet it was only after making these social investments that the company's financial fortunes turned the corner, with happy and inspired employees and customers an indisputable part of the reason. Kaymen and Hirshberg realized they had the opportunity to show all of American business that social and fiscal responsibility could peacefully — and symbiotically — coexist.

So, going back to Stonyfield's dance with CEP, PR has never been the point. In fact, some of Hirshberg's colleagues in management worry about the increased public attention accompanying the award. They know that those who broadcast their business ideals these days also invite the media to take target practice. But Hirshberg now welcomes the scrutiny. He explains, "We're just one tiny little company. I look at the world my three young children are inheriting and I have a real heavy heart about that. At the same time, just to sort of fix things at Stonyfield doesn't do a whole lot for them. What does do a whole lot for them is if by fixing things at Stonyfield I inspire other businesses to say 'Oh yeah, of course!'

Toward that end, Hirshberg guided the company into making several important moves after the original CEP nomination. For one, Stonyfield engaged the architect William McDonough (see page 283) and several energy-efficiency specialists to design a new office space projected to be as pleasant and healthful a place to work as it is state of the art environmentally, with passive solar heating, energy-efficient lighting, fresh air circulated to every desk, non-toxic building materials, and so on. Hirshberg placed one additional requirement on the designers: that every socially driven design innovation pay its cost back in four to five years. "Executive don't get it about these things unless they pay for themselves, and that's how it should be," he says. Fortunately, the health and cost efficiencies embedded in the design allow him to make his point. Stonyfield is also constructing a new visitor center to more effectively spread its message about blending social and fiscal responsibility.

Stonyfield took another big leap by hiring an outside party to monitor its environmental performance and recommend improvements. Many major corporations have submitted to environmental audits, but generally only to ensure minimal compliance with environmental regulations. Stonyfield selected an auditor that shares its own goals of zero net environmental harm. Here, too, the changes made in response to the audit also returned dollars to the company's coffers (see page 275).

But the audit was just step one in what Hirshberg plans will be a regular comprehensive auditing of not just the company's environmental record but its progress toward other social goals, such as creating an ideal workplace for employees. As of this writing, the only major company regularly auditing its social performance is Ben & Jerry's, which in the absence of third-party social auditors has had to create its own process (see page 293). But Hirshberg has committed himself to helping develop a third-party tool through his participation in organizations such as Businesses for Social Responsibility and the Social Venture Network, and committed his company to employing it annually.

Hirshberg became co-chair of the Social Venture Network in 1993. That too fits into the master plan of putting Stonyfield's business recipe in the display case. Says Gary, "I elected to take that position because I now feel that we have kind of polished and refined our formula, not just in the environmental arena but even how we manage ourselves, how we are structured staff-wise, profits-wise [10 percent of pretax profits go to environmental causes], gain-sharing wise. If you came and interviewed anybody at my company, you would find a strikingly high degree of satisfaction." In the accounting department as well, for Stonyfield is the fastest-growing company in its field.

If social responsibility and profitability are so wonderfully compatible, why haven't more companies figured that out for themselves? Opines Hirshberg, "Most businesses haven't made social issues their priority. We're just limited by our imaginations. If businesses can be helped to understand that the solutions to these problems are in their best interests and therefore make them a priority, I'm really confident that it will happen."

COMPANY: REEBOK

Policy/Practice: Financial and organizational support for the Witness program, a collaborative effort with the Lawyers Committee for Human Rights and musician Peter Gabriel to help international activists record and report human-rights violations.

> **Bottom Line:** Gritty commitment to an issue most multinationals barely even acknowledge.

Well before she saw Reebok in action with the Witness program, a bold effort to document international human-rights abuses, Mary Daly sensed that this shoe manufacturer was a different kind of company. In 1989, she enlisted its support for Amnesty International's Human Rights Now concert tour. The traveling show headlined such superstar artists as Peter Gabriel and Bruce Springsteen, an awesome promotional opportunity for the young company, but Daly "went back and said, 'We will let you give us this money but you can have no signage, the artists will not wear your clothes, and you have to take a second role to the overall mission.' They agreed to all these conditions."

Reebok impressed Daly further when it subsequently made human-rights consciousness-raising the major work of its foundation to validate its long-term commitment to the issue. As its initial effort, the foundation established the Reebok Human Rights awards program to celebrate the achievements of young human rights activists around the world.

So Daly, with co-conspirator Gabriel, made bigger plans still for the company. On a 1986 Amnesty concert tour, Daly had told Gabriel of her frustration at seeing the press turn down human-rights stories she brought them because she had no accompanying visuals: "He was carrying around a hand-held video camera — kind of a new idea at that point — and shooting everything on the tour and he was very clear the technology was getting simpler." Simple enough, in fact, to soon enable the next leap forward in human-rights awareness: putting camcorders in the hands of human-rights groups. They nurtured the idea for years; after Reebok established the Human Rights awards, Gabriel communicated the concept to Reebok Foundation head Sharon Cohen, the catalyst behind the awards effort, in a fax.

"Of course, it's always thrilling to get a personal note

from Peter Gabriel. Then I read it and saw that he wanted to work with us on this project," recalls Cohen. But after investigating the proposal with human-rights groups, she uncovered a host of difficulties. For one thing, cameras weren't enough — activists needed fax machines and computers with modems as well. For another, there was the daunting challenge of exporting these technologies to Third World countries with, says Cohen, "their unstable electricity, problems of getting the film back out, and of course protecting people whose lives are already in danger."

"I had just a huge list of obstacles," Cohen recalls, "and I went to Paul Fireman [Reebok chairman/CEO] and laid out the problems to him. He looked at me — this is why I love working for this company — with a smile and said, 'So you're saying if we don't do it, nobody else will.' I said, 'That's what I'm saying.' And he said, 'I guess we have to do it, don't we?'"

On Gabriel's advice, the program was named Witness. Reebok then brought the New York–based Lawyers Committee for Human Rights into the picture to house the program, because a vital issue in human-rights documentation is the credibility of the footage, a standard that the committee's legal expertise could help ensure. Finally, Reebok and the committee recruited Daly, with her years of dedication to the issue, as a consultant.

Those issues dispensed with, Cohen started hunting down cameras and other hardware for the program. She expected Reebok's influence to open doors at major manufacturers and spring loose whatever was needed. She quickly learned otherwise: "With the exception of our friends at Polaroid, the other twenty-four companies that we approached said, 'We've got our mission, we give them to inner-city schools,' and so forth, worthy causes which from a foundation point of view I can understand. But I also realized that these activists in many instances are trying to expose the injustices of governments around the world, and for global companies, this is a problem. This is why in fact not many companies do anything in the area of human rights."

And why Reebok's courage shines like a floodlight. As a company that has its product assembled overseas in low-wage countries, Reebok had its own human-rights issues to face. Says Daly, "When they became involved in funding a rock 'n roll tour, they had no idea it was going to be an opportunity for them to take a look at their labor practices, and to create the human-rights standards [the company's Levi Strauss–like standards for overseas contractors — see page 165]. They've not only become more sensitive to the problem, but they also did something about it and they've kind of done the right thing at every step, even though it's made their work harder. It's not an easy marriage for them."

Much of the credit, Daly says, goes to Cohen herself, who far from simply writing checks, effectively midwifed Witness into existence. It was Cohen who did the research, got the requisite parties together over a table, elucidated the issues, hammered the disparate ideas into a program, and then secured Reebok's full-fledged commitment.

Daly also credits Cohen and Reebok with lending their corporate expertise to make the program successful: "They're a marketing company and they think 'audience' all over the place. Reebok was very helpful in creating the Witness logo, packaging the brochure, and preparing the materials and video that engage people in the program." Reebok has also showed the Lawyers Committee how to plan and target Witness events and in general made them a more promotion-savvy organization overall. And yet Daly, who now serves the committee as a consultant, notes that the committee's executive director, Michael Posner, would be on the company's tail in a flash if he found it guilty of human-rights violations of its own, "and they know that from the get-go based on who Mike is."

Has Witness itself made a major human-rights impact yet? That's difficult to answer, said Daly when we spoke in late 1994, because the program was still young and "it's also hard in the human-rights arena to ever claim a victory." However, a Witness camera documented evidence, later shown on

CNN, of Burmese children being sold into sexual slavery in the brothels of Thailand. Another Witness surreptitious video-taping led to an hour-long episode of ABC's "Turning Point" on bonded child labor in Indian carpet factories. Witness cameras also captured evidence of mass execution in the war in the former Yugoslavia that could later serve as evidence in the prosecution of war crimes.

With most hardware makers remaining out of the picture, Witness still hurts for equipment and videotape, although some of Reebok's vendors, such as the Leo Burnett ad agency, have donated, and employees and outside parties — even one high school class — have pitched in, too. As of late 1994, the program had placed roughly seventy cameras, and an equal number of fax machines, in about sixty-five countries. (Fittingly, Reebok's director of human-rights programs, Doug Cahn, gave Witness its first camera when he brought in his camcorder from home.) Other problems come with the territory. "The relationships you develop with these human rights groups are complicated," says Daly. "You deal with many languages and cultures, and different kinds of organizations all over the world. So in fact it's harder than we thought it was in the beginning."

But Reebok has clearly signed on for the long haul, says Daly: "They've been a real partner in coming up with solutions." Notes Cohen, "This is a really tough project. We knew that from the beginning because it was breaking new ground. But like the Lawyers Committee and Peter, we're here to make Witness work, whatever that might take."

COMPANY: HOME DEPOT

Policy/Practice: Environmentally conscious mass-market retailing.

Bottom Line: Good environmental ethics is also good retailing.

Mark Eisen was out of work but not ideas when he approached Home Depot in the home center chain's Atlanta headquarters just prior to Earth Day, 1990: "My background in retail consulting trained me to watch major trends. And very simply, I saw the environmental trend as not a flash in the pan but a very long-term fundamental change. I walked into the office saying 'I think you guys, the home centers, are more fundamentally tied to the environment than any other retailer and could be doing something about it.'"

Little did he know that the impending Earth Day had turned the thoughts of Home Depot's management in much the same direction. So Eisen had himself a job: "And now, hopefully you can look back and say we've really expanded the game in the big picture."

Indeed. Under Eisen's leadership as manager of environmental marketing, Home Depot, the world's largest home center corporation with over $12 billion in annual sales, is helping to green the hardware and home center industries as well as speeding the diffusion of environmental consumerism to the masses. Plus, the company's setting a potent example for mass retailers of all types by using its monolithic purchasing power and customer reach to effect positive social change.

Eisen has no budget and only a secretary for staff. It's the Home Depot way — any cost Eisen added would just add cost for the customer, and Home Depot's business is built on low-margin, volume pricing. But what Eisen does have at his disposal is that awesome buying and market capacity, and that makes all the difference. Suppliers will jump through all sorts of hoops to sell to Home Depot, so after first identifying what he feels are true alternative products, he requires their manufacturers to validate through a certification outfit called Scientific Certification Systems (SCS) any environmental claims they make to Home Depot customers. As a result of that process, many suppliers have improved their products. And as

Eisen says, "When they clean them up for Home Depot, that cleans them up for everybody else."

Because of Home Depot's leadership, Eisen points out, the American hardware industry now has more certified products than some otherwise environmentally progressive nations. As of this writing, thirty of these reduced-impact products — from recycled content flooring to spray paints certified for no detectable VOCs (volatile organic compounds) to soybean fertilizer — line Home Depot's shelves.

And Home Depot is pushing the envelope further still in wood products. Several of its northern California stores now offer pine shelving from a supplier that harvests its forests selectively instead of the clear-cut-and-replant approach that has typified contemporary forestry and outraged ecologists and lay environmentalists alike. Many more stores offer a mahogany door harvested in a manner that preserves, not destroys, rain forest. While sustainably harvested forest products aren't available in sufficient quantities to supply anywhere near the whole chain, Home Depot is also angling to offer its customers wood in its commodity bins — that is, structural wood like two-by-fours and plywood — certified as coming from "well-managed" forests. Because of the amount of lumber it buys to stock its empire (about 340 stores as of the end of 1994), its efforts could have a transformative effect on the entire forest industry.

Of course, viewed from afar, Home Depot's foray into alternative, eco-friendly products might appear to be just a cynical attempt to snatch market share from "green marketers." Environmental awareness has spawned countless niche businesses that offer products like unbleached toilet paper and organic cotton T-shirts to folks willing to pay premium prices to relieve their environmental guilt. But Home Depot's project differs in almost every respect from theirs and, arguably, makes far greater impact.

For one thing, Home Depot, unlike most green marketers, isn't preaching to the already converted. Home Depot caters to the masses, who buy for *value,* not *values.* Sure, polls suggest that many mainstream shoppers prefer to buy greener, too, but only if they don't have to pay extra for it. And they often don't at Home Depot, because the company's merchants have often found creative ways to whittle down or eliminate the usual premiums and, therefore, customer resistance. For example, by buying directly from a company, Collins Pine, that had been solely a commodity supplier, Home Depot was able to eliminate middlemen and offer without a price premium the selectively harvested wood shelving mentioned above.

For all of Eisen's efforts, no one will ever mistake Home Depot for an "eco-store." Instead of pushing its alternative products on customers, it simply denotes them with educational labeling and lets the customer choose. For example, a relatively environmentally friendly weed killer will share a shelf with a far more pernicious, but immensely popular one. Such juxtapositions provoke many a sneer from environmental purists, but Eisen says they miss the point. If its customers demand destructive mass-market products and Home Depot doesn't carry them, they'll take their business elsewhere. Net result: there's just as much herbicide leaching from lawns into groundwater and one of America's most conscientious companies begins dying on the vine.

Not every Eisen initiative has worked out as planned. In 1993, Home Depot opened a drive-through recycling center, Recycling Depot, in the parking lot of one of its Atlanta stores. Recycling Depot paid its patrons for everything from household recyclables to aluminum window frames and discarded plumbing pipe hauled in by the pickup load by contractors. So strong were metal prices at the time that Eisen expected they would carry the entire enterprise, making Recycling Depot as profitable as the home centers themselves. Once he proved his thesis, Home Depot would cookie-cutter the concept at all its stores. But the thesis hasn't proved out; the collapse of aluminum prices and cyclical nature of recycling markets in general has drastically scaled back and slowed the entire project.

Despite this one setback, Eisen and Home Depot have more than made their point — to their industry and to the business community at large. By moving proactively instead of waiting for the environmental crisis to force them to react, they have transformed a threat into an economic opportunity. They've used creativity and market forces to foster private certification, perhaps saving the company and its supplier industries from stifling regulations down the line. And they've carved out a new path of social enterprise. "Retailers that aren't taking social advantage of their purchasing leverage aren't being as responsible as they could be," says Eisen. "What we're doing could be happening in every industry. Maybe one day, every big company will have somebody with a job like mine."

Socially Appropriate Product/Service

Company: Natural Cotton Colours

Policy/Practice: Creating a valuable organic product, and promoting its advantages to expand the organic movement.

Bottom Line: What to wear to a sustainable future.

While pursuing their entomology degrees in the 1970s, Sally Fox and a friend used to swap daydreams about buying farms and living the pastoral life. One day, her companion suggested jokingly that Sally, whose hobby is hand spinning, grow colored cotton. "Then later," Fox recalls, "while attending a hand-spinning conference, I saw some really reddish brown cotton from Guatemala and I went, 'Oh, my God!'"

Unbeknownst to Fox until that moment, the Toltecs and Aztecs had cultivated colored cotton in the Americas for thousands of years. Europeans then carried it to China, Africa, and India, where the original khaki cloth was made from brown cotton. A fascinated Fox hit the library and soon found another heritage of colored cotton in the American South, amongst Cajun hand spinners and African slaves, who were allowed to grow brown cotton that wouldn't compete with their owners' commercial whites. Over the centuries, however, the original variety of Toltec hues had dropped back to a few browns. Little did Fox know that history would select her to restore the palette.

Fast-forward to 1982 and Fox is working for a California cotton breeder trying to develop an insect-resistant plant. Among the varieties she plans to test is a small bag of seeds and brownish lint from the USDA's archives. The fiber quality is terrible, but the intrigued Fox carries a few seeds home to her mother's backyard garden in Menlo Park, hoping a little selective breeding might produce some novelty cotton for her and her fellow hobbyists.

Some novelty. After years of painstaking breeding and some seat-of-the-pants business education, Fox today presides over a $5.5 million company, Natural Cotton Colours, that produces cotton in an impressive array of chic earth-tones — greens, browns, and reddish-browns — for such popular manufacturers as Levi Strauss, The Gap, L.L. Bean, and Land's End. But Fox's scheme is broader than creating fashion curiosities, for her cotton grows organically, bringing a little more hope to a pesticide-overdosed planet.

Fox explains that while conventional cotton is not itself heavily sprayed, the sheer number of acres devoted to its cultivation make it one of the most pesticide-intensive crops. Those pesticides not only find their way into the bodies of farmworkers and neighbors in the regions where cotton is farmed but also into the rest of us through our meat, milk, and cheese. Notes Fox, "Probably for every 1,000 pounds of cotton fiber produced, there are 2,500 pounds of cotton seed that are harvested and fed to dairy and feedlot cattle. So unless you're a strict vegetarian, your life is affected by what happens in the cotton industry."

The environmental impacts of cotton dyeing and bleaching are no less devastating. Fox says that nearly all of the toxic wastes produced by textile mills come from the dyeing and bleaching processes as does most of the energy usage.

Of course, it's precisely because of the fortunate overlap between environmental and economic benefits that Fox Fibre is catching on with textile mill operators. Dyeing also happens to be the most expensive of the textile processes; the cost of treating the toxic residue of dyeing and bleaching for regulatory purposes runs up the bill even higher. Fox's customers don't have to pay those tabs. That allows them to more effectively compete with mills in low-wage countries where environmental laws also tend to be lax or nonexistent. In fact, with Fox's young company able to work with only select customers, she favors mills in industrialized countries with high environmental standards and jobs to protect. That hasn't hurt her relationship with domestic mill owners, either.

Fox began her organic cotton farming on one-quarter of an acre in 1985. As of 1994, some 40,000 acres of white cotton are farmed organically in addition to Fox's 5,000, primarily because Fox has cajoled, advised, and encouraged other farmers to make the switch, and supported them with customer referrals when they do. Although for both economic and cultural reasons, farmers tend to be slow to adapt to the more labor-intensive organic methods, those that have followed Fox's lead have seen immediate benefits: lower production costs, safer work, and healthier plants and soil. Another plus is the increased mental stimulation of organic methods. "A lot of farmers have become bored with the lack of intellectual challenge in [chemical agriculture]," Fox explains.

The long-term effects of her organic evangelism could reach further still. Cotton growers rotate their crops with alfalfa, wheat, and beans, making possible such developments as organic dairies. Since cotton growers farm far more acres than do most food farmers, organic cotton agriculture is the express route to increasing the acreage in organic certification. Which in turn gives a boost to organic compost and biological pest control companies, helping them gear up to compete with chemical companies. Which in turn inspires university agricultural departments to devote more energy to organic research. "I feel that cotton is the key to the organic farming movement," says Fox, who adds with hard-earned pride, "My cotton was really very instrumental in getting it going."

Fox also foresees the time when her cotton is the commodity from which most browns, greens, and khaki cotton textiles will be created, permanently removing a huge amount of cotton from the dye-and-pollute cycle. While the colors of cotton, which Fox describes as "a miniature tree," are limited to the range of colors available in wood, Fox points out that today, her manufacturing customers can achieve all the colors available in a number of red-brown, brown, beige, and green spectrums by mixing them with each other or with white. And she continues to develop new hues, with mutations holding out still further possibilities.

By the way, Fox's colors intensify rather than fade with washing, an advantage over not only dyed fabrics but also previous colored plants. They make for softer fabrics than dyed textiles, as well. And it turns out that the brown colors have intrinsic fire retardant properties, which makes them a natural for such applications as upholstery and children's sleepwear.

In 1993, Natural Cotton Colours won the first-ever United Nations Environmental Programme Award for its contribution to the future of the environment and the agriculture and textile industries; the Edison Award as the most innovative company of that year; and *Good Housekeeping* magazine's Green Award. It may be impossible to predict what the fashion industry will throw at us in the future, but it's less difficult to figure that a big part of that future will belong to Sally Fox and her Fox Fibre.

COMPANY: SEVENTH GENERATION

Policy/Practice: First pioneering the development and marketing of environmentally responsible household products, and now pioneering their entry into the mass market.

> **Bottom Line:** The resourceful thinking that made dozens of household goods planet friendly is now making them wallet friendly.

When Jeffrey Hollender helped direct-mail veteran Alan Newman take over a small environmental products mail-order business in 1988, his head was filled with big ideas. He and Newman would expand the catalog, which then featured only energy-conservation devices, to include a broad range of ecologically benign household products, from toilet paper to dishwashing liquid to bedding. Marketing would be a slam dunk, because millions of environmentally conscientious consumers were clamoring for just what the company planned to offer. Those consumers would put the business, which had never made money, on its feet and lead the mass market to the company's doors.

When I spoke to chairman/CEO Hollender in mid-1994, Newman had long since left the company and the business — which he and Newman renamed Seventh Generation — still hadn't made money. But Hollender's ideas were bigger than ever, out of necessity. Turns out those millions of consumers — or most of them, anyway — were a phantom, so Hollender is now chasing the mass market directly.

Seventh Generation — named for the Great Law of the Iroquois Confederacy, which states "In every deliberation, we must consider the impact on the next seven generations" — isn't dying on the vine. It's just taking longer to reach profitability than originally planned. In fact, although growth was nominal for several years in the mid-1990s, it does do over $7 million in sales, a huge bump from its modest beginnings. Just as important, it's delivered on its primary mission, developing and marketing a broad range of eco-friendly, everyday household goods: toilet tissue, napkins, and facial tissue made from 100 percent post-consumer recycled, unbleached paper; dishwashing liquid, laundry detergent, and dishwasher detergent with no phosphates or chlorine; trash bags from 100 percent recycled plastic (minimum 80 percent post-consumer); and on and on. As the environmental crisis deepens and consumers' awareness of their ability to impact it spreads, Seventh Generation products or some very much like theirs will grace vast numbers of kitchen and bathroom shelves.

But the company did seriously err at the start, admits Hollender, because "we focused on a market that was smaller than we thought it was, and we spent a lot of marketing dollars trying to chase too few consumers." Not that Hollender need apologize for the miscalculation. Consumer polls had shown for several years that up to about 25 percent of the marketplace was willing to pay more for products that damaged the earth less. These same consumers tended to be more affluent, so ostensibly they could afford the premium they offered to pay.

Problem is, they were fibbing. When push came to shove, most of them shopped for value and convenience just like everybody else. That killed Seventh Generation's business plan. As a small, new company, it was hampered by economies of scale, product development costs, and, often, the higher prices it had to pay for alternative raw materials. To recover those costs, it had to price products above the mainstream competition's. As a company that sold through mail order and health food stores, it was also asking consumers to not only buy non-traditional products and pay more for them but also buy those products in non-traditional places. For most consumers, that was simply asking too much. When sales plateaued in 1991, Hollender and the company's investors knew that something else had to be tried — mainstream supermarkets and mainstream pricing.

As 1994 came to a close, Seventh Generation announced that its products would be appearing in New England's Star Markets, Purity, and Big Y stores, and on a test basis, also in some eastern A & P, Top's Markets, and Wegman's Markets stores. The announcement followed the company's prodigious effort to not only secure shelf space but also overhaul its pricing considerations so it could compete with widely recognized brands. Says Hollender, "We went back to all our manufacturers and said, 'Will you be partners with us in this expanded distribution? Will you give us pricing as if we were already in that business because if we don't have competitive pricing, we won't get in the first place and we can't afford to take it all out of our own margin. In some cases, we found new manufacturers. In some cases, we reformulated the products." But all the haggling and reformulating paid off, as Seventh Generation was able to lower prices from 10 to 50 percent, depending on product, which opened the door to the mainstream market.

But Seventh Generation paid a price, too — environmentally. Says Hollender, "We become increasingly subject to making trade-offs to provide a product that is attractive to a somewhat less committed consumer, and those trade-offs are something that we live with every day. For instance, all dish detergents on the market contain chlorine, phosphates, and petroleum cleaning agents, all three of which we're against. When we reformulated our detergent, we couldn't come up with a product that worked and cost what we thought was appropriate without using a petroleum surfactant, although we were able to eliminate the chlorine and the phosphates. We went ahead and marketed that product, disclosing that it has petroleum ingredients in it."

However, Hollender feels no need to apologize: "In a purist sense, you could argue that we should have waited until we solved the technical problems or we should have put the [unreformulated] product out there even though it didn't work as well or cost more. But we made the decision that if we could get people to use a product that didn't have chlorine or phosphates, that was a step in the right direction." Seventh Generation doesn't use petroleum surfactants in any of its other cleaning products.

Having bridged the price issue, Seventh Generation faces a tougher challenge still in winning mainstream consumers' trust. Green cleaning products have a bad and not always undeserved reputation for underperforming their more noxious brand-name competitors. If you care more about getting your sink clean than what happens after you rinse the mess down the drain, then most green cleaners are going to finish a poor second. Seventh Generation has attempted to overcome the credibility gap by having its products tested against major brands by a third-party lab and publishing the results on its packaging. Claims Hollender, "For example, our laundry powder is about 98 percent as effective as Tide but it is 17 percent more effective than Arm & Hammer. Our window cleaner is more effective than Windex." But he acknowledges that consumers may not always take the time to wade through all the performance and environmental text on a Seventh Generation box.

For all the company's resourcefulness in attacking its business problems, Hollender is prouder still of its environmental accomplishments. Seventh Generation has made a special project of finding product uses for post-consumer waste materials that have low recycling value because those are the most likely to end up in landfills. For instance, most recycled tissue paper is made with office and computer paper waste, which is in high demand in recycling markets. Seventh Generation found a way to make tissue from telephone book and corrugated waste, of which there was a market glut. The company even found a way to make tissue from discarded juice drink boxes, previously thought to be unrecyclable.

Still, Hollender has no illusion that Seventh Generation products are saving the planet. Nor does he try to convince consumers otherwise: "I think that our products in general do represent major leaps forward for the environment. However, they're far from perfect so I don't want to say that we've solved the problem. Talk about a product like paper towels. Yes, it's great that we don't use bleach, that we use 100 percent post-consumer fiber, that we have a condensed roll that can ship in a truck using half the space and thus creating half the pollution. I can say lots of wonderful things about the product, but people shouldn't be using paper towels." But Seventh Generation has stopped telling its customers to only use them when necessary, another concession to investors and mainstream marketing.

For all the compromises, Hollender is confident that the move to supermarkets is the right one, not only for Seventh Generation stockholders but also for reducing the average household's planetary impact, still the company's primary mission. Nor does he think that the company's red-ink past portends anything about the future: "A company like Procter and Gamble spends $50 million to put a single product into a test market. Our company has lost collectively around $10 million over six years. Considering that we've developed twenty-seven products that are about to enter the supermarkets, that we've built a strong brand name, that we've built a catalog business that does $7 million in sales, that hasn't been a bad investment. Since we dropped our prices, we've seen continued growth for the first time in four years. So I think we're in the very early stages of what looks like a successful evolution."

COMPANY: FENTON COMMUNICATIONS

Policy/Practice Providing public relations and advertising services for socially responsible clients only.

Bottom Line: Values on Madison Avenue — now, there's a concept!

A quick read of David Fenton's résumé provides ample fodder for cynicism about the 1960s generation: Dropped out of high school during the Vietnam War years and became a photographer for the antiwar movement's Liberation News Service. Moved to Ann Arbor, Michigan, and helped start an underground newspaper. Became involved with an alternative political party, the Human Rights Party, which won control of Ann Arbor's city council. Produced a series of antinuclear concerts at Madison Square Garden featuring such for-the-people artists as Jackson Browne, Bonnie Raitt, and Bruce Springsteen.

So what's Fenton doing now? Public relations. Right on!

But now take a look at his client list. A few samples: Natural Resources Defense Council, Greenpeace, American Council for an Energy Efficient Economy, Public Citizen, Institute for Policy Studies, TransAfrica, Seventh Generation, Calvert Social Investment Fund, Nelson Mandela and the African National Congress, the British Labor Party. If you detect a discernible social slant to Fenton Communications' clientele, your antennae are in excellent working order. The firm refuses all business that's out of joint with its progressive values. Insists Fenton, "I'd rather quit before compromising that, go into another line of work, sell shirts to Bloomingdale's, anything."

Fenton has never studied PR. In fact, he never returned to high school. But he received some rather elite on-the-job training. He learned public relations, he says, from activist Abbie Hoffman in 1968, "when I was a teenage dropout running around the revolution. He was a real inspiration because he understood the impact of television and media on politics better than anybody." Fenton began to apply what he learned while working with the Human Rights Party, and then joined the staff of *Rolling Stone* magazine as its public relations director in the late 1970s. The concert production sharpened his skills; after a short time freelancing, he opened Fenton Communications in 1982, with Ralph Nader and *Mother Jones* magazine among his first clients.

Although you may not know Fenton's company, you almost certainly know some of its work. Engaged by the Death Penalty Information Center, the firm as been journalists' main source for information on racial bias in the application of the death penalty. When Nelson Mandela made his triumphant first visit to the United States, Fenton's company donated its services to promote the tour, providing what he estimates as $150,000 worth of staff time.

And if you stopped buying apples in 1989 to protect your family from the pesticide Alar, thank Fenton Communications, along with client Natural Resources Defense Council

(NRDC), for alerting you to Alar's dangers. The firm arranged for an NRDC report linking Alar to cancer to be released on CBS's "60 Minutes," and orchestrated actress Meryl Streep's visibility as a spokesperson for the issue, which led to her testimony about Alar before Congress. The campaign shriveled consumer apple purchases to a skinny core until Alar's manufacturer withdrew the chemical from the market.

The Alar saga continues today, a battle, as Fenton portrays it, of principled versus unprincipled PR. In recent years, the press has widely reported that the Alar scare was overblown and that the pesticide presented no threat to the public. Fenton stands by his firm's original work: "The mainstream toxicologists are with us completely on this. The EPA has completely banned Alar. The chemical and agricultural industries mounted a very purposeful misinformation campaign to try to convince elite opinion makers that Alar was never dangerous, and the media fell for it. But that battle isn't over yet."

Fenton Communications also works with business clients, but only ideals-driven companies or companies pushing a socially positive product need apply. As for green marketers making unsubstantiated claims, Fenton asserts: "I'm very suspicious of that stuff. I'll call my friends at Green Seal and the environmental auditors that I know and talk to them about it first." In the early 1990s, Fenton was approached by a biotechnology company that had invented a process for vaccinating plants against some species of caterpillars to eliminate the need for certain pesticides: "We investigated this process with some independent scientists and determined that the organism they were creating was very safe to eat — it was just proteins — and that it had no persistence in the environment, so we decided to work on it. But we spent two days at their corporate headquarters grilling their scientists, and at one point the CEO looked very perplexed. He thought he had asked us to come out so he could hire us and we were putting him through the third degree."

Fenton fiercely protects his company's reputation "because it's our primary currency. That we're so choosy about who we work on gives us a very unique credibility with journalists, because we're not harassing them with nonsense. We stand for something and we check our information out before we bring it to them, so that's a very precious thing, and I wouldn't sacrifice or dilute it." The firm also draws the line on what it considers unethical tactics, even in the service of causes it supports. Fenton points to the common practice in mainstream PR of putting together phony coalitions made to appear as authentic grassroots groups: "You'll see something like the Coalition for Healthy Lands and it turns out to be cattle people who want to graze the rivers until they die. I wouldn't touch anything like that, I can't claim perfection but I can claim intent."

Not that Fenton Communications is above finessing the system. Says David, "We almost never have a big budget. We're accustomed to guerrilla tactics." One of those tactics is to create television ads so dramatic and emotional that they become news themselves, which can generate hundreds of thousands of dollars of free air time. For example, for the Alar campaign, says Fenton, "We made a television ad with Meryl Streep washing broccoli in the sink and saying, 'The government says I have to wash the broccoli. What's wrong with it?' That ad was seen by many people all over the country and we never paid a penny to buy time for that. We didn't have it."

Fenton Communications doesn't just wait for organizations representing causes it considers vital to show up on its doorstep. It originates some issue campaigns in-house and then seeks foundation support to finance them. "A lot of our Central American human-rights work was funded that way. So was much of our anti-apartheid work and our work for the emerging nuclear freeze movement in the early eighties." The firm does not, however, often work pro bono, says Fenton: "I think the PR industry needs to develop a pro bono tradition like the law firms have. But it's difficult for us to do that because we're working for small companies and nonprofits and publishers and none of them pay a lot. Still, we do frequently work many, many staff hours beyond what we get paid when we care a lot about something." Fenton Communications financed the Mandela tour by asking its other clients to pay normal rates for a month while the firm put most of its time into the tour. They agreed, enthusiastically, says Fenton.

Fenton shares something else with other 1960s activists who have remained true to their values — lower economic expectations. "We've been profitable for the last nine years. We haven't had a payroll problem in that amount of time, and we have no bank or investor debt, so the company's healthy, I guess. But nor can we look many months down the road with the security of knowing where the income is going to come from." He isn't contemplating changing anything, however: "I think I got damaged at the cellular level along the way so I can't sell out in that regard."

ACTIVISM

COMPANIES: VARIOUS (SEE BELOW)

Policy/Practice: Taking forceful public stands on controversial issues.

Bottom Line: The way these business leaders see it, it's riskier not to speak up.

Most of the ethical business initiatives detailed in the present work justify themselves, either hypothetically or in fact, in terms of classic enlightened self-interest. However, in early 1991, several progressive companies took a step that however enlightened, could hardly be dismissed as self-interested: protesting America's impending participation in the Persian Gulf war. It was a dramatic demonstration that often principled business is simply about . . . principle.

The background: In 1990, several progressive retail business leaders joined hands as a group called Act Now to educate and organize their customers to act on important social issues. They chose as their first issue fuel efficiency, with its profound implications for both the environment and militarism in the Middle East. Targeting a Senate bill that would require automakers to improve mileage performance, the group circulated a card that their customers could send to their senators requesting support for the legislation.

A few months later, Saddam Hussein's forces invaded Kuwait, the United States formed a United Nations–led coalition that threatened to blow the Iraqis into so many grains of sand, and the fuel-efficiency issue assumed a far more urgent dimension. The board of Ben & Jerry's, one of the original Act Now companies, decided that a public statement about the conflict was at least as forceful a gesture toward energy and peace as anything Act Now was doing. On New Year's Eve of that year, with the United Nations' deadline for an Iraqi pullout set at January 15, B & J's Ben Cohen and Liz Bankowski made a list of possible signatories and began contacting them by phone and fax.

Shortly thereafter, Ben & Jerry's and their hastily gathered group of eighteen co-signers affixed their logos to a full-page ad in the national edition of the *New York Times*. The ad was in the form of a letter titled "An Unnecessary War" and addressed to President Bush and Congress. It began in moderate, respectful terms, asking that patient diplomacy and economic sanctions against Iraq be given a chance to work and applauding the president for his support of sanctions to that point. It also acknowledged the difficulties involved in holding the U.N. coalition together. Then it began hitting between the eyes:

. . . those difficulties are small when weighed against the enormous human suffering war will bring to hundreds of thousand of troops and civilians.

We further urge you to begin work immediately *[their emphasis] on a National Energy Policy based on conservation and development of safe, alternative energy sources. We can eliminate the need to import* any *[their emphasis] oil from Iraq and Kuwait by improving average auto fuel efficiency by a mere three miles per gallon!*

The price of gasoline should never be a reason to send our sons and daughters off to die in a foreign war.

Signees besides Ben & Jerry's included Stonyfield Farm, San Francisco baker and dessert maker Just Desserts, Patagonia, the *Utne Reader,* the *LA Weekly,* Working Assets Funding Service, Rhino Entertainment, *Business Ethics* magazine, Paul Newman/Kayso Productions, Conservatree Paper, *Hemmings Motor News,* and several other companies. While many of the above names are closely identified with the progressive business movement, that doesn't negate the fact that all participating companies were putting market share and employee support at risk, considering the patriotic wave then washing over the American public. Indeed, Bush's prosecution of the war would eventually propel him to a 90 percent approval rating.

Bankowski, then a Ben & Jerry's board member and now the company's director of social mission development as well, says that the company did in fact worry about offending some employees: "We did have people from one of our plants who were in the National Guard and served in the Persian Gulf. We didn't want to do anything to be disrespectful or nonsupportive of that role." The board posted its intention to take the stand; it didn't, however, put it up for a company-wide vote. Says Bankowski: "Our board reserves the right to take positions on public issues that we see as important and are tied to who we are, and peace has been one of those."

It is not unusual, of course, for companies to involve themselves in politics. Corporations do it all the time, through lobbying and PAC contributions, but nearly always behind the scenes and for narrow corporate ends, not the general good. Increasingly, once exposed, they risk the wrath of issue-sensitive consumers. Following the November 1994 elections, several Latino organizations called for a boycott of the Disney corporation and other large companies that had contributed to Governor Pete Wilson's immigrant-bashing reelection campaign in California. In Oregon, state employees organized an informal boycott of business contributors to a conservative state legislator after a mean-spirited initiative that he authored narrowly passed, slashing their compensation by 6 percent.

Although Ben & Jerry's has far more overtly taken controversial political positions, it has never suffered the backlash that companies did in the above-mentioned circumstances. Nor, I assume, did the other signees of the Gulf War ad. For one, Elliot Hoffman, president of Just Desserts, told me that despite an on-air mauling by a conservative radio talk show host and the inevitable few nasty letters, his company's participation in the ad only bonded his customers and employees even more tightly to the company. Bankowski says that biannual employee surveys show that Ben & Jerry's workforce not only supports the company's activism but, like Just Desserts' employees, takes pride in it, even if staff doesn't unanimously support every company stand. Customer mail is overwhelmingly positive as well. I hear similar things from Gary Hirshberg, CEO of Stonyfield Farm, which is based in conservative New Hampshire. Note that these companies ostensibly sell to many, many people who don't share their taste in politics, and hire some (in Stonyfield's case, many) as well.

What's the message here? Apparently it matters far less what stand your company takes than in whose interest it takes it. Unlike the usual corporate campaign contributor, none of the Gulf War ad signees expressed themselves in a way that pitted one set of stakeholders, stock owners, against all others.

Jim Kelly's experience certainly supports that conclusion. In 1992, Kelly, president of Portland, Oregon–based Rejuvenation Lamp & Fixture, and his brother John convinced forty businesses, including several major Northwest retail chains and the Portland Trailblazers basketball team, to add their logos to a full-page ad in the Portland *Oregonian* urging voters to defeat the statewide anti-gay ballot initiative. The initiative lost, with the Portland-area vote decisive, but nearly half the voters, presumably including many Rejuvenation patrons, backed it.

Kelly lost neither sleep nor business over the matter, which was only the latest instance of his company standing on principle over profit: "In fifteen years, I can only think of one negative incident. Someone wrote me a nasty letter saying that they didn't realize we gave money to 1% for Peace, and they thought it was all a bunch of hogwash. We've had many people who appreciate that in us and said that was part of the reason they did business with us. Obviously we don't take stands on issues like abortion, where you could get firebombed or something. But I think businesses have power and ability to make change. Yes, there's some risk in taking those stands but there's also a lot to gain."

SECTION IV

Planet

ENERGY EFFICIENCY

COMPANY: J. C. PENNEY

Policy/Practice: Designing new buildings and retrofitting old ones for maximum cost-efficient energy savings.

Bottom Line: Energy usage — and pollution — cut by more than half.

Like most other Americans in business, the folks who run J. C. Penney used to take for granted the prodigious amounts of energy their operation consumed. The wake-up call came in 1973, when the Organization of Petroleum Exporting Countries (OPEC) flexed its political muscles and cut off oil shipments to the United States, Japan, and western Europe. Suddenly, Penney had to sweat not only the price of the energy that fueled its stores but the very security of the supply.

OPEC lifted its boycott in March of 1974, most of the nation went back to its energy-guzzling ways, and the words *energy efficiency* — so much a part of the national vocabulary in the previous months — all but vanished from collective memory. J. C. Penney was one of very few businesses to get the boycott's secondary message — security issues aside, energy usage is a huge, untapped source of easy cost savings. Before the decade ended, the chain had instituted an energy-efficiency program. Today, through aggressive retrofitting and energy-conscious design of new buildings, J. C. Penney stores burn less than half the power they did in the early 1970s, says energy programs manager Alan Rose.

Of all the "win-win" social business practices, energy efficiency's wins are perhaps the most clear-cut. The monetary advantages, although not immediate, show up soon thereafter — Rose says Penney's up-front investment in hardware pays back in "as little as a year on some things and typically around thirty to thirty-six months." Performance-wise, Penney's lighting is better, and heating and cooling just as good as before.

The social win is largely environmental, because at the other end of the wire to your light switch or air conditioner is an electric utility belching foul smoke up its stacks, generating radioactive waste, or in the case of hydroelectric plants, wreaking havoc on habitats and fish stocks. If other companies did what Penney does, the nation wouldn't need as many power plants as it does now, and we wouldn't need to burn as much fuel in the ones we keep on-line. For instance, as of early 1993 Penney estimated its energy improvements had saved the consumption of 43 million gallons of oil or 540 million pounds of coal.

There's even a payoff in international competitiveness. Because it has no domestic oil supply, Japan long ago committed itself to energy efficiency. Its radically lower energy costs per unit of production are now a significant factor in its manufacturers' ability to compete with ours. The same is true in environmentally progressive western Europan nations such as Germany and Sweden.

But Rose admits that Penney probably is less driven by such lofty considerations than it is by the effect of energy efficiency on its medium- and long-term bottom line. To Penney's leaders, the innovations of Rose's department make undeniable fiscal sense.

To maximize the savings, Penney takes a systems approach to energy usage, realizing that the greatest gains come not from add-on changes but from the interrelationships between lighting, heating, cooling, and insulation, as well as from operation and maintenance of the equipment. For example, the company retrofits lighting in a store before buying a new air-chilling unit because reducing lighting consumption reduces the heat the lights throw off and thus the need to cool the air. Rose: "In a store that we ran some numbers on, we were able to buy a chiller that was twenty-five tons smaller just due to the fact that we reduced lighting load."

You don't have to be a techno-geek to understand that you can reap other efficiency gains by installing equipment that adjusts the amount of air cooled or heated to the load need at the time. Penney accomplishes this by mounting variable-frequency drives on its HVAC (heating/cooling) motors and sometimes replacing the motors themselves with more efficient models. Nor do you have to have an economics doctorate to understand that state, national, and international mandates on reducing CFC emissions are raising the cost of CFC refrigerants, which is why Penney is switching over now to non-CFC chillers that also run more efficiently.

Indoor air-quality for employees is a charged issue these days, and Penney has attacked this problem in the most energy-wise manner, as well. Rose points out that whatever air you introduce into a building for ventilation purposes will have to be heated or cooled, so "we use a sensor that senses CO_2 in the space, which is pretty much a barometer of how many bodies we've got wandering around in there. We control the volumes of outside air coming into the store based on those levels, which is much more efficient than just dumping x amount of air in regardless of occupancy."

Although Penney is always installing fresh technology as it seeks to keep its energy systems state of the art, Rose says, "We haven't had any major problems — a few glitches here and there, but it's performed well for us." So he's constantly scanning the field for new and better ideas because while he's proud of what his programs have accomplished for the company so far, he thinks he can do much more.

Rose says he's frequently contacted by other companies looking to replicate Penney's savings. But the questions tend to cease once they hear the up-front price tag. Rose just shakes his head: "Most of us are more worried about what the operating statement is going to look like at the end of the month as opposed to what it could look like five years down the road. I don't think we at Penney have any more or less capital to invest. It's just that our priorities might be a tad different."

COMPANY: SOUTHWIRE

Policy/Practice: Establishing an energy-efficiency management system.

Bottom Line: Unless you already have an efficiently managed company, the hardware won't make much of a difference.

If you think energy efficiency is just a matter of buying some new devices and getting some engineering wizard to install them, then it probably won't do for your company what it did for Southwire. Take it from Jim Clarkson, Southwire's energy manager who helped the company reverse a business crisis in the 1980s with a comprehensive energy overhaul. If you're trying to conserve energy over any meaningful period of time, says Clarkson, your company better be managing itself efficiently as well: "It's a culture. If you're good, you're good all over. If you're bad, you're bad all over. And the good guys eat the bad guys."

Thanks to its combined energy and management smarts, Southwire, a major electric wire and cable maker based in Carrollton, Georgia, has been breakfasting on bad guys for years. But until it solved the energy puzzle, it almost got eaten itself. In the late 1970s, fast-rising energy costs overwhelmed Southwire's competitive edge over its international rivals. In

France, Italy, and the Far East, new companies were entering the marketplace with newer, far more efficient equipment, helped in some cases by their government's policies favoring capital investment. For example, most came on-line with five-wire drawing machines compared to Southwire's older model, which drew a single wire. On top of Southwire's energy and technology problems, a worldwide overcapacity of wire caused prices to plummet. Domestic rivals like Kaiser and General Electric simply dropped out of the business because, explains Clarkson, "they were conglomerates that simply didn't want to accept a 2 percent return on capital." Southwire had little choice but to stay in the game — wire was all it made.

Energy costs and wire prices weren't Southwire's only headache at the time. The company was having quality and productivity problems and was highly leveraged besides in a time of rising interest rates. But management realized that energy savings were the easiest and quickest way out of the mess. Energy typically contributes about 10 to 11 percent to the cost of converting raw materials to wire, but by 1980 Southwire's percentage had risen to about 22, devouring the company's profit margin. As both the most out-of-control cost and the one most easily slashed, energy was an obvious target. So the company hired Clarkson, teamed him up with some Southwire engineers, and unleashed them to hunt down the savings.

Realizing that you can't control what you can't measure, Clarkson's group began metering energy use throughout the operation, then analyzing the data. That gave them figures that few other companies, including their rivals, had. Clarkson sighs as he recalls a conversation with the energy manager at a government power plant who told him she didn't have permission to buy meters, only equipment that saved energy: "I happen to think meters save more money than any other device that we have.

"The real key in any energy program is to see to it that there's proper allocation of costs back to the [decision makers] that ran them up, see that it's reported back to them, see that their management knows, and ask them 'How did you do last quarter and how did that compare to the quarter before and why is this different and what you are doing about it, and report back to me next quarter.' Once that sort of system's in place, a lot of things can start happening."

A rough sample of those things: During a single year when their wire production *increased,* Southwire's steam usage fell by half. An analysis of the company's copper-melting process led to a 25 percent cut in energy cost. Overall, from 1980 to 1987, Southwire's Btus per pound of production dropped by 50 percent and helped end the company's fiscal crisis.

In December of 1987, Southwire bought a plant from a competitor that was going under. It has bought a plant every year since then, giving it as of this writing seventeen plants scattered over ten states. It is now the largest wire maker in the United States, and as it has continued to grow, energy efficiency plays an ever larger role. Energy use comprises less than 5 percent of the cost of Southwire's wire making these days, but the company now does its own aluminum making and energy is the biggest single cost factor — from 40 to 60 percent, depending on aluminum prices — in that process.

Energy efficiency also helps Southwire offset the cost of plant acquisitions. In fact, you really begin to understand the effect a federal energy-efficiency initiative could have on U.S. competitiveness when you examine Southwire's achievements relative to its competition. Many of the ailing operations that Southwire takes over failed in part because of poor energy management. Clarkson: "At our old plants, it's pretty darn hard to squeeze another 1 or 2 percent a year out of a plant that has already cut 50 percent. But we buy a new plant and we're just heroes. We can show the plant manager how to knock ten to twenty thousand dollars a month off the energy bill immediately."

Obviously, much of Southwire's early savings came from equipment purchases. Energy-saving options on the equipment cost the company more, but Clarkson says in almost every case — "except for a couple of fly-by-night outfits" — the outlay was worth it.

However, many of what were then options are now standard-issue, so Southwire keeps its competitive-energy edge in other ways. For example, the company achieved the steam usage savings mentioned above by checking for and repairing leaks, upgrading insulation, and other maintenance operations. It also bought equipment — such as the hallowed five-wire drawing machine — that made more product per unit of energy. In fact, says Clarkson, "frequently the same thing that would save energy would increase quality and productivity and vice versa." Of course, the company has reconfigured its office lighting and heating/air conditioning, too. However, those usages comprise a tiny slice of its overall energy pie.

Clarkson also cautions those who would follow in Southwire's footsteps to figure human factors into the energy equation. He says he and the other energy engineers have at times been so focused on buying the right equipment that they've neglected the people responsible for using it: "We would put a speed controller on a pump and then later find out this thing isn't working because nobody really knows what it's for and they don't know how to fix it and they aren't convinced it's going to work anyway. That's kind of like the Lone Ranger riding into town, shooting some bad guys, and riding off into the sunset. While you're there, you have to train the local sheriff and go back once a year and help him out."

Of course, the most crucial human factor is that top management understand and support the initiative. Clarkson credits his bosses for much of his team's success, in particular management's willingness to buy hardware that may not pay back for a year or two. But he's also learned over the years to approach them with the right ideas at the right point in the business cycle: "When we were making money, our banks would let us reinvest in the business, so I'd focus on getting equipment in. During bad times, the banks wouldn't let us have any money, so then I focused on operations. Besides, during good times you tell management how you can nitpick energy, and they don't care. They're busy trying to make wire and get it out the door. You say it costs more and they say 'Yeah, I know but I've got an order to fill.' During bad times, they're starving and trying to find any way to cut costs, so then you can get their attention on improving processes."

For all its energy ingenuity, Southwire has bled some red ink in recent years. "We're in a tough business," says Clarkson, noting that the company suffered in both 1992 and 1993, when aluminum and copper prices plunged worldwide. But Clarkson knows his message has appeal come rain or shine: "This stuff is real predictable — we put in this gizmo, we'll save this much money — whereas if you make a little more wire, you're not sure you're going to make any money on it."

Despite the indisputable logic of energy efficiency, however, Clarkson cautions that it's no panacea for struggling companies: "I don't think you can go to a plant that has high turnover and disgruntled employees and bad housekeeping and just graft this onto them. I believe energy efficiency is indigenous, part of a culture of good management. Energy is just like any other challenge that faces businesses throughout, and the same tools are used to solve it that are used to solve anything else."

PACKAGING

COMPANY: ODWALLA

Policy/Practice: Taking responsibility for the recycling of its packaging and other solid wastes.

Bottom Line: One company that recycles as if the planet depended upon it.

Executives rarely know what's in store two months ahead for their company, much less what the future holds years from now. But the outlines of business's long-range environmental future are already showing through in some areas, and one of those is packaging. With the raw-material base continuing to shrink and landfills continuing to fill up, government here will eventually require retailers and manufacturers to take full responsibility for recycling their packaging, as some governments in Europe already do.

When that hammer falls, it won't fall on Odwalla, a fresh juice company based in Davenport, California, that's tougher on itself environmentally than any legislature will ever be. Then again, it's run by an environmentalist — Greg Steltenpohl, Odwalla's chair and CEO since its inception in 1980, who came to the company with an environmental studies degree from Stanford University and a knowledge of how companies and governmental bodies worldwide were dealing with ecological issues.

Of course, Greg's background wasn't much help on the packaging issue. From the first carrot peeled at Odwalla, he was worrying about how to mitigate the environmental impact of the operation's plastic juice bottles, because no one in business or government had ever fully addressed plastics recycling. "Responsibility essentially stopped on the shelf," he recalls. "Everyone was relying on consumers, who in many cases really didn't have any avenues for recycling. So even if they wanted to take the extra step to find the right place to put it, in many communities that wasn't possible."

One of those communities was Santa Cruz, where Odwalla first began selling. Santa Cruz had a curbside recycling program but it didn't cover plastics. Says Steltenpohl, "We approached the city and asked why, and the reply was there wasn't a market for the material." Determined to invent whatever was needed, the company set up its own recycling infrastructure, first establishing a route collection system with its own trucks and drivers, then setting up a storage facility at the city's recycling center, where the plastic could be held until it became marketable. With a little research, Odwalla discovered next that by first sorting, milling, and grinding the plastic into flakes, it could find markets for the stuff. The commodity sales in turn fed income to help offset the costs of the program.

After operating the program for two years, Odwalla returned to Santa Cruz and asked the city to add the program to its ongoing collection system. This time the officials consented because, says Steltenpohl, recycled plastics markets had expanded, new legislation was mandating more recycling, and "we'd shown the entrepreneurial problems could be solved."

Odwalla has long since expanded its territory into other western states. It has also expanded its packaging recycling efforts with the same entrepreneurial drive and resourcefulness it demonstrated in Santa Cruz. Most of the cities in which Odwalla juices are sold now have plastic recycling programs in place, but not always at curbside. So Odwalla has researched the recycling alternatives for every community in which it sells, and maintains a hot line and database so it can direct consumers to the proper site or option in their area.

Odwalla applies the same level of ingenuity and commitment to the rest of its solid-waste stream. Most of the organic wastes from its juicing process — 60,000 pounds per week as of late 1994 — is sold as animal feed; Odwalla shaves and dries the remainder for herbs and teas, and plans to increase the portion used for human consumption to help fund other environmental initiatives that are less cost efficient. The company is also developing a rigorous recycled-content purchasing policy to help expand markets for recycled materials, including using recycled plastic pallet wrap for shipping juice by truck. It has begun a cycle of regular eco-audits as well, so it can measure and thus better control its other wastes.

Meanwhile, the company continues to search out a still better fate for its juice bottles. "Long-term, we're really looking for an alternative to plastic for our bottles," says Steltenpohl. "We're putting some R and D effort into looking at the potential for a cornstarch derivative or something that would be organic and truly biodegradable, not just solar degradable into tiny plastic pieces. We're also looking at cleaner alternatives to the amount of gums and glues on our labels, and being more conscious on our purchase of ink types."

Through its participation in several business networks, including the Social Venture Network, Odwalla has been able to influence other companies with what it has learned about reducing packaging and other environmental impacts. But Steltenpohl seems just as impressed with the efforts of his own workforce to squeeze a little more environmental performance from their juice company: "When employees see what the company is willing to do, it really deepens their commitment and their own strategic inquiry. And that's really the power because where the rubber meets the road is in every purchasing decision and all the employees who either throw things away or decide to spend the extra second putting them over in another pile."

COMPANY: APPLEBROOK FARMS

Policy/Practice: Introducing environmentally responsible bulk packaging to a mail-order business.

Bottom Line: A special gift surprise — for the company! — in every box.

Applebrook Farms' consumers don't care a whit about the company's environmental posture. But their "purchasing agents" do, which owner/founders Mark Albion and Paul Birnholz figured might help them out of a troubling packaging dilemma. You see, Applebrook, based in Westford, Vermont, makes all-natural dog biscuits — sold both by mail order and in retail stores — for health-conscious pooches. Conscientious businesspeople that they are, Albion and Birnholz wanted to ease the impact their product's packaging made on the planet. They knew their customers would happily support their efforts if — big if — they didn't have to sacrifice convenience or cost. Unfortunately, their first attempts at solving the problem had run smack up against precisely those barriers.

For instance, they investigated using a canister made from unbleached cardboard, but it required the use of an expensive inside wrapper that threatened to push the retail price past the doggie threshold. During the Christmas season, they tried marketing biscuits in "stocking stuffers" made from 100 percent biodegradable cellulose bags, but the packaging tended to degrade ahead of schedule after shipping and repeated handling.

Enter the company's Back to Bulk! program, an attempt to go greener by flat-out eliminating as much packaging as possible. In 1992, Applebrook offered its mail-order customers substantially reduced prices — from $6.00 to $3.25 per pound — to switch their purchases from bags to bulk shipments by the box, promising to have refillable containers available by the following year. The savings inherent in reduced packaging costs covered most of the price break; Applebrook kicked in part of its profit margin to sweeten the deal. About 500 customers bit, but the best was yet to come because over the next year one hidden advantage after another began revealing itself to the company.

About six months into Back to Bulk!, Albion and Birnholz noticed that customers were buying lots more biscuits per transaction — up from $35 worth annually to nearly $100. Only three explanations for that, the duo figured — customers were buying more for themselves, buying for other people as well, and handing out more samples to new dogs. The last factor was especially key because, says Albion, "we knew from experience that once we get this product into people's hands and dogs' mouths — especially finicky hounds — we have them. We have a core group that will absolutely go to the ends of the earth to get our products." Sure enough, word of mouth increased the original 500 customers to 1,200 "just from Back to Bulk!," says Albion. "We started building over $100,000 in revenue from that one program."

As they analyzed the phenomenon, Albion and Birnholz saw the whole packaging package in 3-D relief. Reducing the amount of packaging material also dropped the labor needed to wrap the biscuits; both factors reduced costs to Applebrook. The company could then pass its savings to customers as lower prices, encouraging them to pass out samples to new dogs, which in turn spurred the word-of-mouth campaign. "And then the third thing the initiative did," says Albion, "was to change the ability to advertise the product. That is, it gave us more market presence. The canisters put it out there on the counter. Before, people would tend to keep the packaged product in the refrigerator or shoveled away somewhere. This brought it out front and center like a cookie jar."

Back to Bulk! accomplished yet one more thing for Albion personally — it gave the former Harvard Business School prof a great teaching story. Albion explains that Applebrook isn't his primary occupation — he spends most of his time advising major corporations on the benefits of socially responsible practices and values. He and Birnholz, senior partner in an accounting firm, started Applebrook in late 1990 as something of a plaything in which they could test their ideas about ideals-driven business, create some jobs for hard-up Vermonters, and, oh yes, get Birnholz's irresistible doggie treats to the canine masses.

"We weren't strategically smart about Back to Bulk!," Albion admits. "We just sort of fell into it from being really disgusted with our environmental issues around packaging." That's not quite how he tells it when he relates the story to Fortune 500 CEOs, but small matter. The tale still shows how an environmental practice returned immediate dollars to the bottom line and simultaneously increased the visibility of the product. "That's one of the strongest examples I have, quite frankly," he exclaims.

Like most business tales, of course, this one also includes a few cautionary notes. What worked so well for mail-order customers didn't pan out at all in retail stores. Again, says Albion, "It's one thing to get a consumer to change how they buy the product, quite another to change the way retailers are going to retail. We had this vision that we were going to get retailers to carry Applebrook Farm canisters and keep a lot of inventory in the back. Except for a few small retailers, that just wasn't going to happen," so Applebrook focused more of its energy on mail order, where it was making all of its money anyway.

One more problem — several customers took the Back to Bulk! price drop in exactly the opposite spirit in which it was offered. "What the price break really said to people is, 'Do you realize that half of what you've been paying is the packaging?'" Albion says with a sigh. "But they got it differently. Some people thought we had been ripping them off by not selling in bulk before." After tiring of fielding the angry phone calls, the company began including an explanatory paragraph — on a no-bigger-than-necessary piece of paper, of course — with every shipment.

Problems solved, Back to Bulk! continues to move more dog biscuits for Applebrook. Dogs are happier because, at its lower price, their owners offer more of the product to them. And Albion and Birnholz get to yap about their happy little accident, although they generally resist the urge to brand it a howling success.

TRANSPORTATION

COMPANY: 3M

Policy/Practice: Providing vans to employees who pool their transportation to and from work.

Bottom Line: A new TQM: traffic quality management.

3M has a ways to climb before it tops any list of "green" companies, but the giant manufacturer is certainly farther up the slope than many of its industrial brethren. Its well-publicized Pollution Prevention Pays (3P) program, created in 1975, has averted in its first nineteen years more than 600,000 tons of pollution, saved the company $700 million in the process, and spurred imitators throughout the corporate world. Product-wise, the company touts that its Never Rust Soap Pad is made from recycled plastic bottles and non-phosphorus soap that won't pollute waterways.

More quietly, since 1973 3M has encouraged employees to reduce traffic congestion and air pollution by riding to work together in company-provided vans. In typical 3M style, the program runs on employee initiative. Volunteer drivers, called "pool coordinators," recruit their passengers, and if they recruit well, they clear some money from the deal. Riders pay sixty dollars per month for up to a fifteen-mile round trip, which covers the gas, maintenance, and depreciation of the vehicles. If drivers of twelve-passenger vans carry at least eight passengers, they don't pay the monthly. If they get two more to ride, the company pays them the $120 in extra fares. (Drivers can also choose to drive minivans. They pay a flat twenty-five dollars per month to drive those.)

The company urges employees to take part in the program with positive incentives such as free parking in underground or covered spaces, a not inconsiderable privilege in brutal Minnesota winters. Still, participation tends to vary with the price of gas. Out of the 12,000 employees at 3M's St. Paul headquarters, roughly 650 employees were riding in just under 100 vans as of late 1994. Explains employee transit manager Terry Ployhart, "Gas is at reasonable cost at this point and people do enjoy driving themselves to work and being autonomous. Where we've seen large peaks in our program has been during the energy crisis. At one particular time, the number of vans out on the street all of a sudden doubled." The company operates van-pooling at eight 3M sites besides St. Paul.

Obviously, 3M lays out some cash to run the van pool program — primarily, the price of the vans and administrative costs. But they may well be getting much or all of that back in employee performance. A company study revealed that ride sharers were less likely to use sick leave and more likely to manage their time well during the workday. And chuckles Ployhart, who oversees the pools, everyone who's in the program arrives on time.

INTERNATIONAL STANDARDS

COMPANY: H. B. FULLER

Policy/Practice: Establishing uniformly high environmental, health, and safety standards for domestic and international operations.

Bottom Line: A company that reads its own warning labels.

Environmental activists have long decried the way multinational corporations with noxious manufacturing processes export their production to Third World nations where environmental laws are lax and enforcement laxer. On the surface, H. B. Fuller would seem to be exactly the type of company they worry about. The St. Paul, Minnesota–based corporation makes all kinds of nasty stuff — adhesives, sealants, coating, paints, and other specialty chemicals — and operates on dozens of locations in Latin America and Asia/Pacific in addition to Europe and North America.

But Fuller is neither an ordinary chemical company nor an ordinary multinational. Long acknowledged by business ethics experts as a model corporate citizen, Fuller holds its international units to the same environmental standards it enforces in America, where laws are relatively tough. And its American standards and performance not only far exceed the average for its industry but stand apart in the corporate universe as a whole.

Always reflective about its stakeholder relationships, the company, which went public in 1968, reexamined and codified its social responsibilities in 1978. However, just six years later Fuller executives urgently revisited their worldwide environmental and safety practices. The reason was an international incident that made knees quiver in boardrooms across the nation: Bhopal.

The almost incomprehensible suffering — over 4,000 residents killed and 200,000 injured — caused by a chemical leak at a Union Carbide plant in Bhopal, India, obsessed chairman/CEO Tony Andersen, says Joe Pellish, Fuller vice president for environment, health, and safety: "Everything that was published on the subject, Tony read or had access to. It became almost a fetish with him. Bottom line, he posed the question, What if that happened to us?"

With that query as an organizing principle, Andersen mobilized talent from throughout the company to focus on the problem. A management committee drawn from Fuller operations all over the world generated a series of recommendations that were approved by Fuller's board, which further directed that by 1990, the company have in place the ability to immediately address any potential adverse effects of a hazardous chemcial release on the surrounding environment and populations. The board also established a permanent Worldwide Environment, Health, and Safety (WEHS) Committee; formed a WEHS oversight committee at the senior management level; and ordered that every Fuller facility worldwide undergo assessment by corporate staff once every three years in addition to periodic assessments by area WEHS coordinators.

Since that time, the WEHS Committee has met annually. With input from manufacturing and technical managers from throughout the company's international network, it has consistently upgraded the WEHS standards as well as their implementation and enforcement. As for assessments, in 1993 alone 88 environmental, health, or safety audits were conducted in 62 facilities, 21 of those outside the United States.

If you want to measure a company's environmental commitment, start with its attitude toward regulatory compliance. Companies like Fuller set such high standards for themselves that compliance is almost irrelevant. For instance, to prevent undetected leaks of stored liquids into soil and groundwater, the company has in recent years aggressively replaced underground raw-material storage tanks with aboveground tanks and secondary containment structures. In the United States, regulations would have required Fuller to have removed all of its underground tanks by 1998. Beams Pellish, "I'm pleased to tell you we were up and out with all of our U.S. tanks by 1993." In Latin America — where regulatory control is, to put it mildly, relaxed — the company had removed dozens of tanks as of this writing, with the remaining tanks scheduled to be removed by year-end 1994.

Fuller also impresses with the way it has met the board's directive on emergency preparedness. The company's primary objective, of course, remains prevention and it has been remarkably successful in that regard. For instance, its worst recent year for chemical spills was 1993, with eight incidents totaling 510 gallons — peanuts for a company this size — and the company has never been cited for a serious violation of government regulations, a rare claim in Fuller's business.

Still, should the company's multilayered prevention program fail and a leak to the outside occur, Fuller appears to be up to the challenge. Managers at all facilities have developed "pre-emergency plans," essentially rehearsals for disaster. Through regular reviews of the plans, managers keep employees familiarized with their roles in an emergency situation. They also give local emergency "responders," such as fire departments, copies of the plans, and encourage them to tour the facilities to better understand the emergency procedures and types of materials stored and manufactured on-site. At many of the larger facilities, Fuller conducts mock-disaster drills in concert with local emergency responders.

Pellish stands over the operation like a commander over an army, and he has a modern commander's tools, including a software package called CAMEO™ (Computer Aided Management of Emergency Operations). The guts of the system is a database covering every one of Fuller's manufacturing, warehouse, and lab facilities around the world. The company has stuffed the database with crucial information — key contact names, details about bulk storage and equipment, and a diagram of each building and its general contents — that Fuller personnel and/or outside responders can immediately access should an emergency occur.

But CAMEO doesn't sit idle in the meantime. In fact, says Pellish, the system's primary value is its wargame-like ability to model accidental releases and their consequences: "We could, for example, hypothetically drop a 150-pound cylinder of chlorine gas that we used to use in chlorinating products, and by inserting the temperature, location, structure, and other elements that are in the model, we can predict the plume and show you on a screen where it's going to go. We've screened in all of our locations in the world, including local area maps. So if I'm sitting here in the Twin Cities and our facility in Columbia Heights had a leak, I can mark the spot of the spill, calculate where it's going, and identify vulnerability zones — a school close by or a hospital or nursing home buildings or other high-density populations." Pellish admits that the database is currently more useful in the United States but Fuller has exported it to European operations to begin working with emergency responders there with a goal of expanding its use worldwide.

None of the above would mean much, however, without two final factors: dedicated participation by senior management and emphasis by same — in a manner obvious to every employee — of caution over productivity and profits. Fuller documents, whether prepared for shareholders or employees, consistently convey this ordering of priorities. As for executive involvement, Pellish reports directly to the CEO, and the oversight committee, he notes, includes Tony Andersen, president/COO Walter Kissling, two senior vice presidents, and two other vice presidents: "We've been doing some bench-marking with some of our cohorts and they're amazed that we get this sort of attention." The oversight committee meets on average two to three times a year.

In 1993, Fuller became the first specialty chemical company and only the second Fortune 500 company to affirm the CERES Principles, the rigorous ten-point environmental code of business conduct authored by the Coalition for Environmentally Responsible Economies, which Social Venture Network member Joan Bavaria co-chairs. Of course, the CERES Principles weren't much of a stretch for Fuller, because its own WEHS principles approximated the CERES approach. The company has since modified WEHS to incorporate CERES concepts that weren't represented so that WEHS today, Pellish says, is essentially the CERES guidelines adapted to Fuller particulars.

Not that Fuller is without fault in these areas, or claims to be. The company is caught with its competition in a wrenching period of transition. For example, what were once considered acceptable methods of toxic disposal, such as deep-well injections, are considered environmental anathema today. Like other chemical companies, Fuller continues to search for and develop more appropriate technology and processes, but operates today in an uncomfortably compromised manner.

Some of its smaller failings have been almost comical for a company so fervently trying to do the right thing. In the early days of the WEHS initiative, the WEHS Committee conducted a series of paper surveys to discover what emergency procedures were already in place. Pellish recalls, "It shocked us to find out that there wasn't even a basic audible fire-alarm system at some facilities. So we recommended an immediate mandate such that within ninety days all facilities have at least an air horn that could warn the people to get the heck out." It just goes to show that even a greenish company like Fuller can miss the forest for the trees.

Sustainable Development

Company: Stonyfield Farm

Policy/Practice: Environmental monitoring and response.

Bottom Line: A double-green return on investment.

Stonyfield Farm may well be America's greenest business citizen, but not everyone in management shared president/CEO Gary Hirshberg's enthusiasm for auditing the company's environmental performance in 1994. After all, *Newsweek* magazine had just finished mauling Ben & Jerry's after the Vermont ice-cream maker published the results of its annual social audit. Never mind that B & J is the only notable American employer to regularly audit its social behavior. Forget that auditor Paul Hawken concluded that the company still deserved its big-hearted reputation. The reporter pounced on the company's every self-acknowledged failing and threw it back in its face. Now some of Stonyfield's leaders feared Stonyfield might be volunteering for its own spanking.

Gary pressed his view and won them over. "If you can't measure it, you can't manage it," he insisted. And when the audit turned up some embarrassing numbers — for example, two and a half pounds of water consumed for every pound of yogurt produced — Gary embraced them as a "big, big opportunity. We now have a baseline of data we can work from. Until the audit, we were flailing away in the dark."

Environmental auditing is no longer unusual in American business, but Stonyfield's reasons for doing it still are. Most companies undergo environmental audits to assure themselves they are meeting regulatory standards. Stonyfield wasn't worried about compliance — it was already sailing far above that hurdle. Its goal was much more utopian: canceling out to the greatest degree possible the total ecological cost of its operation. The audit would allow it to do that with much greater precision.

Of course, first Stonyfield needed to find an auditor that tested for something beyond the regulatory minimums. They hired an outfit called GreenAudit, which promotes environmental goals that match Stonyfield's. Like other auditors, GreenAudit tests for regulatory compliance, but it also looks for the degree to which a company's actions meet its own stated standards as well as for other opportunities for the company to proactively reduce its impact.

After a protracted review of Stonyfield's operation, GreenAudit's final report confirmed the value of Stonyfield's efforts to date, stating that "Stonyfield Farm is an environmentally superior company." However, the report also cautioned that the company fell short of "full environmental excellence." In other words, Stonyfield still had more that it could do. No news there, but Gary and sister Nancy, Stonyfield's environmental coordinator, were thrilled to know exactly how to start closing the gaps. Six months later, GreenAudit returned for a midyear review and found that 90 percent of the recommended actions it had listed were under way at the company.

The lengths to which Stonyfield will go to walk its talk will appear to many observers obsessive, even mad. However, Gary answers that this is what it takes to make a business operate sustainably. For instance, Stonyfield heats its yogurt with propane, which despite being the cleanest-burning of the fossil fuels, still sends carbon dioxide, the primary global-warming culprit, wafting up the factory's stacks. Using numbers generated by the audit, Stonyfield has calculated the number of trees it would have to plant to capture the equivalent amount of CO_2 emitted, added in the CO_2 exhaled by its delivery trucks, and is now considering investing in sufficient tree-planting to cancel its "debt."

Gushes Gary, "Rain forest destruction is a disaster not just because of the tree burning, which releases huge amounts of carbon in the atmosphere, but because of that loss of CO_2-fixing material. If the companies that were destroying forest committed to replacing that carbon-fixing material elsewhere, you would have a truly revolutionary concept. I'm not recommending more destruction, but you get the idea."

With audit results in hand, Stonyfield has also moved to recapture its waste heat, clean up the few remaining effluents in its wastewater, and upgrade the EPA-approved cleaning compounds used in the plant to even greener alternatives suggested by the auditor. GreenAudit also noted that while management's commitment to ecological operation was unassailable, it fell shy in terms of formalizing policies, assigning responsiblity, and fully communicating those policies and responsibilities to all employees. Stonyfield started putting those systems in place as soon as the report was issued.

The above initiatives exist alongside such ongoing efforts as the company's years of work trying to create a national recycling infrastructure for its plastic packaging; its philanthropic support of environmentalism; its purchasing from farmers committed to sustainable agriculture methods; its empowerment of employees to make environmental improvements; its prodigious efforts to educate consumers about environmentalism; and on and on. Stonyfield has even begun to investigate acquiring land around the plant so food for employees can be grown with compost from the production wastes.

Of course, the first question that most executives might ask Hirshberg is, who's minding the store while you're running around saving the planet? The quick answer is that the company has maintained a 45 percent top-line growth rate over the previous six years. But Gary is also quick to point out that the improvements inspired by the audit — more efficient use of energy, waste reduction, packaging reduction, and pollution prevention — also reduce costs in the fairly short term: "As [GreenAudit CEO] David Mager went through the audit at our mid-year review, every single audit item — and he went through some pretty wide-ranging stuff — put dollars back into our bottom line. If reporters want to read the results of our audit, I invite them to focus on *that*."

COMPANY: HERMAN MILLER

Policy/Practice: Bottom-up environmentalism, top-down ethical commitment.

Bottom Line: A forward-looking environmental stance that not only leads its industry ethically but positions the company for sales leadership in a more environmentally conscientious future.

Companies that depend on wood supplies have led the charge against conservationism in recent years, claiming that its economic costs are being ignored. But in the late 1980s, Bill Foley and Bob Johnston of furniture manufacturer Herman Miller saw firsthand the conservationists' point. The Zeeland, Michigan–based company had been having trouble maintaining supplies of rosewood and teak. As Foley and Johnston began to research the matter, their inquiry led them straight to their employer's uncomfortable role in tropical rain forest destruction. Quite simply, foreign harvests of prime rain forest hardwoods, partially driven by demand from manufacturers like

Miller, had gone so far beyond nature's ability to regenerate new trees that purchasers like Miller were already experiencing shortages.

Since its founding in 1923, Herman Miller has demonstrated a concern for doing business with the best interests of all of its stakeholders in mind. It also takes pride in a four-decade tradition of participatory management, which among other things empowers employees to make environmental policy recommendations. Emboldened by the company's conscientious culture, Foley and Johnston pressed forward, taking the results of their study to the company's environmental steering committee, the Environmental Quality Action Team (EQAT). After investigating further, EQAT members swallowed hard and recommended that the company no longer purchase woods — rain forest and otherwise — that weren't harvested in a sustainable manner, meaning not only the replacement of harvested trees but consideration for the wider ecological aspects of forest regeneration.

It was a gutsy move because Miller's ethical heritage notwithstanding, EQAT's recommendation messed with company heritage of another stripe. Some of Miller's furniture pieces are so well regarded that they stand on exhibit in the Smithsonian Institution and other major museums of design. One of those pieces, the Eames lounge chair, depended upon rosewood veneer, a tropical rain forest product, for its distinctive appearance.

Despite fears that the new policy would kill the $2,000-plus chair, management adopted the mandate anyway and it stands today, the first of its kind in the industry. Through its activities with the Tropical Forest Foundation and several established environmental groups, the company now promotes its sustained-yield ideals to architectural and interior design firms as well as other furniture makers. It has also worked with Congress and the United Nations to help shape policies and regulations that would increase the value of standing forests and help ensure their survival.

As for the Eames chair, Miller now makes it from native American cherry and walnut. Environmental affairs manager

Paul Murray notes, "People without a wood background wouldn't really notice the difference, although we specify it in our labeling." And while some customers expressed alarm that the company would tinker with such a classic product, Murray adds that "the sales of the chair haven't really changed much."

So it goes with most of Miller's environmental undertakings. "We don't have a huge staff here in environmental affairs, but we feel we have 5,000 environmentalists working for us," says Murray. "Whatever concept you want to talk about is fair game." He adds that about two-thirds of Miller's environmental initiatives originate with employee suggestions, with the others flowing from his department:

"We believe here that the best business solutions come from the people that work with the products, and we're finding that true in the environmental arena at well. The people generating waste are the best ones to solve the waste problems. The best ones to deal with emissions are the ones in the areas where the emissions begin. We've become a national leader in recycling. That's because employees on the floor will ask, 'Why are we throwing this away?'"

Whether they originate in employee suggestions or in Murray's department, Miller's environmental initiatives are as comprehensive, well conceived, and of course financially rewarding as any you'll find in corporate America. Instead of paying to dispose of them, Miller now sells leather trimmings to luggage makers to make attaché cases, and vinyl scraps to stereo and car makers to use as sound-deadening material. In total, Miller's ability to swap or sell recyclable materials has been worth nearly a quarter of a million dollars a year.

The company saves more still through internal recycling efforts, such as reusing solvents. Its packaging-reduction efforts have saved it over $1.4 million. Miller also operates a trash-to-energy plant in Zeeland that supplies heat and energy to the main facility. The plant burns wood scraps and sawdust that might otherwise end up in a landfill, saving about $350,000 in energy and landfill costs in the process.

The cost-cutting advantages of a green agenda like

Miller's may rouse cynics to point fingers, but money alone doesn't begin to explain some of Miller's actions. For example, in 1991 a state regulatory agency was pressing the company to buy — at a cost of about $800,000 — two incinerators that would collect and burn nearly all the toxic solvents escaping from the spray booths on its wood-finishing line. According to Murray, the incinerators' performance exceeded what the federal Clean Air Act required and what any of its competitors were doing, so Miller's attorneys told CEO Richard Ruch that they felt the agency's request could be successfully fought. Ruch turned to Murray, then the finishing manager, for his opinion. Murray replied that, legal considerations aside, "'I live downwind and it's the right thing to do.' You know, he signed that day for the incinerator expense. That really showed me that this company takes what it's saying about being an environmental leader real seriously."

Indeed, from a sheer conceptual standpoint, many of Miller's environmental initiatives point beyond reduced impact toward the elusive goal of true sustainability. For instance, the shuttling of fabric discards to companies that use them for feedstock represents a "closing of loops," which is the crème de la crème of recycling. In 1984, the company formed a subsidiary, Phoenix Designs, that buys back used Miller furniture and reconditions it for resale. Miller has also adopted the notion of cradle-to-grave environmental impact, favoring materials and processes that are energy efficient to use and emit minimal pollutants and product designs that disassemble easily so that parts can be reused or recycled.

Not that Miller has yet reached green nirvana, as Murray is the first to concede. But Miller has set its sights high; for example, it has eliminated all ozone-depleting chemicals from its manufacturing and set a goal of zero waste to landfills by the end of 1995.

Murray is matter-of-fact about the company's environmental commitments: "We're told as employee-owners that we're to do the right thing. But I wouldn't claim in any way, shape, or form that our initiatives are just for the environment. They're also for the future of the company." Miller's management knows that some business customers are demanding environmental performance from their suppliers much as Miller now screens its vendors. In the public sector, the U.S. government, a major furniture purchaser, is currently developing environmental standards for suppliers, and many foreign governments far exceed the United States' progress in this area. These mandates aside, environmental commitments help differentiate Miller from its competition to environmentally concerned individual consumers as well.

But ultimately, Miller realizes the economic justification for its stewardship is more basic still. Says Murray, "Take our wood program. If we don't stay concerned about where our wood is coming from, eventually there won't be any wood. We want to make sure our company survives."

FACILITY DESIGN

COMPANY: WILLIAM McDONOUGH & PARTNERS, ARCHITECTS

Policy/Practice: Designing environmentally responsible and healthful commercial buildings.

Bottom Line: Changing the architecture of architecture.

Bill McDonough earns his living as an architect and educator but his talks and writings suggest he's a frustrated sea captain because his favorite metaphors concern ships. One of those metaphors comes from a story about Ralph Waldo Emerson, who in 1831 traveled to Europe on a sailboat when his wife died. After coming home on a steamship, he noted how he had missed the "aeolian kinetic" — that is, the force of the wind — on the return passage. In a talk he gave before the Social Venture Network in Santa Barbara in 1992, McDonough added his own observations on the difference between the two vessels:

"Emerson went over on a solar-powered vehicle that was recyclable, and the people operating the vehicle were working in the open air with the forces of nature in a way that had been developed over millennia. On the return, he traveled in a steel bucket that put oil slicks on the water, spewed smoke in the air, and the people operating it were shoveling coal in the dark. This is a matter of design, and most specifically, it's a matter of design ethics."

"Design ethicist" might in fact be a better professional title for McDonough, for whom the term *architect* seems far too restrictive. It is exactly for the ethical context that he brings to his work that such conscientious organizational citizens as furniture maker Herman Miller, Stonyfield Farm Yogurt, and the Environmental Defense Fund have engaged his services. When you need to put up a building but worry as much about its cost to the ecology as its cost in dollars; when you think of your building as a place that should support both the health and productivity of the people inside, not just contain them; William McDonough & Partners, Architects — who also design everything from fabrics to industrial centers to urban plans — is the firm most likely to top your list.

"We're not interested in being the best green architects in the world," exclaims McDonough when we speak in late 1994. "We're interested in being the best architects, period, and I don't understand how one could separate those two anyway." At this point in our history, he says, if you the architect propose a project that specifies "profligate waste" — precious rain forest resources like mahogany, inefficient use of energy, or needlessly toxic materials — "you're negligent and you're aesthetically dubious."

But McDonough also realizes the realities of this point in history, and one of those is that with the advent of cheap energy, most architects have forgotten how to take advantage of the site's natural attributes, in particular the contributions the sun can make to heat or lighting. "I've spoken to thousands of architects," he told a New York audience in 1993, "and when I ask the question, 'How many of you know how to find true South?' I rarely get a raised hand."

Needless to say, a McDonough building always faces south if possible, flooding it with natural light to both reduce energy use and provide a healthful and psychically nurturing workplace. Windows are sized and placed to maximize the light's penetration into the building's interior. The heavy thermal mass in the walls of a McDonough structure stores the coolness of the night and releases it during the day, reducing the air conditioning load; in winter, it soaks up heat from the sun, cutting the pull on the building's heaters. These are not McDonough inventions. They are techniques of the ancients, employed in everything from adobe huts to Gothic cathedrals.

But those who hire the guy get far more than just a scavenger of history. In fact, they get someone whose ways of working, both conceptually and operationally, are so far out of the mainstream that they must be met at least halfway by the client's own openness or the working relationshp will collapse at the onset.

Take, for instance, one of McDonough's latest ideas, "looking at buildings as if they were trees." In practical terms, that means topping structures with roofs planted with succulents or grasses to absorb water, so the building doesn't contribute to a city's storm runoff problem; the roof then releases the water slowly back to the atmosphere like, yes, a tree. If the roof vegetation is sprayed with water — gray water captured from waste outflows, of course — it can also provide cooling through evaporation, depending on the climate. The vegetation also supplies insulation and protects the roof membrane from ultraviolet degradation and thermal shock, says McDonough, "so it extends the life of the roof — we don't know how long but at least twice — which adds value, of course." At the building's base, McDonough designs parking lots that drain through the asphalt, again mitigating runoff but also allowing rainfall to recharge groundwater and the biology in the soil system as it would do if the building were a massive tree trunk under a permeable canopy.

A project that McDonough developed for Wal-Mart illustrates another of his key ideas. A few years ago, the company hired his firm to help it create a model environmentally considerate store, various features of which could be incorporated in subsequent Wal-Mart construction. McDonough configured the space so the store, in Lawrence, Kansas, could be "recycled" as residential apartments once it completed its commercial life. "If you design for housing, you've got your [human] proportions right," explains McDonough, which neatly facilitates several other of his goals as well. For example, raising ceilings to housing height creates more space for hot air to rise away from people, reducing cooling requirements. And, again, allowing the daylight to reach people deeper inside the building drops artificial lighting needs.

Outside, the store features xeriscape landscaping that requires little water; a wastewater and runoff-recovery system to provide that water; a solar-powered exterior sign; and a parking lot made from recycled asphalt. The inside systems include state-of-the-art energy-efficient design that dropped utility requirements by 54 percent, and equipment that operates without CFCs. McDonough had the building constructed without CFC use as well, and moved Wal-Mart off its usual steel construction to wood, dropping the Btu use from 300,000 to 40,000 per square foot in the process. Finally, he arranged for all of the wood to be sustainably harvested.

McDonough designs as much for human as planetary health. In particular, he has assaulted sick building syndrome with a vengeance. During the 1970s energy crisis, commercial builders began sealing off windows and work spaces to lower utility bills. The thinking was seriously flawed because the health and performance consequences of the design change likely overwhelm the energy savings. In sealed buildings, infectious bacteria, secondhand tobacco smoke, and chemical toxins get trapped in the airstream and circulate via the heating and cooling systems. McDonough's buildings deliver fresh air to every employee in the space through personal, adjustable outlets. He uses the least toxic materials possible, such as carpets with water-based glues. And he makes one other revolutionary design change as well — the windows open.

For many potential clients, of course, the big question remains, Do McDonough designs cost more? McDonough won't deny that in some cases, up-front costs might be slightly higher, but only from the narrowest point of view: "From a fiduciary position, if you're telling me that you don't want to deal with productivity or health issues, or you don't want to look at energy operating costs, then you don't understand where you're spending your money. But the managers will change over time. They will recognize those values — that's why we're building the model."

LANDSCAPING

COMPANY: BANK ONE

Policy/Practice: Xeriscaping — i.e., landscaping with drought-resistant, native plants.

Bottom Line: The perfect aesthetic match for a low-rainfall region, and the water and maintenance savings pay for it.

In at least one respect, water and money crises don't much differ — you give first aid in both cases by cutting off all unnecessary outflows. Maybe that's why the folks at a bank in Tucson, Arizona, took to the concept of xeriscaping ahead of most businesses and residents in their parched region.

In the mid-1980s, an organization called Southern Arizona Water Resources Association (SAWARA) formed to deal with Tucson's vital water issues, one of which was the wasteful watering of outdoor landscaping. As in other parts of the water-poor American Southwest, many people had landscaped their homes and businesses with lush grasses, tall trees, and other plants native to much wetter parts of the planet. The amount of water it took to sustain those landscapes threatened to deprive Tucson of fresh water for far more vital uses: drinking, washing, toilets, agriculture, industrial uses, and so on. SAWARA hoped to break Tucsonans of their bad landscaping habits by creating a model project that showcased the practical, attractive alternative — xeriscaping.

Xeriscaping, in its best applications, is champagne living on a beer budget. The logic is as elegant as it is simple — plants native to a desert region need only modest amounts of water, and to many eyes offer a satisfactory array of bright colors and other aesthetic features that consumers demand. But SAWARA knew it had to make its case financially, as well — that is, the savings in water and maintenance costs would have to compensate for the considerable investment of relandscaping before it could convince businesses and home-owners to start tearing out their lawns.

Michael Hard, a division head for Valley National Bank of Arizona, participated in those SAWARA meetings and wanted his company to take a lead role in showing other Tuc-sonans, particularly other Tucson businesses, how to save water for both their own and the city's good. And he had just the place for SAWARA's demonstration project — the bank's Tucson Services Center, an operations center on eleven acres in Tucson's south side with landscaping that soaked up water like a sponge. Hard took the idea back to his people, and after doing some figuring, they volunteered the site for a xeriscap-ing makeover. In February 1986, the bank announced a con-test for the best design that could be accomplished for $100,000, an amount Valley National's numbers showed could be recouped in the acceptable payback period of about seven years.

From there, the project proceeded like, well, water flow-ing downhill. A University of Arizona landscape architecture graduate student won the contest and its $1,000 prize and the massive project, involving the removal of 168,000 square feet of turf, took root. Final cost: an under-budget $98,450. But the real savings showed up in the water and maintenance sav-ings, which exceeded Valley National's expectations. Between the two costs, Hard says, the bank saved about $14,400 an-nually, and beat the payback period as well.

Valley National wasn't the only entity attempting to

change Tucson's landscaping customs. SAWARA worked with local nurseries to stock and feature some of the most attractive varieties of native plants. The local botanical garden pitched in with a demonstration residential garden and, says Hard, "the public sector took a major role in this, too — they redid roads, and made sure they put in desert landscaping in the medians, the intersections, and critical entrances to the city."

But the bank played a big part in the effort and it paid off in, if not revolution, some significant progress. "Having lived here since then, I see far more desert landscaping used than ever before," says Hard. Especially when he visits his company's own Arizona facilities — Valley National's management was sufficiently impressed with the xeriscape experiment to mandate that all the corporation's renovation utilize xeriscaping. And although Valley National became part of Columbus, Ohio–based Banc One Corporation in a 1993 merger (when it changed names to Bank One), the policy remains in effect.

What was a good idea in Tucson, of course, makes increasing sense in many other areas of the United States, not to mention other countries, as freshwater shortages become more and more commonplace around the world. So Hard acknowledges that the bank project is a good lesson for business landscaping projects everywhere: "Not only were we able to participate in something important for the community, but it made hard-core business sense, too. You don't often get those kinds of opportunities."

Organization & Accountability

SOCIAL AUDITING

COMPANY: BEN & JERRY'S

Policy/Practice: Auditing its all-around social performance.

Bottom Line: An idealistic innovation becomes a critical managing tool.

When Ben & Jerry's crafted its social mission statement in the mid-1980s, co-founder Ben Cohen wanted to make sure that the company backed it with some means of holding itself accountable for the ideals it had just declared to the world. Thus was born the social audit, not only at Ben & Jerry's but also in America, for no significant American company had ever attempted such a thing. In 1988, the company began a tradition of publishing in its annual report the audit's findings, including those places where goals and behavior didn't match up.

With a cynical, predatory press tracing its every misstep, the wider progressive business movement now recognizes that its continued credibility depends upon greater accountability. So in retrospect, the audit idea appears downright prescient. But Liz Bankowski, B & J's director of social mission development, is even happier about another unintended result:

"The audit allows a look at the company that is critical and not just to its social responsibility but to all parts of its mission. Our last social performance audit [1993] probably played an even bigger part in triggering changes in our company than other [non-social] audits. So in that sense it was an important tool for managing this company."

While a number of high-ideals companies were preparing to follow Ben & Jerry's lead as of the end of 1994, the ice-cream maker remained the only major American company with a social audit process in place. But it's the company's willingness to publicly call itself on the carpet that really bull-dozes the envelope. Snipe if you wish at B & J's social posture, but you can hardly accuse them of self-promotion while they're tattling on themselves.

Take for instance, the audit review published in the 1993 annual report. Yes, the text includes auditor Paul Hawken's conclusion that "there has been no change or retreat from the values that informed the company's earliest days. If anything, they are more entrenched than ever." But those remarks follow bracing reports about quality problems with some company products and employee injuries (the latter persisting, Hawken notes, despite the company's earnest attempts to address problems uncovered in the 1992 audit). The audit also includes Hawken's insinuation that, despite an in-place profit-sharing plan, a company like this should be doing still more to gain-share with its employees.

"We got on all of those things [after Hawken reported them to management]," says Bankowski. "The point of the audit is not just to say, *mea culpa, mea culpa*. We did a stock-option award to everyone in the company, we've made real strides in the safety issue, and that's of course what the audit is there for."

With no model to follow, B & J had to make up the audit process as it went along. The first few audits were conducted internally, with outside experts on social-minded business such as Control Data founder William Norris reviewing and reporting the results to shareholders. The company objectified the process further in 1991, when it hired Milton Moskowitz to both gather the data and write the report. In 1992, B & J engaged green business pioneer Hawken for the job. It rehired him in 1993 and for the foreseeable future to develop the process along more consistent lines than it had in the past.

B & J gives Hawken — as they did Moskowitz before him — full access to all company records and to any individuals he wishes to interview. The company publishes the report in its entirety, editing only for corrections of fact, and then only with the auditor approving changes. That said, the process can't yet be compared to its financial namesake. As Hawken noted in the 1992 report, a true audit would require the company to keep an accurate, updated paper trail on its social behavior. The absence of such records makes the current process more a survey of the company's business citizenship, but that's still a groundbreaking action in American commerce.

Ben & Jerry's still struggles with the best way to capture the information it wants the audit to cover. B & J has always reported its audit in narrative form, and while Bankowski thinks that the report could include more hard data than it has, there will always be a need for more nuanced comments: "When you look at gender equity, that's quantifiable. So is solid-waste reduction. But when we attempted to source peaches from black family-owned farms in the South, that doesn't get quantified as anything but a failure. But it wasn't a failure, because we went the distance to try to source in a way that would have really helped a community in need. So I think the narrative form is really important in capturing that kind of thing."

The social audit assumed vastly greater importance in 1994 after a flood of negative press swirled about the Body Shop, in some sense the Ben & Jerry's of the United Kingdom. Many progressive business leaders have suggested that if the Body Shop had audited its own social performance, it would not have been so open to the frontal assault by muckraking journalist John Entine that catalyzed the media ambush. Apparently, the Body Shop reached the same conclusion in the story's wake for, like Ben & Jerry's, it hired a business responsibility expert, Stanford professor Kirk Hanson, to assess its social behavior. The audit will take place in 1995.

Not that a social audit insulates a company from bad press. In a July 1993 story, *Newsweek* reporter Carolyn Friday jumped all over Hawken's scattered negative findings in the 1993 Ben & Jerry's audit, conveniently neglecting to mention his glowing overall conclusion and also failing to acknowledge the company for telling on itself. But says Bankowski, *Newsweek*'s slam "was hardly a blip on our screen. We thought it was rather amusing that they quoted from our audit and didn't say that this was in the company's own assessment of itself. But beyond that, it didn't concern us at all. We feel absolutely that disclosure is the better thing to do because we want to make sure that what we say and do are the same. We can't control expectations people have externally and internally, and we know that oftentimes those go way beyond what we said."

Nevertheless, Bankowski and her B & J colleagues do sometimes worry that in publishing the audit for the *Newsweek*s and John Entines to peruse, they may have done the rest of the movement a disservice: "I think to the extent companies are subscribing to socially responsible practices, they need to have a way of assessing their own behaviors so they can check in and set a reasonable agenda of stuff they need to work on, not to have it all out there in their annual report. It's an interesting debate, because clearly your customers have a right to know, too. If you make [your social mission] part of who you are, if you lead with it in the marketplace like we do, our customers have to know that we are scrutinizing ourselves, and I don't know how they would know if we didn't disclose it.

"The thing that concerns me, though, is I don't know if we're going to make this a more accessible movement for business [with a more public] process." Full social disclosure goes way beyond traditional business ethics, she notes, and that could be counterproductive: "I think we have to be careful not to make the conditions of membership so intimidating that we discourage companies from moving more in the realm of socially responsible actions."

GOVERNANCE

COMPANY: RHINO ENTERTAINMENT

Policy/Practice: Involving employees in fundamental company decisions and processes outside their work function.

Bottom Line: A great place to be a grunt.

It sometimes seems that Rhino Entertainment, a Los Angeles, California–based company specializing in popular music and video reissues, harbors almost as many going committees as Congress. But no one's complaining that this group isn't getting things done, or that it's out of touch with the people, or even that all it cares about is money. Employee participation in decision making, of course, has been on the rise for years in American business, through what is generally called teamwork. But that concept should not be confused with what goes on at Rhino. At most corporations with teams, frontline employees participate in decisions formerly made by supervisors or middle management but they generally have no more input into fundamental company decisions than they did under the pre-teamwork structure.

Rhino, by contrast, has spawned a comparatively dizzying number of ways for employees to not only communicate their thoughts to top management but also to contribute to vital company processes outside their daily work function. In Rhino-ese, this is called "how the insane run the asylum," and by all appearances, the crazies are doing themselves proud.

Effectively, Rhino's committee structure supplies the "walk" to match the company's talk because it was established to both embody and carry out the pledges contained in the company's mission statement. The first plank of that statement articulates Rhino's business mission. But most of the remainder deals with workplace and social issues — "personal and professional growth" of the workforce, "the free exchange of ideas," "fair play," "a sense of pride," "ethical behavior," and "a sense of social and environmental responsibility." The roster of committees seems to do a pretty fair job of covering that ambitious ground, without weighing the company down. Says Shannon Brown, who as Rhino's minister of culture oversees the teams, "We find places where things could be better, go at them with people who want to work on the problems, set some goals, hopefully achieve them, and then move on."

Take for instance, the Benefit and Compensation Committee. Created as an extension of the human resources department to attract fresh ideas from throughout the company, the committee undertook management's goal of creating a performance-based profit-sharing system. Result: the Rhino By Objective process (see page 10) crafted from an idea suggested by vice president for human resources Sharon Foster. Mission accomplished, the committee disbanded.

The committees current at Rhino as of my conversation with Brown in early 1995 all served ongoing functions. The Building Aesthetics Team formed to facilitate the company's move into new quarters, help with space allocation, and so forth. It has stayed together to address any issues arising about the new building — comfort, friendliness, decor, and so on. The *Rhino Reader* team manages the company's in-house newsletters. Rhino even has a virtual committee, the Information and Communication Team. That group oversees the company's e-mail system that, among other things, now serves as a cyberspace forum in which any team or individual can raise issues and draw input from throughout the company. In fact, says Brown, the committee itself rarely meets in person anymore, conducting its business by e-mail.

The Women's Product Development Team is Rhino's testimony to the crossover between high-diversity standards and opening new markets. Until the team formed, men had made most of the artists and repertoire decisions at Rhino, which led to a catalog dominated by male artists. The company built its considerable success on the strength of that catalog, but when management decided to pursue women's markets, it only made sense to ask female Rhinos from outside A & R to contribute to the process. That gave women input into some of the most important, and fun, decisions the company makes.

Brown says that the Social and Environmental Responsibility Team (SERT), headed by vice president of A & R Gary Stewart, "is probably the team that drives us most here. It oversees so much of who we are." Indeed, just for starters, the committee manages Rhino's extensive employee volunteerism program. The company offers up to four hours a month of paid company time — or compensatory time if the employees volunteer outside of work hours — to those who work on community-service projects and gives an additional week off between Christmas and New Year's to all who have completed at least sixteen hours of community service during the year. Employees can volunteer for any organization or cause that moves them, but SERT also organizes formal Rhino service activities. Most of those take place at a local urban community center called the Al Wooten, Jr., Heritage Center that Rhino has effectively adopted. Many Rhinos, as company employees refer to themselves, volunteer there regularly, and Brown says about 60 percent of the employees spent at least some time there during 1994.

Also on SERT's heaping plate: Rhino's office recycling system and eco-audit; a Bucks-A-Week Club, through which employees can request that from one or more dollars be diverted from their weekly salary to a homeless organization; and a roughly once-a-month speakers program. Past topics for the latter have included ballot initiatives, children's issues, sexual orientation in the workplace, and old-growth forests.

About a third of Rhino's workforce belonged to one team or another when Brown and I spoke in early 1995, but committee involvement is hardly the be-all and end-all of Rhino employee participation. The company holds open forums every couple of months where executives share financial progress reports and other management issues with the entire workforce. (For those employees who want to understand company finances in greater detail, the finance department holds seminars every six months.) The forums conclude with an open dialogue during which any employee can contribute. The company also provides a private suggestion box for those who don't feel comfortable speaking up publicly.

Employees can also get themselves heard by top management through their department heads or team leaders, who meet regularly with Rhino owners Richard Foos and Harold Bronson. On top of all that, ownership's doors are always open to any employee, by appointment. Says Brown, "I started here as a receptionist four years ago. I'm one of the best examples of what this place is all about and how it can absolutely open doors if you're interested in getting involved. There's no limit really as to what you can take part in."

And that includes helping the company set its future course. Through what Rhino calls the Big Idea Program, employees can write up their pet mega-suggestion and drop it into one of several mailboxes scattered throughout the building. Brown takes the suggestions to the relevant department heads to see if they are worthwhile pursuing and the company awards the employee with the best idea of the year with a four-figure check. Stewart runs his own idea program, soliciting suggestions for new Rhino releases: "I call it the More Brains Blowout. We get together every four months — any employees that want to come — and I just get out the butcher paper and let them roll with ideas."

Exactly what all this stuff means to Rhino depends upon whom at the company you talk to. Both Brown and Stewart acknowledge that when people have work to get out, voluntary participation tends to fall by the wayside, and a great number of Rhino-ites just do their work and go home under any circumstance. As Stewart says, "I would say our structure creates the possibility for people who really want to [be involved] but it doesn't create the probability and I think that's about all you can do at this level." Nor does he think that a more participatory, turned-on work environment necessarily makes for a more productive one. He suggests that Rhino's culture is what it is because its owners have chosen to redefine that as a bottom-line, even if it diverts energy from more traditional business considerations.

To Brown, the synergy between employee input and company output is obvious and essential: "I am amazed in the four years that I've been here how productivity has gone up as we've evolved our internal policies. Rhino has always been successful but we've had some amazing years the last few. I can't believe that has more to do with external issues than the fact that we have a very happy group here."

About the Author

Alan Reder is the author of *In Pursuit of Principle and Profit: Business Success Through Social Responsibility* (Tarcher/Putnam, 1994) and co-author (with Jack A. Brill) of *Investing from the Heart: The Guide to Socially Responsible Investing and Money Management* (Crown, 1992). A member of the Social Venture Network, he lives in Rogue River, Oregon, with his wife Hyiah, daughter Ariel, and son Ajene.

About the Social Venture Network

BY PAM SOLO, EXECUTIVE DIRECTOR

Eight years ago, a group of investors, venture capitalists, and businesspeople gathered in Boulder, Colorado, to found the Social Venture Network (SVN). The mission then, as it is now, was to bring together people from the business community who are committed to changing the way the world does business and to using the business vehicle to help build a just and sustainable society. In a sense, SVN was a natural outgrowth of decades of activism by shareholders and religious groups to make business more responsive to the welfare of all of its stakeholders, not just its owners. As part of this larger movement, SVN members have been national and international leaders in showing how to bring social responsiveness into daily business practice and how to use enterpreneurial creativity to address social needs.

In its brief history, SVN has grown to more than 450 members and spawned such other important organizations as SVN Europe, Business for Social Responsibility, and Students for Socially Responsible Business. Membership in SVN is by application. The goal of the membership policy is to create a balanced and stimulating community of entrepreneurs, investors, corporate leaders, public-interest innovators, and intellectuals committed to the SVN mission. For more information, contact:

The Social Venture Network
1388 Sutter Street, Ste. 1010
San Francisco, CA 94109
Voice (415)771–4308
Fax (415)771–0535